BUSINESS/SCIENCE/TECHNOLOGY DIVISION
CHICAGO PUBLIC LIBRARY
400 SOUTH STATE STREET
CHICAGO, IL 60605

International Financial Reporting Standards

A Practical Guide

Fifth Edition

Hennie van Greuning

D1501174

THE WORLD BANK
Washington, D.C.

© 2009 International Bank for Reconstruction and Development and the World Bank

1818 H Street, NW Washington, DC 20433

Telephone: 202-473-1000

Internet: www.worldbank.org

E-mail: feedback@worldbank.org

All rights reserved.

1 2 3 4 5 13 12 11 10 09

The findings, interpretations, and conclusions expressed herein are those of the author(s) and do not necessarily reflect the views of the Board of Executive Directors of the World Bank or the governments they represent.

The World Bank does not guarantee the accuracy of the data included in this work. The boundaries, colors, denominations, and other information shown on any map in this work do not imply any judgment on the part of the World Bank concerning the legal status of any territory or the endorsement or acceptance of such boundaries.

Rights and Permissions

The material in this work is copyrighted. Copying and/or transmitting portions or all of this work without permission may be a violation of applicable law. The World Bank encourages dissemination of its work and will normally grant permission promptly.

For permission to photocopy or reprint any part of this work, please send a request with complete information to the Copyright Clearance Center, Inc., 222 Rosewood Drive, Danvers, MA 01923, USA, telephone 978-750-8400, fax 978-750-4470, www.copyright.com.

All other queries on rights and licenses, including subsidiary rights, should be addressed to the Office of the Publisher, World Bank, 1818 H Street NW, Washington, DC 20433, USA, fax 202-522-2422, e-mail pubrights@worldbank.org.

ISBN: 978-0-8213-7727-7

eISBN: 978-0-8213-7899-1

DOI: 10.1596/978-0-8213-7727-7

Library of Congress Cataloging-in-Publication Data has been requested.

Contents

R0422102979

THE CHICAGO PUBLIC LIBRARY

PART & CHAPTER	STANDARD NUMBER	TITLE	PAGE
PART V		**DISCLOSURE**	

Foreword

The publication of this fifth edition coincides with the convergence in accounting standards that has been a feature of the international landscape since the global financial crisis of 1998. The events of that year prompted several international organizations, including the World Bank and the International Monetary Fund, to launch a cooperative initiative to strengthen the global financial architecture and to seek a longer-term solution to the lack of transparency in financial information. International convergence in accounting standards under the leadership of the International Accounting Standards Board (IASB) and the Financial Accounting Standards Board (FASB) in the United States has now progressed to the point where more than 100 countries currently subscribe to the International Financial Reporting Standards (IFRS).

In the U.S., the August 2008 announcement that the SEC proposes that IFRS reporting begin with 2014 filings, subject to certain interim milestones being met, will no doubt accelerate convergence. The AICPA response was positive in stating that one set of master standards will ultimately lead to investment comparisons on a worldwide basis as well as enable cross border transactions to be more transparent and reliable. From December 2009 onwards one can therefore expect limited early use by entities in the U.S. By 2011 the SEC will determine whether to require mandatory adoption of IFRS for all U.S. issuers by 2014.

The rush toward convergence continues to produce a steady stream of revisions to accounting standards by both the IASB and FASB. For accountants, financial analysts, and other specialists, there is already a burgeoning technical literature explaining in detail the background and intended application of these revisions. This book provides a non-technical, yet comprehensive, managerial overview of the underlying materials.

The appearance of the fifth edition of this book—already translated into 15 languages in its earlier editions—is therefore timely.

Each chapter briefly summarizes and explains a new or revised IFRS, the issue or issues the standard addresses, the key underlying concepts, the appropriate accounting treatment, and the associated requirements for presentation and disclosure. The text also covers financial analysis and interpretation issues to better demonstrate the potential effect of the accounting standards on business decisions. Simple examples in most chapters help further clarify the material. It is our hope that this approach, in addition to providing a handy reference for practitioners, will help relieve some of the tension experienced by nonspecialists when faced with business decisions influenced by the new rules. The book should also assist national regulators in comparing IFRS to country-specific practices, thereby encouraging even wider local adoption of these already broadly accepted international standards. It also forms the basis of a securities accounting workshop offered several times each year to World Bank Treasury clients in central banks and other public sector funds.

Kenneth G. Lay, CFA
Treasurer
The World Bank
Washington, D.C.
January 2009

Acknowledgments

The author is grateful to Ken Lay, vice president and treasurer of the World Bank, who has supported this fifth edition as a means to assist our client countries with a publication to facilitate understanding the International Financial Reporting Standards (IFRS) and emphasize the importance of financial analysis and interpretation of the information produced through application of these standards.

Charles Hattingh of PC Finance Research (South Africa) has provided invaluable insights into the complexities and implementation problems of IFRS.

The Stalla Review for the CFA® exam made a significant contribution to a previous edition by providing copyright permission to adapt material and practice problems from its textbooks and questions database.

I am grateful to the International Accounting Standards Committee Foundation for the use of its examples in chapter 12 (IAS 41–Agriculture). In essence, this entire publication is a tribute to the output of the International Accounting Standards Board. Deloitte Touche Tohmatsu also allowed the use of two examples from its publications.

Colleagues in the World Bank Treasury shared their insights into the complexities of applying certain standards to the treasury environment. I benefited greatly from hours of conversation with many colleagues, including Hamish Flett and Richard Williams.

Despite the extent and quality of the inputs that I have received, I am solely responsible for the contents of this publication.

Hennie van Greuning
January 2009

THE WORLD BANK TREASURY
Washington, D.C.

Introduction

This text, based on four earlier editions that have already been translated into 15 languages, is an important contribution to expanding awareness and understanding of International Financial Reporting Standards (IFRS) around the world, with easy-to-read summaries of each standard and examples that illustrate accounting treatments and disclosure requirements.

TARGET AUDIENCE

A conscious decision has been made to focus on the needs of executives and financial analysts in the private and public sectors who might not have a strong accounting background. This publication summarizes each standard (whether it is an IFRS or an International Accounting Standard) so managers and analysts can quickly obtain a broad overview of the key issues. Detailed discussion of certain topics has been excluded to maintain the overall objective of providing a useful tool to managers and financial analysts.

In addition to the short summaries, most chapters contain basic examples that emphasize the practical application of some key concepts in a particular standard. This text provides the tools to enable an executive without a technical accounting background to (1) participate in an informed manner in discussions relating to the appropriateness or application of a particular standard in a given situation, and (2) evaluate the effect that the application of the principles of a given standard will have on the financial results and position of a division or of an entire enterprise.

STRUCTURE OF THIS PUBLICATION

Each chapter follows a common outline to facilitate discussion of each standard:

1. **Objective of Standard** identifies the main objectives and the key issues of the standard.

2. **Scope of the Standard** identifies the specific transactions and events covered by a standard. In certain instances, compliance with a standard is limited to a specified range of enterprises.

3. **Key Concepts** explains the usage and implications of key concepts and definitions.

4. **Accounting Treatment** lists the specific accounting principles, bases, conventions, rules, and practices that should be adopted by an enterprise for compliance with a particular standard. Recognition (initial recording) and measurement (subsequent valuation) are specifically dealt with, where appropriate.

5. **Presentation and Disclosure** describes the manner in which the financial and nonfinancial items should be presented in the financial statements, as well as aspects that should be disclosed in these financial statements—keeping in mind the needs of various users. Users of financial statements include investors, employees, lenders, suppliers or trade creditors, governments, tax and regulatory authorities, and the public.

6. **Financial Analysis and Interpretation** discusses items of interest to the financial analyst in chapters where such a discussion is deemed appropriate. None of the discussion in these sections should be interpreted as a criticism of IFRS. Where analytical preferences and practices are highlighted, it is to alert the reader to the challenges still remaining along the road to convergence of international accounting practices and unequivocal adoption of IFRS.

7. **Examples** are included at the end of most chapters. These examples are intended as further illustration of the concepts contained in the IFRS.

The author hopes that managers in the client private sector will find this format useful in establishing accounting terminology, especially where certain terms are still in the exploratory stage in some countries.

CONTENT INCLUDED

All of the accounting standards issued by the International Accounting Standards Board (IASB) through December 31, 2008, are included in this publication. The IASB texts are the ultimate authority—this publication merely constitutes a summary.

About the Author

Hennie van Greuning is a senior adviser in the World Bank's Treasury and has previously worked as a sector manager for financial sector operations in the Bank. He has been a partner in a major international accounting firm and a controller in a central bank, in addition to heading bank supervision in his home country. He is a CFA Charterholder and qualified as a Chartered Accountant. He holds doctoral degrees in both accounting and economics. He is the coauthor of *Analyzing and Managing Banking Risk*, *Risk Analysis for Islamic Banks*, and *International Financial Statement Analysis*.

Part I

Financial Statement Presentation

Chapter One

Framework for the Preparation and Presentation of Financial Statements

1.1   OBJECTIVE

An acceptable coherent framework of fundamental accounting principles is essential for preparing financial statements. The major reasons for providing the framework are to

- identify the essential concepts underlying the preparation and presentation of financial statements;
- guide standard setters in developing accounting standards;
- assist preparers, auditors, and users to interpret the International Financial Reporting Standards (IFRS); and
- provide principles, as not all issues are covered by the IFRS.

The framework sets guidelines and should not be seen as a constitution, as there are certain instances where individual standards vary from the principles established in this chapter.

1.2   SCOPE OF THE FRAMEWORK

The existing framework deals with the

- objectives of financial statements,
- qualitative characteristics of financial statements,
- elements of financial statements,
- recognition of the elements of financial statements,
- measurement of the elements of financial statements, and
- concepts of capital and capital maintenance.

The framework is not a standard, but it is used extensively by the International Accounting Standards Board (IASB) and by its International Financial Reporting Interpretations Committee (IFRIC).

1.3   KEY CONCEPTS

Objective of Financial Statements

1.3.1   The **objective** of financial statements is to provide information about the **financial position** (balance sheet), **performance** (income statement), and **changes in financial position** (cash flow statement) of an entity. This information should be useful for making economic decisions by the users of the financial statements, who cannot dictate the information they should be getting.

1.3.2   Financial statements also show the results of **management's stewardship** of the resources entrusted to it. This information, along with other information in the notes to the financial statements, assists users of financial statements in predicting the entity's future cash flows and, in particular, their timing and certainty. To meet this objective, financial statements provide information about an entity's

- assets;
- liabilities;
- equity;
- income and expenses, including gains and losses;
- contributions by and distributions to owners in their capacity as owners; and
- cash flows.

1.3.3   **Fair presentation** is achieved through the provision of useful information (full disclosure) in the financial statements, whereby **transparency** is secured. If one assumes that fair presentation is equivalent to transparency, a secondary objective of financial statements is to secure transparency through full disclosure and provide a fair presentation of useful information for decision-making purposes.

Qualitative Characteristics

1.3.4   Qualitative characteristics are the attributes that make the information provided in financial statements useful to users:

- **Understandability.** Information should be readily understandable by users who have a basic knowledge of business, economic activities, and accounting, and who have a willingness to study the information with reasonable diligence.

- **Relevance.** Relevant information influences the economic decisions of users, helping them to evaluate past, present, and future events or to confirm or correct their past evaluations. The relevance of information is affected by its nature and materiality.

- **Reliability.** Reliable information is free from material error and bias and can be depended upon by users to represent faithfully that which it either purports to represent or could reasonably be expected to represent. The following factors contribute to reliability: faithful representation, substance over form, neutrality, prudence, and completeness.

- **Comparability.** Information should be presented in a consistent manner over time and in a consistent manner between entities to enable users to make significant comparisons.

1.3.5   The following are the underlying assumptions of financial statements (see figure 1.1 at the end of the chapter):

- **Accrual basis.** Effects of transactions and other events are recognized when they occur (not when the cash flows). These effects are recorded and reported in the financial statements of the periods to which they relate.

- **Going concern.** It is assumed that the entity will continue to operate for the foreseeable future.

1.3.6   The following are **constraints** on providing relevant and reliable information:

- **Timeliness.** Undue delay in reporting could result in loss of relevance but improve reliability.
- **Benefit versus cost.** Benefits derived from information should exceed the cost of providing it.

1.3.7   **Balancing qualitative characteristics.** To meet the objectives of financial statements and make them adequate for a particular environment, providers of information must balance the qualitative characteristics in such a way that best meets the objectives of financial statements.

1.3.8   The application of the principal qualitative characteristics and the appropriate accounting standards normally results in financial statements that provide **fair presentation.**

1.4   ACCOUNTING TREATMENT

Elements of Financial Statements

1.4.1   The following elements of financial statements are directly related to the measurement of the financial position:

- **Assets.** Resources controlled by the entity as a result of past events and from which future economic benefits are expected to flow to the entity
- **Liabilities.** Present obligations of an entity arising from past events, the settlement of which is expected to result in an outflow from the entity of economic benefits
- **Equity.** Assets less liabilities (commonly known as shareholders' funds)

1.4.2   The following elements of financial statements are directly related to the measurement of performance:

- **Income.** Increases in economic benefits in the form of inflows or enhancements of assets, or decreases of liabilities that result in an increase in equity (other than increases resulting from contributions by owners). Income embraces revenue and gains.
- **Expenses.** Decreases in economic benefits in the form of outflows or depletion of assets, or incurrences of liabilities that result in decreases in equity (other than decreases because of distributions to owners).

Initial Recognition of Elements

1.4.3   A financial statement element (assets, liabilities, equity, income, and expenses) should be **recognized** in the financial statements if

- it is **probable** that any future economic benefit associated with the item will flow to or from the entity, and
- the item has a cost or value that can be **measured with reliability.**

Subsequent Measurement of Elements

1.4.4 The following bases are used to different degrees and in varying combinations to **measure** elements of financial statements:

- Historical cost
- Current cost
- Realizable (settlement) value
- Present value (fair market value)

Fair value has to be used to measure financial instruments, but it is optional for valuing property, plant and equipment, intangible assets, and agricultural products.

Capital Maintenance Concepts

1.4.5 Capital and capital maintenance include

- **Financial capital** is synonymous with net assets or equity; it is defined in terms of nominal monetary units. Profit represents the increase in nominal money capital over the period.
- **Physical capital** is regarded as the operating capability; it is defined in terms of productive capacity. Profit represents the increase in productive capacity over the period.

1.5 PRESENTATION AND DISCLOSURE: TRANSPARENCY AND DATA QUALITY

1.5.1 In forming a safe environment for stakeholders, corporate governance rules should focus on creating a culture of transparency. Transparency refers to making information on existing conditions, decisions, and actions accessible, visible, and understandable to all market participants. Disclosure refers more specifically to the process and methodology of providing the information and of making policy decisions known through timely dissemination and openness. Accountability refers to the need for market participants, including the relevant authorities, to justify their actions and policies and to accept responsibility for both decisions and results.

1.5.2 Transparency is a prerequisite for accountability, especially to borrowers and lenders, issuers and investors, national authorities, and international financial institutions. In part, the case for greater transparency and accountability rests on the need for private sector agents to understand and accept policy decisions that affect their behavior. Greater transparency improves economic decisions taken by other agents in the economy. Transparency also fosters accountability, internal discipline, and better governance, while both transparency and accountability improve the quality of decision making in policy-oriented institutions. Such institutions—as well as other institutions that rely on them to make decisions—should be required to maintain transparency. If actions and decisions are visible and understandable, the costs of monitoring can be lowered. In addition, the general public is better able to monitor public sector institutions, shareholders and employees have a better view of corporate management, creditors monitor borrowers more adequately, and depositors are able to keep an eye on banks. Poor decisions do not go unnoticed or unquestioned.

1.5.3 Transparency and accountability are mutually reinforcing. Transparency enhances accountability by facilitating monitoring, while accountability enhances transparency by providing an incentive for agents to ensure that their actions are disseminated properly and understood. Greater transparency reduces the tendency of markets to place undue emphasis on positive or negative news and thus reduces volatility in financial markets. Taken together, transparency and accountability also impose discipline that improves the quality of decision making in the public sector. This can result in more efficient policies by improving the private sector's understanding of how policy makers may react to events in the future. Transparency forces institutions to face up to the reality of a situation and makes officials more responsible, especially if they know they will have to justify their views, decisions, and actions. For these reasons, timely policy adjustment is encouraged.

1.5.4 The provision of transparent and useful information on market participants and their transactions is an essential part of an orderly and efficient market; it also is a key prerequisite for imposing market discipline. For a risk-based approach to bank management and supervision to be effective, useful information must be provided to each key player: supervisors, current and prospective shareholders and bondholders, depositors and other creditors, correspondent and other banks, counterparties, and the general public. Left alone, markets may not generate sufficient levels of disclosure. Although market forces normally balance the marginal benefits and costs of disclosing additional information, the end result may not be what players really need.

1.5.5 The public disclosure of information is predicated on the existence of quality accounting standards and adequate disclosure methodology. The process normally involves publication of relevant qualitative and quantitative information in annual financial reports, which are often supplemented by biannual or quarterly financial statements and other important information. Because the provision of information can be expensive, disclosure requirements should weigh the usefulness of information for the public against the costs of providing it.

1.5.6 It is also important to time the introduction of information well. Disclosure of negative information to a public that is not sufficiently sophisticated to interpret it could damage an entity (especially if it is a financial institution). In situations where low-quality information is put forth or users are not deemed capable of properly interpreting what is disclosed, public requirements should be phased in carefully and tightened progressively. In the long run, a full-disclosure regime is beneficial, even if some immediate problems are experienced, because the cost to the financial system of not being transparent is ultimately higher than the cost of revealing information.

1.5.7 The financial and capital market liberalization of the past decades brought increasing volatility to financial markets and, consequently, increased the information needed to ensure financial stability. With the advance of financial and capital market liberalization, pressure has increased to improve the usefulness of available financial sector information through the formulation of minimum disclosure requirements. These requirements address the quality and quantity of information that must be provided to market participants and the general public.

1.5.8 Transparency and accountability are not ends in and of themselves; nor are they panaceas to solve all problems. They are designed to improve economic performance and the working of international financial markets by enhancing the quality of decision making and risk management among market participants. In particular, transparency does not change the nature of banking or the risks inherent in financial systems. Although it cannot prevent financial crises, transparency may moderate the responses of market participants to bad news by helping them to anticipate and assess negative information. In this way, transparency helps to mitigate panic and contagion.

1.5.9 A dichotomy exists between transparency and confidentiality. The release of proprietary information may enable competitors to take advantage of a particular situation, a fact that often deters market participants from full disclosure. Similarly, monitoring bodies frequently obtain confidential information from financial institutions, which can have significant market implications. Under such circumstances, financial institutions may be reluctant to provide sensitive information without the guarantee of client confidentiality. However, both unilateral transparency and full disclosure contribute to a regime of transparency. If such a regime were to become the norm, it would ultimately benefit all market participants, even if in the short term it would create discomfort for individual entities.

1.5.10 In the context of public disclosure, financial statements should be easy to interpret. Widely available and affordable financial information supports official and private monitoring of a business's financial performance. It promotes transparency and supports market discipline, two important ingredients of sound corporate governance. Besides being a goal in itself, in that it empowers stakeholders, disclosure could be a means to achieve better governance. The adoption of internationally accepted financial reporting standards is a necessary measure to facilitate transparency and contribute to proper interpretation of financial statements.

1.5.11 In the context of fair presentation, no disclosure is probably better than disclosure of misleading information. Figure 1.1 shows how transparency is secured through the IFRS framework.

Figure 1.1 Transparency in Financial Statements Achieved through Compliance with IASB Framework

---

OBJECTIVE OF FINANCIAL STATEMENTS

To provide a fair presentation of

- Financial position
- Financial performance
- Cash flows

TRANSPARENCY AND FAIR PRESENTATION

- Fair presentation is achieved through providing useful information (full disclosure), which secures transparency.
- Fair presentation equates with transparency.

SECONDARY OBJECTIVE OF FINANCIAL STATEMENTS

To secure transparency through a fair presentation of useful information (full disclosure) for decision-making purposes

ATTRIBUTES OF USEFUL INFORMATION

Existing Framework

- Relevance
- Reliability
- Comparability
- Understandability

Alternative Views

- Relevance
- Predictive value
- Faithful representation
- Free from bias
- Verifiable

Constraints

- Timeliness
- Benefit vs. cost
- Balancing the qualitative characteristics

UNDERLYING ASSUMPTIONS

Accrual basis   Going concern

EXAMPLE: FRAMEWORK FOR THE PREPARATION AND PRESENTATION OF FINANCIAL STATEMENTS

EXAMPLE 1.1

Chemco Inc. produces chemical products and sells them locally. The corporation wishes to extend its market and export some of its products. The financial director realizes that compliance with international environmental requirements is a significant precondition if the company wishes to sell products overseas. Although Chemco already has established a series of environmental policies, common practice expects an environmental audit to be done from time to time, which will cost approximately $120,000. The audit would encompass the following:

- Full review of all environmental policy directives
- Detailed analysis of compliance with these directives
- Report containing in-depth recommendations of those physical and policy changes that would be necessary to meet international requirements

The financial director of Chemco has suggested that the $120,000 be capitalized as an asset and then written off against the revenues generated from export activities so that the matching of income and expenses will occur.

EXPLANATION

The costs associated with the environmental audit can be capitalized only if they meet the definition and recognition criteria for an asset. The IASB's framework does not allow the recognition of items in the balance sheet that do not meet the definition or recognition criteria.

To recognize the costs of the audit as an asset, it should meet both the

- definition of an asset, and
- recognition criteria for an asset.

For the costs associated with the environmental audit to comply with the **definition of an asset**, the following should be valid:

i) The costs must give rise to a resource controlled by Chemco.

ii) The asset must arise from a past transaction or event, namely the audit.

iii) The asset must be expected to give rise to a probable future economic benefit that will flow to the corporation, namely the revenue from export sales.

The requirements of (i) and (iii) are not met. Therefore, Chemco cannot capitalize the costs of the audit because of the absence of fixed orders and detailed analyses of expected economic benefits.

To **recognize** the costs as an asset in the balance sheet, they must comply with the recognition criteria (see §1.4.3), namely

- The asset should have a cost that can be measured reliably.
- The expected inflow of future economic benefits must be probable.

To properly measure the carrying value of the asset, the corporation must be able to demonstrate that further costs will be incurred that would give rise to future benefits. However, the second requirement poses a problem because of insufficient evidence of the probable inflow of economic benefits and would therefore again disqualify the costs for capitalizing as an asset.

Chapter Two

First-Time Adoption of IFRS (IFRS 1)

2.1 OBJECTIVE

Specific issues occur with the first-time adoption of IFRS. IFRS 1 aims to ensure that the entity's first financial statements (including interim financial reports for that specific reporting period) under IFRS provide a suitable starting point, are transparent to users, and are comparable over all periods presented.

2.2 SCOPE OF THE STANDARD

IFRS 1 applies when an entity adopts IFRS for the first time by an explicit and unreserved statement of compliance with IFRS. The standard specifically covers

- comparable (prior period) information that is to be provided,
- identification of the basis of reporting,
- retrospective application of IFRS information, and
- formal identification of the reporting and the transition date.

IFRS requires an entity to comply with each individual standard effective at the reporting date for its first IFRS-compliant financial statements. Subject to certain exceptions and exemptions, IFRS should be applied retrospectively. Therefore, the comparative amounts, including the opening Statement of Financial Position for the comparative period, should be restated from national generally accepted accounting principles (GAAP) to IFRS.

2.3 KEY CONCEPTS

2.3.1 The **reporting date** is the Statement of Financial Position date of the first financial statements that explicitly state that they comply with IFRS (for example, December 31, 2005).

2.3.2 The **transition date** is the date of the opening Statement of Financial Position for the prior year comparative financial statements (for example, January 1, 2004, if the reporting date is December 31, 2005).

2.4 ACCOUNTING TREATMENT

Opening Statement of Financial Position (Balance Sheet)

2.4.1 The opening IFRS Statement of Financial Position as of the transition date should recognize all assets and liabilities whose recognition is required by IFRS, but not recognize items as assets or liabilities whose recognition is not permitted by IFRS.

2.4.2 With regard to **event-driven fair values**, if fair value had been used for some or all assets and liabilities under a previous GAAP, these fair values can be used as the IFRS "deemed costs" at date of measurement.

2.4.3   When preparing the opening Statement of Financial Position,

- **Recognize** all assets and liabilities whose recognition is required by IFRS. Examples of changes from national GAAP are derivatives, leases, pension liabilities and assets, and deferred tax on revalued assets. Adjustments required are debited or credited to equity.

- **Remove** assets and liabilities whose recognition is not permitted by IFRS. Examples of changes from national GAAP are deferred hedging gains and losses, other deferred costs, some internally generated intangible assets, and provisions. Adjustments required are debited or credited to equity.

- **Reclassify** items that should be classified differently under IFRS. Examples of changes from national GAAP are financial assets, financial liabilities, leasehold property, compound financial instruments, and acquired intangible assets (reclassified to goodwill). Adjustments required are reclassifications between Statement of Financial Position items.

- Apply IFRS in **measuring** assets and liabilities by using estimates that are consistent with national GAAP estimates and conditions at the transition date. Examples of changes from national GAAP are deferred taxes, pensions, depreciation, or impairment of assets. Adjustments required are debited or credited to equity.

2.4.4   **Derecognition** criteria of financial assets and liabilities are applied prospectively from the transition date. Therefore, financial assets and financial liabilities that have been derecognized under national GAAP are not reinstated. However,

- All derivatives and other interests retained after derecognition and existing at the transition date must be recognized.

- All special purposed entities (SPEs) controlled as of the transition date must be consolidated.

Derecognition criteria can be applied retroactively provided that the information needed was obtained when initially accounting for the transactions.

2.4.5   Cumulative foreign currency translation differences on translation of financial statements of a foreign operation can be deemed to be zero at transition date. Any subsequent gain or loss on disposal of operation excludes pretransition-date translation differences.

Recognition of Assets

2.4.6   With regard to **property plant and equipment**, the following amounts can be used as IFRS deemed cost:

- Fair value at transition date

- Pretransition-date revaluations, if the revaluation was broadly comparable to either fair value, or (depreciated) cost adjusted for a general or specific price index

2.4.7   With regard to **investment property**, the following amounts can be used as IFRS "deemed cost" under the cost model:

- Fair value at transition date

- Pretransition-date revaluations, if the revaluation was broadly comparable to either fair value, or (depreciated) cost adjusted for a general or specific price index

If a fair value model is used, no exemption is granted.

2.4.8 With regard to **intangible assets,** the following amounts can be used as deemed cost, provided that there is an active market for the assets:

- Fair value at transition date
- Pretransition-date revaluations if the revaluation was broadly comparable to either fair value, or (depreciated) cost adjusted for general or specific price index

2.4.9 With regard to **defined benefit plans,** the full amount of the liability or asset must be recognized, but deferrals of actuarial gains and losses at the transition date can be set to zero. For posttransition-date actuarial gains and losses, one could apply the corridor approach or any other acceptable method of accounting for such gains and losses.

2.4.10 Previously recognized **financial instruments** can be designated as trading or available for sale—from the transition date, rather than initial recognition.

2.4.11 Financial instruments comparatives for International Accounting Standard (IAS) 32 and IAS 39 need not be restated in the first IFRS financial statements. Previous national GAAP should be applied to comparative information for instruments covered by IAS 32 and IAS 39. The major adjustments to comply with IAS 32 and IAS 39 must be disclosed, but need not be quantified. Adoption of IAS 32 and IAS 39 should be treated as a change in accounting policy.

2.4.12 If the liability portion of a **compound instrument** is not outstanding at the transition date, an entity need not separate equity and liability components, thereby avoiding reclassifications within equity.

2.4.13 Hedge accounting should be applied prospectively from the transition date, provided that hedging relationships are permitted by IAS 39 and that all designation, documentation, and effectiveness requirements are met from the transition date.

Business Combinations

2.4.14 It is not necessary to restate pretransition-date **business combinations.** If any are restated, all later combinations must be restated. If information related to prior business combinations are not restated, the same classification (acquisition, reverse acquisition, and uniting of interests) must be retained. Previous GAAP carrying amounts are treated as deemed costs for IFRS purposes. However, those IFRS assets and liabilities that are not recognized under national GAAP must be recognized, and those that are not recognized under IFRS must be removed.

2.4.15 With regard to business combinations and resulting **goodwill,** if pretransition-date business combinations are not restated, then

- goodwill for contingent purchase consideration resolved before the transition date should be adjusted,
- any non-IFRS acquired intangible assets (not qualifying as goodwill) should be reclassified,
- an impairment test should be carried out on goodwill, and
- any existing negative goodwill should be credited to equity.

2.4.16 **Foreign currency translation** and pretransition-date goodwill and **fair value adjustments** should be treated as assets and liabilities of the acquirer, not the acquiree. They are not restated for postacquisition changes in exchange rates—either pre- or posttransition date.

Exemptions

2.4.17 Following are the exemptions related to the retroactive application of IFRS:

- Business combinations prior to the transition date
- Fair value or revalued amounts, which can be taken as deemed costs
- Employee benefits
- Cumulative foreign currency translation differences, goodwill, and fair value adjustments
- Financial instruments, including hedge accounting

2.5   PRESENTATION AND DISCLOSURE

2.5.1 A statement should be made to the effect that the financial statements are being prepared in terms of IFRS for the first time.

2.5.2 Prior information that cannot be easily converted to IFRS should be dealt with as follows:

- Any previous GAAP information should be prominently labeled as not being prepared under IFRS.
- Where the adjustment to the opening balance of retained earnings cannot be reasonably determined, that fact should be stated.

2.5.3 Where IFRS 1 permits a choice of transitional accounting policies, the policy selected should be stated.

2.5.4 The way in which the transition from previous GAAP to IFRS has affected the reported financial position, financial performance, and cash flows should be explained.

2.5.5 With regard to reporting date **reconciliations** from national GAAP (assume December 31, 2005), the following must be disclosed:

- Equity reconciliation at the transition date (January 1, 2004) and at the end of the last national GAAP period (December 31, 2004)
- Profit reconciliation for the last national GAAP period (December 31, 2004)

2.5.6 With regard to interim reporting reconciliations (assume interim reporting date to be June 30, 2005, and reporting date to be December 31, 2005), the following must be disclosed:

- Equity reconciliation at the transition date (January 1, 2004), at the prior year comparative date (June 30, 2004), and at the end of the last national GAAP period (December 31, 2004)
- Profit reconciliation for the last national GAAP period (December 31, 2004) and for the prior year comparative date (June 30, 2004)

2.5.7 **Impairment** losses are disclosed as follows:

- Recognized or reversed on transition to IFRS
- IAS 36 disclosures as if recognized or reversed in the period beginning on the transition date

2.5.8 Use of fair values as **deemed costs** is as follows:

- Disclosed aggregate amounts for each line item
- Disclosed adjustment from national GAAP for each line item

Chapter Three

Presentation of Financial Statements (IAS 1)

3.1 OBJECTIVE

The objective of this standard is to prescribe the basis for presentation of general purpose financial statements and what is necessary for these statements to be in accord with IFRS. The key issues are to ensure comparability both with the entity's financial statements of previous periods and with the financial statements of other entities. It also enables informed users to rely on a formal, definable structure and facilitates financial analysis.

3.2 SCOPE OF THE STANDARD

IAS 1 outlines

- what constitutes a complete set of financial statements (namely, Statement of Financial Position, Statement of Comprehensive Income, statement of changes in equity, cash flow statement, and accounting policies and notes);
- overall requirements for the presentation of financial statements, including guidelines for their structure;
- the distinction between current and noncurrent elements; and
- minimum requirements for the content of financial statements.

An updated IAS was issued in September 2007. Performance reporting and the reporting of comprehensive income are major issues dealt with, and voluntary name changes are suggested for key financial statements. These name changes are mentioned in paragraph 3.4.4 below. While the suggested new names are used throughout this publication, certain IFRS titles still contain the old names (for example, IAS 10, Events after the balance sheet date). In such cases the official title is used.

3.3 KEY CONCEPTS

3.3.1 **Fair presentation.** The financial statements should present fairly the financial position, financial performance, and cash flows of the entity. Fair presentation requires the faithful representation of the effects of transactions, other events, and conditions in accordance with the definitions and recognition criteria for assets, liabilities, income, and expenses set out in the framework. The application of IFRS is presumed to result in fair presentation.

3.3.2 Departure from the requirements of an IFRS is allowed only in the extremely rare circumstance in which the application of the IFRS would be so misleading as to conflict with the objectives of financial statements. In such circumstances, the entity should disclose the reasons for and the financial effect of the departure from the IFRS.

3.3.3 **Current assets** are

- assets expected to be realized or intended for sale or consumption in the entity's normal operating cycle,
- assets held primarily for trading,
- assets expected to be realized within 12 months after the Statement of Financial Position date, and
- cash or cash equivalents, unless restricted in use for at least 12 months.

3.3.4 **Current liabilities** are

- liabilities expected to be settled in the entity's normal operating cycle,
- liabilities held primarily for trading, and
- liabilities due to be settled within 12 months after the Statement of Financial Position date.

3.3.5 **Noncurrent assets and liabilities** are expected to be settled more than 12 months after the Statement of Financial Position date.

3.3.6 The portion of **noncurrent interest-bearing liabilities** to be settled within 12 months after the Statement of Financial Position date can be classified as noncurrent liabilities if

- the original term is greater than 12 months,
- it is the intention to refinance or reschedule the obligation, or
- the agreement to refinance or reschedule the obligation is completed on or before the Statement of Financial Position date.

3.4 ACCOUNTING TREATMENT

3.4.1 Financial statements should provide information about an entity's financial position, performance, and cash flows that is useful to a wide range of users for economic decision making.

3.4.2 **Departure from the requirements** of an IFRS is allowed only in the extremely rare circumstance in which the application of the IFRS would be so misleading as to conflict with the objectives of financial statements. In such circumstances, the entity should disclose the reasons for and the financial effect of the departure from the IFRS.

3.4.3 The **presentation and classification** of items should be consistent from one period to another unless a change would result in a more appropriate presentation, or a change is required by the IFRS.

3.4.4 A complete set of financial statements comprises the following:

- Statement of Financial Position (Balance Sheet)
- Statement of Comprehensive Income (Income Statement)
- Statement of changes in equity
- Cash flow statement
- Accounting policies and notes

Entities are encouraged to furnish other related financial and nonfinancial information in addition to the financial statements.

3.4.5 **Fair presentation**. The financial statements should present fairly the financial position, financial performance, and cash flows of the entity.

The following aspects should be addressed with regard to **compliance** with the IFRS:

- Compliance with the IFRS should be disclosed.
- Compliance with **all** requirements of each standard is compulsory.
- Disclosure does not rectify inappropriate accounting treatments.
- Premature compliance with an IFRS should be mentioned.

3.4.6 Financial statements should be presented on a going-concern basis unless management intends to liquidate the entity or cease trading. If not presented on a going-concern basis, the fact and rationale for not using it should be disclosed. Uncertainties related to events and conditions that cast significant doubt on the entity's ability to continue as a going concern should be disclosed.

3.4.7 The **accrual basis** for presentation should be used, except for the cash flow statement.

3.4.8 **Aggregation** of immaterial items of a similar nature and function is allowed. Material items should not be aggregated.

3.4.9 Assets and liabilities should not be **offset** unless allowed by the IFRS (see chapter 32 [IAS 32]). However, immaterial gains, losses, and related expenses arising from similar transactions and events can be offset.

3.4.10 With regard to **comparative information**, the following aspects are presented:

- Numerical information in respect of the previous period
- Relevant narrative and descriptive information

3.5   PRESENTATION AND DISCLOSURE

3.5.1 Financial statements should be clearly identified and distinguished from other types of information. Each component of the financial statements should be clearly identified, with the following information prominently displayed:

- Name of reporting entity
- Own statements (distinct from group statements)
- Reporting date or period
- Reporting currency
- Level of precision

Statement of Financial Position (Balance Sheet)

3.5.2 The **Statement of Financial Position** provides information about the financial position of the entity. It should distinguish between major categories and classifications of assets and liabilities.

3.5.3 **Current or noncurrent distinction.** The Statement of Financial Position should normally distinguish between current and noncurrent assets, and between current and noncurrent liabilities. Disclose as current amounts to be recovered or settled within 12 months.

3.5.4 **Liquidity-based presentation.** Where a presentation based on liquidity provides more relevant and reliable information (for example, in the case of a bank or similar financial institution), assets and liabilities should be presented in the order in which they can or might be required to be liquidated.

3.5.5. **Current assets** are

- assets expected to be realized or intended for sale or consumption in the entity's normal operating cycle
- assets held primarily for trading
- assets expected to be realized within 12 months after the Statement of Financial Position date, and
- cash or cash equivalents unless restricted in use for at least 12 months.

3.5.6 **Current liabilities** are

- liabilities expected to be settled in the entity's normal operating cycle,
- liabilities held primarily for trading, and
- liabilities due to be settled within 12 months after the Statement of Financial Position date.

3.5.7 **Long-term interest-bearing liabilities** to be settled within 12 months after the Statement of Financial Position date can be classified as noncurrent liabilities if

- the original term of the liability is greater than 12 months,
- it is the intention to refinance or reschedule the obligation,
- the agreement to refinance or reschedule the obligation is completed on or before the Statement of Financial Position date.

3.5.8 **Capital** disclosures encompass the following:

- The entity's objectives, policies, and processes for managing capital
- Quantitative data about what the entity regards as capital
- Whether the entity complies with any capital (adequacy) requirements
- Consequences of noncompliance with capital requirements, where applicable
- For each class of share capital
  - number of shares authorized
  - number of shares issued and fully paid
  - number of shares issued and not fully paid
  - par value per share, or that it has no par value
  - reconciliation of shares at beginning and end of year
  - rights, preferences, and restrictions attached to that class
  - shares in the entity held by the entity itself, subsidiaries, or associates
  - number of shares reserved for issue under options and sales contracts

3.5.9 Table 3.1 shows the **minimum information** that must appear on the face of the **Statement of Financial Position**:

Table 3.1 Minimum Information for the Statement of Financial Position

Assets	Liabilities and Equity
Property, plant, and equipment	Trade and other payables
Investment property	Provisions
Intangible assets	Financial liabilities
Financial assets	Current tax liabilities
Investments accounted for using the equity method	Deferred tax liabilities
Biological assets	Reserves
Deferred tax assets	Minority interest
Inventories	Parent shareholders' equity
Trade and other receivables	Liabilities included in disposal groups held for sale (see IFRS 5)
Current tax assets	**Equity**
Cash and cash equivalents	Non-controlling interests
Assets held for sale (see IFRS 5)	Issued capital and reserves attributable to owners of the parent
Assets included in disposal groups held for sale	

3.5.10 **Other information** that must appear on the face of the **Statement of Financial Position or in notes** includes the following:

- Nature and purpose of each reserve
- Shareholders for dividend not formally approved for payment
- Amount of cumulative preference dividend not recognized

Statement of Comprehensive Income

3.5.11 Information about performance of the entity should be provided in a single Statement of Comprehensive Income or in two statements: a separate income statement followed immediately by a statement displaying components of other comprehensive income. **Minimum information** on the face of the **Statement of Comprehensive Income** includes the following:

- Revenue
- Finance costs
- Share of profits or losses of associates and joint ventures
- Tax expense
- Discontinued operations
- Profit or loss
- Each component of other comprehensive income
- Total comprehensive income
- Profit or loss attributable to non-controlling interests
- Profit or loss attributable to owners of the parent

- Comprehensive income attributable to non-controlling interests as well as to owners of the parent

3.5.12 **Other information** on the face of the **Statement of Comprehensive Income or in notes** includes:

- Analysis of expenses based on nature or their function (see the example at the end of the chapter)
- If expenses are classified by function, disclosure of the following is required:
    - Depreciation charges for tangible assets
    - Amortization charges for intangible assets
    - Employee benefits expense
    - Dividends recognized and the related amount per share

IFRS no longer allows the presentation of any items of income or expense as extraordinary items.

Statement of Changes in Equity

3.5.13 The **statement of changes in equity** reflects information about the increase or decrease in net assets or wealth.

3.5.14 **Minimum information** on the face of the **changes in equity** statement includes the following:

- Profit or loss for the period
- Each item of income or expense recognized **directly** in equity
- Total of above two items showing separately the amounts attributable to minority shareholders and parent shareholders
- Effects of changes in accounting policy
- Effects of correction of errors

3.5.15 **Other information** on the face of the **changes in equity statement or in notes** includes the following:

- Capital transactions with owners and distributions to owners
- Reconciliation of the balance of accumulated profit or loss at beginning and end of the year
- Reconciliation of the carrying amount of each class of equity capital, share premium, and each reserve at beginning and end of the period

Other

3.5.16 For a discussion of the **cash flow statement,** refer to IAS 7 (chapter 4).

3.5.17 **Accounting policies and notes** include information that must be provided in a systematic manner and cross-referenced from the face of the financial statements to the notes:

- **Disclosure of accounting policies**
    - Measurement bases used in preparing financial statements
    - Each accounting policy used, even if it is not covered by the IFRS

- Judgments made in applying accounting policies that have the most significant effect on the amounts recognized in the financial statements
- **Estimation Uncertainty**
    - Key assumptions about the future and other key sources of estimation uncertainty that have a significant risk of causing material adjustment to the carrying amount of assets and liabilities within the next year

3.5.18 **Other disclosures** include the following:

- Domicile of the entity
- Legal form of the entity
- Country of incorporation
- Registered office or business address, or both
- Nature of operations or principal activities, or both
- Name of the parent and ultimate parent

3.6 FINANCIAL ANALYSIS AND INTERPRETATION

3.6.1 Financial analysis applies analytical tools to financial statements and other financial data to interpret trends and relationships in a consistent and disciplined manner. In essence, the analyst is in the business of converting data into information, thereby assisting in a diagnostic process that has as its objective the screening and forecasting of information.

3.6.2 The financial analyst who is interested in assessing the value or creditworthiness of an entity is required to estimate its future cash flows, assess the risks associated with those estimates, and determine the proper discount rate that should be applied to those estimates. The objective of the IFRS financial statements is to provide information that is useful to users in making economic decisions. However, IFRS financial statements do not contain all the information that an individual user might need to perform all of the above tasks, because the statements largely portray the effects of past events and do not necessarily provide nonfinancial information. IFRS financial statements do contain data about the past performance of an entity (its income and cash flows) as well as its current financial condition (assets and liabilities) that are useful in assessing future prospects and risks. The financial analyst must be capable of using the financial statements in conjunction with other information to reach valid investment conclusions.

3.6.3 The **notes** to financial statements are an integral part of the IFRS financial reporting process. They provide important detailed disclosures required by IFRS, as well as other information provided voluntarily by management. The notes include information on such topics as the following:

- Specific accounting policies that were used in compiling the financial statements
- Terms of debt agreements
- Lease information
- Off-Statement of Financial Position financing
- Breakdowns of operations by important segments
- Contingent assets and liabilities

■   Detailed pension plan disclosure

3.6.4   **Supplementary schedules** can be provided in financial reports to present additional information that can be beneficial to users. These schedules include such information as the five-year performance record of a company, a breakdown of unit sales by product line, a listing of mineral reserves, and so forth.

3.6.5   The management of publicly traded companies in certain jurisdictions, such as the United States, is required to provide a **discussion and analysis** of the company's operations and prospects. This discussion normally includes the following:

■   A review of the company's financial condition and its operating results

■   An assessment of the significant effects of currently known trends, events, and uncertainties on the company's liquidity, capital resources, and operating results

■   The capital resources available to the firm and its liquidity

■   Extraordinary or unusual events (including discontinued operations) that have a material effect on the company

■   A review of the performance of the operating segments of the business that have a significant impact on the business or its finances

The publication of such a report is encouraged, but is currently not required by IFRS.

3.6.6   Ratio analysis is used by analysts and managers to assess company performance and status. Ratios are not meaningful when used on their own, which is why trend analysis (the monitoring of a ratio or group of ratios over time) and comparative analysis (the comparison of a specific ratio for a group of companies in a sector, or for different sectors) is preferred by financial analysts. Another analytical technique of great value is relative analysis, which is achieved through the conversion of all Statement of Financial Position (or Statement of Comprehensive Income) items to a percentage of a given Statement of Financial Position (or Statement of Comprehensive Income) item.

3.6.7   Although financial analysts use a variety of subgroupings to describe their analysis, the following classifications of risk and performance are often used:

■   **Liquidity.** An indication of the entity's ability to repay its short-term liabilities, measured by evaluating components of current assets and current liabilities.

■   **Solvency.** The risk related to the volatility of income flows, often described as business risk (resulting from the volatility related to operating income, sales, and operating leverage) and financial risk (resulting from the impact of the use of debt on equity returns as measured by debt ratios and cash flow coverage).

■   **Operational efficiency.** Determination of the extent to which an entity uses its assets and capital efficiently, as measured by asset and equity turnover.

■   **Growth.** The rate at which an entity can grow as determined by its retention of profits and its profitability measured by return on equity (ROE).

■   **Profitability.** An indication of how a company's profit margins relate to sales, average capital, and average common equity. Profitability can be further analyzed through the use of the Du Pont analysis.

3.6.8 Some have questioned the usefulness of financial statement analysis in a world where capital markets are said to be efficient. After all, they say, an efficient market is forward looking, whereas the analysis of financial statements is a look at the past. However, the value of financial analysis is that it enables the analyst to gain insights that can assist in making forward-looking projections required by an efficient market. Financial ratios serve the following purposes:

- They provide insights into the microeconomic relationships within a firm that help analysts project earnings and free cash flow (which is necessary to determine entity value and creditworthiness).

- They provide insights into a firm's financial flexibility, which is its ability to obtain the cash required to meet financial obligations or to make asset acquisitions, even if unexpected circumstances should develop. Financial flexibility requires a firm to possess financial strength (a level and trend of financial ratios that meet or exceed industry norms); lines of credit; or assets that can be easily used as a means of obtaining cash, either by selling them outright or by using them as collateral.

- They provide a means of evaluating management's ability. Key performance ratios, such as the ROE, can serve as quantitative measures for ranking management's ability relative to a peer group.

3.6.9 Financial ratio analysis is limited by the following:

- **The use of alternative accounting methods**. Accounting methods play an important role in the interpretation of financial ratios. Ratios are usually based on data taken from financial statements. Such data are generated via accounting procedures that might not be comparable among firms, because firms have latitude in the choice of accounting methods. This lack of consistency across firms makes comparability difficult to analyze and limits the usefulness of ratio analysis. The various accounting alternatives currently found (but not necessarily allowed by IFRS) include the following:
  - First-in-first-out (FIFO) or last-in-first-out (LIFO) inventory valuation methods
  - Cost or equity methods of accounting for unconsolidated associates
  - Straight-line or accelerated-consumption-pattern methods of depreciation
  - Capitalized or operating lease treatment

  IFRS seeks to make the financial statements of different entities comparable and so overcome these difficulties.

- **The homogeneity of a firm's operating activities**. Many firms are diversified, with divisions operating in different industries. This makes it difficult to find comparable industry ratios to use for comparison purposes. It is better to examine industry-specific ratios by lines of business.

- **The need to determine whether the results of the ratio analysis are consistent**. One set of ratios might show a problem, and another set might prove that this problem is short term in nature, with strong long-term prospects.

- **The need to use judgment**. The analyst must use judgment when performing ratio analysis. A key issue is whether a ratio for a firm is within a reasonable range for an industry, and the analyst must determine this range. Although financial ratios are used to help assess the growth potential and risk of a business, they cannot be used alone to directly value a company or determine its creditworthiness. The entire operation of the business must be examined, and the external economic and industry setting in which it is operating must be considered when interpreting financial ratios.

3.6.10 Financial ratios mean little by themselves. Their meaning can only be gleaned by using them in the context of other information. In addition to the items mentioned in 3.6.9 above, an analyst should evaluate financial ratios based on the following:

- **Experience.** An analyst with experience obtains a feel for the right ratio relationships.
- **Company goals.** Actual ratios can be compared with company objectives to determine if the objectives are being attained.
- **Industry norms (cross-sectional analysis).** A company can be compared with others in its industry by relating its financial ratios to industry norms or a subset of the companies in an industry. When industry norms are used to make judgments, care must be taken, because
  - Many ratios are industry specific, but not all ratios are important to all industries.
  - Differences in corporate strategies can affect certain financial ratios. (It is a good practice to compare the financial ratios of a company with those of its major competitors. Typically, the analyst should be wary of companies whose financial ratios are too far above or below industry norms.)
- **Economic conditions.** Financial ratios tend to improve when the economy is strong and to weaken during recessions. Therefore, financial ratios should be examined in light of the phase of the economy's business cycle.
- **Trend (time-series analysis).** The trend of a ratio, which shows whether it is improving or deteriorating, is as important as its current absolute level.

3.6.11 The more **aggressive the accounting methods**, the lower the quality of earnings; the lower the quality of earnings, the higher the risk assessment; the higher the risk assessment, the lower the value of the company being analyzed (see table 3.2).

Table 3.2 Manipulation of Earnings via Accounting Methods That Distort the Principles of IFRS

Financial Statement Item	Aggressive Treatment (bending the intention of IFRS)	"Conservative" Treatment
Revenue	Aggressive accruals	Installment sales or cost recovery
Inventory	FIFO-IFRS treatment	LIFO (where allowed—not allowed per IFRS anymore)
Depreciation	Straight line (usual under IFRS) with higher salvage value	Accelerated-consumption-pattern methods (lower salvage value)
Warranties or bad debts	High estimates	Low estimates
Amortization period	Longer or increasing	Shorter or decreasing
Discretionary expenses	Deferred	Incurred
Contingencies	Footnote only	Accrue
Management compensation	Accounting earnings as basis	Economic earnings as basis
Prior period adjustments	Frequent	Infrequent
Change in auditors	Frequent	Infrequent
Costs	Capitalize	Expense

3.6.12 Table 3.3 provides an overview of some of the **ratios that can be calculated** using each of the classification areas discussed in 3.6.7.

3.6.13 When performing an analysis for specific purposes, various elements from different ratio classification groupings can be combined, as seen in table 3.4.

Table 3.3 Ratio Categories

1. Liquidity	Numerator	Denominator
Current	Current assets	Current liabilities
Quick	Cash + marketable securities + receivables	Current liabilities
Cash	Cash + marketable securities	Current liabilities
Receivables turnover	Net annual sales	Average receivables
Average receivables collection period	365	Receivables turnover
Inventory turnover	Cost of goods sold	Average inventory
Average inventory processing period	365	Inventory turnover
Payables turnover	Cost of goods sold	Average trade payables
Payables payment period	365	Payables turnover
Cash conversion cycle	Average receivables collection period + average inventory processing period − payables payment period	N/A

2. Solvency (Business and Financial Risk Analysis)

	Numerator	Denominator
Business risk (coefficient of variation)	Standard deviation of operating income	Income
Business risk (coefficient of variation) – net income	Standard deviation of net income	Mean net income
Sales variability	Standard deviation of sales	Mean sales
Operating leverage	Mean of absolute value of % change in operating expenses	Percentage (%) change in sales
Debt-equity	Total long-term debt	Total equity
Long-term debt ratio	Total long-term debt	Total long-term capital
Total debt ratio	Total debt	Total capital
Interest coverage	EBIT (Earnings before interest and taxes)	Interest expense
Fixed financial cost coverage	EBIT	Interest expense + one-third of lease payments
Fixed charge coverage	EBIT + lease payments	Interest payments + lease payments + preferred dividends / (1 − tax rate)
Cash flow to interest expense	Net income + depreciation expense + increase in deferred taxes	Interest expense
Cash flow coverage of fixed financial cost coverage	Traditional cash flow + interest expense + one-third of lease payments	Interest expense + one-third of lease payments
Cash flow to long-term debt	Net income + depreciation expense + increase in deferred taxes	Book value of long-term debt
Cash flow to total debt	Net income + depreciation expense + increase in deferred taxes	Total debt
Financial risk	Volatility caused by firm's use of debt	N/A

continued

Table 3.3 Ratio Categories (continued)

3. Operational Efficiency (Activity)

	Numerator	Denominator
Total asset turnover	Net sales	Average net assets
Fixed asset turnover	Net sales	Average total fixed assets
Equity turnover	Net sales	Average equity

4. Growth

	Numerator	Denominator
Sustainable growth rate	Retention rate of earning reinvested (RR) × (ROE)	N/A
RR (retention rate)	Dividends declared	Operating income after taxes
Return on equity – ROE	Net income − preferred dividends	Average common equity
Payout ratio	Common dividends declared	Net income − preferred dividends

5. Profitability

	Numerator	Denominator
Gross profit margin	Gross profit	Net sales
Operating profit margin	Operating profit (EBIT)	Net sales
Net profit margin	Net income	Net sales
Return on total capital	Net income + interest expense	Average total capital
Return on total equity	Net income	Average total equity
Return on common equity	Net income − preferred dividends	Average common equity
Du Pont 1: ROE **ROA x Financial Leverage**	Net income	Equity
Net profit margin	Net income	Revenue
× Asset turnover	Revenue	Average assets
× Financial leverage	Average assets	Average equity
Du Pont 2: ROE	Net income	Equity
Operating profit margin	Operating profit (EBIT)	Revenue
× Interest burden	Earnings before tax (EBT)	Operating profit (EBIT)
× Tax burden	Net income	Earnings before tax (EBT)
× Asset turnover	Revenue	Average assets
× Financial leverage	Average assets	Average equity

Table 3.4 Combining Ratios for Specific Analytical Purposes

Purpose of analysis	Ratio Used					
	Liquidity	Solvency (business and financial risk analysis)	Operational efficiency (activity)	Growth	Profitability	External liquidity
Stock/equity valuation		Debt/equity		Dividend payout rate	Return on equity (ROE)	Market price to book value
		Interest coverage		RR (retention rate)	Return on common equity	Market price to cash flow
		Business risk (coefficient of variation of operating earnings)				Market price to sales
		Business risk (coefficient of variation) — net income				
		Sales variability Systematic risk (beta) Sales/earnings growth rates Cash flow growth rate				
	Current ratio	Total debt ratio	Dividend payout		Asset size	Market value of stock outstanding
	Working capital to total assets	Cash flow to total debt				
Risk measurement		Interest coverage				
		Cash flow to total debt				
		Business risk (coefficient of variation of operating earnings/operating profit margins)				
Credit analysis for bond ratings		Long-term debt ratio	Equity turnover		Net profit margin (ROE)	Market value of stock outstanding
		Total debt ratio	Working capital to sales ratio		Return on assets (ROA)	Par value of bonds
		Cash flow to total debt	Total asset turnover		Operating profit margin	
		Cash flow coverage of fixed financial cost			ROE	
		Cash flow to interest expense				
		Variability of sales/net income and ROA				

continued

Table 3.4 Combining Ratios for Specific Analytical Purposes (continued)

Purpose of analysis	Liquidity	Solvency (business and financial risk analysis)	Operational efficiency (activity)	Growth	Profitability	External liquidity
	Current	Cash flow to total debt	Total asset turnover		ROA	Market value of stock to book value of debt
Forecasting bankruptcy	Cash	Cash flow to LT debt	Working capital to sales ratio		ROA	
		Total debt ratio			EBIT to total assets	
		Total debt and total assets			Retained earnings to total assets	
	Quick (acid test)	Operating leverage	Fixed asset turnover	Sustainable growth rate	Gross profit margin	Number of securities traded per day
	Receivables turnover	Financial risk (volatility caused by firm's use of debt)			Operating profit margin	Bid/asked spread
	Average receivables collection period	Fixed financial cost coverage				Percentage of outstanding securities traded per day
	Inventory turnover	Fixed charge coverage			Return on total capital	
Other—not used above	Average inventory processing period				Return on total capital including leases	
	Payables turnover				Du Pont 1	
	Payables payment period				Du Pont 2	
	Cash conversion cycle					

EXAMPLE: PRESENTATION OF FINANCIAL STATEMENTS

ABC Group – Statement of financial position as at 31 December		
	20X8	20X7
ASSETS		
Non-current assets		
Property, plant and equipment		
Goodwill		
Other intangible assets		
Investments in associates		
Available-for-sale financial assets		
Current assets		
Inventories		
Trade receivables		
Other current assets		
Cash and cash equivalents		
Total assets		
EQUITY AND LIABILITIES		
Equity attributable to owners of the parent		
Share capital		
Retained earnings		
Other components of equity		
Non-controlling interests		
Total equity		
Non-current liabilities		
Long-term borrowings		
Deferred tax		
Long-term provisions		
Total non-current liabilities		
Current liabilities		
Trade and other payables		
Short-term borrowings		
Current portion of long-term borrowings		
Current tax payable		
Short-term provisions		
Total current liabilities		
Total liabilities		
TOTAL EQUITY AND LIABILITIES		

continued

EXAMPLE: PRESENTATION OF FINANCIAL STATEMENTS (continued)

ABC Group—Statement of Comprehensive Income for the Year Ended	20X8	20X7
Revenue		
Cost of sales		
Gross profit		
Other income		
Distribution costs		
Administrative expenses		
Other expenses		
Finance costs		
Share of profit of associates		
Profit before tax		
Income tax expense		
Profit for the year from continuing operations		
Loss for the year from discontinued operations		
PROFIT FOR THE YEAR		
Other comprehensive income:		
Exchange differences on translating foreign operations		
Available-for-sale financial assets		
Cash flow hedges		
Gains on property revaluation		
Actuarial gains (losses) on defined benefit pension plans		
Share of other comprehensive income of associates		
Income tax relating to components of other comprehensive income		
Other comprehensive income for the year, net of tax		
TOTAL COMPREHENSIVE INCOME FOR THE YEAR		

Chapter Four

Cash Flow Statements (IAS 7)

4.1   OBJECTIVE

The cash flow statement is a separate financial statement that provides additional information for evaluating the solvency and liquidity of the entity. Cash flow is also relevant for identifying

- movement in cash balances for the period,
- timing and certainty of cash flows,
- ability of the entity to generate cash and cash equivalents, and
- prediction of future cash flows (useful for valuation models).

4.2   SCOPE OF THE STANDARD

All entities are required to present a cash flow statement that reports cash flows during the reporting period. Either the direct or the indirect method of reporting can be used. Cash and cash equivalents must be defined. Cash flows must be classified as follows:

- Operating activities
- Investing activities
- Financing activities

4.3   KEY CONCEPTS

4.3.1   An entity should present a **cash flow statement** that reports cash flows during the reporting period, classified by operating, financing, and investing activities.

4.3.2   **Cash flows** are inflows and outflows of cash and cash equivalents.

4.3.3   **Cash** comprises

- cash on hand, and
- demand deposits (net of bank overdrafts repayable on demand).

4.3.4   **Cash equivalents** are short-term, highly liquid investments (such as short-term debt securities) that readily convert to cash and that are subject to an insignificant risk of changes in value.

4.3.5   **Operating activities** are principal revenue-producing activities and other activities that do not include investing or financing activities.

4.3.6   **Investing activities** are acquisition and disposal of long-term assets and other investments not included as cash-equivalent investments.

4.3.7   **Financing activities** are activities that change the size and composition of the equity capital and borrowings.

4.4   ACCOUNTING TREATMENT

4.4.1   Cash flows from **operating activities** are reported using either the direct or indirect method:

- The **direct method** discloses major classes of gross cash receipts and gross cash payments (for example, sales, cost of sales, purchases, and employee benefits).
- The **indirect method** adjusts profit and loss for the period for
  - effects of noncash transactions,
  - deferrals or accruals, and
  - investing or financing cash flows.

4.4.2   Cash flows from **investing activities** are reported as follows:

- Major classes of **gross cash receipts** and **gross cash payments** are reported separately.
- The aggregate cash flows from acquisitions or disposals of subsidiaries and other business units are classified as investing.

4.4.3   Cash flows from **financing activities** are reported by separately listing major classes of gross cash receipts and **gross cash payments**.

4.4.4   The following cash flows can be reported on a **net** basis:

- Cash flows on behalf of customers
- Items for which the turnover is quick, the amounts large, and maturities short (for example, purchase and sale of investments)

4.4.5   Interest and dividends paid should be treated consistently as either operating or financing activities. Interest and dividends received are treated as investing inflows. However, in the case of financial institutions, interest paid and dividends received are usually classified as operating cash flows.

4.4.6   Cash flows from taxes on income are normally classified as operating (unless specifically identified with financing or investing).

4.4.7   A foreign exchange transaction is recorded in the functional currency using the exchange rate at the date of the cash flow.

4.4.8   Foreign operations' cash flows are translated at exchange rates on dates of cash flows.

4.4.9   When entities are equity or cost accounted, only actual cash flows from them (for example, dividends received) are shown in the cash flow statement.

4.4.10   Cash flows from joint ventures are proportionately included in the cash flow statement.

4.5   PRESENTATION AND DISCLOSURE

4.5.1   The following should be disclosed:

- Cash and cash equivalents in the cash flow statement and a reconciliation with the equivalent items in the Statement of Financial Position
- Details about noncash investing and financing transactions (for example, conversion of debt to equity)

- Amount of cash and equivalents that are not available for use by the group
- Amount of undrawn borrowing facilities available for future operating activities and to settle capital commitments (indicating any restrictions)
- Aggregate amount of cash flows from each of the three activities (operating, investing, and financing) related to interest in joint ventures
- Amount of cash flows arising from each of the three activities regarding each reported business and geographical segment
- Distinction between the cash flows that represent an increase in operating capacity and those that represent the maintenance of it

4.5.2 The following should be shown in aggregate for either the purchase or sale of a subsidiary or business unit:

- Total purchase or disposal consideration
- Purchase or disposal consideration paid in cash and equivalents
- Amount of cash and equivalents in the entity acquired or disposed
- Amount of assets and liabilities other than cash and equivalents in the entity acquired or disposed

4.6   FINANCIAL ANALYSIS AND INTERPRETATION

4.6.1 The IFRS statement of cash flows shows the sources of the cash inflows received by an entity during an accounting period, and the purposes for which cash was used. The statement is an integral part of the analysis of a business because it enables the analyst to determine the following:

- The ability of a company to generate cash from its operations
- The cash consequences of investing and financing decisions
- The effects of management's decisions about financial policy
- The sustainability of a firm's cash-generating capability
- How well operating cash flow correlates with net income
- The impact of accounting policies on the quality of earnings
- Information about the liquidity and long-term solvency of a firm
- Whether or not the going-concern assumption is reasonable
- The ability of a firm to finance its growth from internally generated funds

4.6.2 Because cash inflows and outflows are objective facts, the data presented in the statement of cash flows represent economic reality. The statement reconciles the increase or decrease in a company's cash and cash equivalents that occurred during the accounting period (an objectively verifiable fact). Nevertheless, this statement must be read while keeping the following in mind:

- There are analysts who believe that accounting rules are developed primarily to promote comparability, rather than to reflect economic reality. Even if this view were to be considered harsh, it is a fact that too much flexibility in accounting can present problems for analysts who are primarily interested in assessing a company's future cash-generating capability from operations.

■ As with Statement of Comprehensive Income data, cash flows can be erratic from period to period, reflecting random, cyclical, and seasonal transactions involving cash, as well as sectoral trends. It can be difficult to decipher important long-term trends from less meaningful short-term fluctuations in such data.

4.6.3 Financial analysts can use the IFRS cash flow statement to help them determine other measures that they wish to use in their analysis—for example, free cash flow, which analysts often use to determine the value of a firm. Defining free cash flow is not an easy task, because many different measures are commonly called free cash flow.

4.6.4 **Discretionary free cash flow** is the cash that is available for discretionary purposes. According to this definition, free cash flow is the cash generated from operating activities, less the capital expenditures required to maintain the current level of operations. Therefore, the analyst must identify that part of the capital expenditure included in investing cash flows that relates to maintaining the current level of operations—a formidable task. Any excess cash flow can be used for discretionary purposes (for example, to pay dividends, reduce debt, improve solvency, or to expand and improve the business). IFRS, therefore, requires disclosure of expenditures as those expenditures that were required to maintain the current level of operations and those that were undertaken to expand or improve the business.

4.6.5 **Free cash flow available to owners** measures the ability of a firm to pay dividends to its owners. In this case, all of the cash used for investing activities (capital expenditures, acquisitions, and long-term investments) is subtracted from the cash generated from operating activities. In effect, this definition states that the firm should be able to pay out as dividends cash from operations that is left over after the firm makes the investments that management deems necessary to maintain and grow current operations.

4.6.6 Generally, the cash generated from operating activities is greater than net income for a well-managed, financially healthy company; if it is not, the analyst should be suspicious of the company's solvency. Growth companies often have negative free cash flows because their rapid growth requires high capital expenditures and other investments. Mature companies often have positive free cash flows, whereas declining firms often have significantly positive free cash flows because their lack of growth means a low level of capital expenditures. High and growing free cash flows, therefore, are not necessarily positive or negative; much depends upon the stage of the industry life cycle in which a company is operating. This is why the free cash flow has to be assessed in conjunction with the firm's income prospects.

4.6.7 Many valuation models use cash flow from operations, thus giving management an incentive to record inflows as operating (normal and recurring), and outflows as related to either investing or financing. Other areas where management discretionary choices could influence the presentation of cash flows follow:

■ **Payment of taxes**. Management has a vested interest in reducing current-year payments of taxes by choosing accounting methods on the tax return that are likely to defer tax payments to the future.

■ **Discretionary expenses**. Management can manipulate cash flow from operations by timing the payment or incurring certain discretionary expenses such as research and development, repairs and maintenance, and so on. Cash inflows from operations can also be increased by the timing of the receipt of deposits on long-term contracts.

- **Leasing**. The entire cash outflow of an operating lease reduces the cash flow from operations. For a capital lease, the cash payment is allocated between operating and financing, thus increasing cash flow from operations.

EXAMPLE 4.1

During the year ending 20X1, ABC Company completed the following transactions:

1. Purchased a new machine for $13.0 million

2. Paid cash dividends totaling $8.0 million

3. Purchased Treasury stock (own shares) totaling $45.0 million

4. Spent $27.0 million on operating expenses, of which $10.0 million was paid in cash and the remainder put on credit

Which of the following correctly classifies each of the above transaction items on the operating, investing, and financing activities on the statement of cash flows?

	Transaction 1	Transaction 2	Transaction 3	Transaction 4
a.	Investing inflow	Operating outflow	Financing outflow	All expenses—operating outflow
b.	Financing outflow	Financing outflow	Investing outflow	Cash paid (only)—operating outflow
c.	Investing outflow	Financing outflow	Financing outflow	Cash paid (only)—operating outflow
d.	Financing inflow	Operating outflow	Financing inflow	Cash paid (only)—operating outflow

EXPLANATION

Choice c. is correct. Each transaction had both the proper statement of cash flow activity and the correct cash inflow or outflow direction.

Choice a. is incorrect. This choice incorrectly classifies the cash flow activities for transactions 1, 2, and 4.

Choice b. is incorrect. This choice incorrectly classifies the cash flow activities for transactions 1 and 3.

Choice d. is incorrect. This choice incorrectly classifies the cash flow activities for transactions 1, 2, and 3.

Note: Dividends are sometimes classified as an operating cash flow.

EXAMPLE 4.2

Gibson Entities had the following financial data for the year ended December 31, 20X2:

	Millions of $
Capital expenditures	75.0
Dividends declared	1.2
Net income	17.0
Common stock issued	33.0
Increase in accounts receivable	12.0
Depreciation and amortization	3.5
Proceeds from sale of assets	6.0
Gain on sale of assets	0.5

Based on the above, what is the ending cash balance at December 31, 20X2, assuming an opening cash balance of $47.0 million?

a. $13.0 million

b. $17.8 million

c. $19.0 million

d. $43.0 million

EXPLANATION

Choice c. is correct. The answer is based on the following calculation:

	Millions of $
Operating cash flow	
Net income	17.0
Depreciation and amortization	3.5
Gain on sale of assets	(0.5)
Increase in accounts receivable	(12.0)
Operating cash flow	8.0
Investing cash flow	
Capital expenditures	(75.0)
Proceeds from sale of assets	6.0
Investing cash flow	(69.0)
Financing cash flow	
Common stock issued	33.0
Financing cash flow	33.0
Net change in cash (8 − 69 + 33)	(28.0)
Beginning cash	47.0
Ending cash	19.0

Note that the dividends had only been declared, not paid.

EXAMPLE 4.3

The following are the abridged annual financial statements of Linco Inc.

Statement of Comprehensive Income for the Year Ending September 30, 20X4	$
Revenue	850,000
Cost of sales	(637,500)
Gross profit	212,500
Administrative expenses	(28,100)
Operating expenses	(73,600)
Profit from operations	110,800
Finance cost	(15,800)
Profit before tax	95,000
Income tax expense	(44,000)
Profit for the period	51,000

Statement of Changes in Equity for the Year Ending September 30, 20X4	Share capital ($)	Revaluation reserve ($)	Accumulated profit ($)	Total ($)
Balance—beginning of the year	120,000		121,000	241,000
Revaluation of buildings		20,000		20,000
Profit for the period			51,000	51,000
Dividends paid			(25,000)	(25,000)
Repayment of share capital	(20,000)			(20,000)
Balance—end of the year	100,000	20,000	147,000	267,000

continued

EXAMPLE 4.3 (continued)

Statement of Financial Position at September 30, 20X4

	20X4 ($)	20X3 ($)
Noncurrent Assets		
Property, plant, and equipment		
Office buildings	250,000	220,000
Machinery	35,000	20,000
Motor vehicles	6,000	4,000
Long-term loans to directors	64,000	60,000
	355,000	304,000
Current Assets		
Inventories	82,000	42,000
Debtors	63,000	43,000
Prepaid expenses	21,000	16,000
Bank	–	6,000
	166,000	107,000
Total Assets	**521,000**	**411,000**
Equity and Liabilities **Capital and Reserves**		
Share capital	100,000	120,000
Revaluation reserve	20,000	–
Accumulated profits	147,000	121,000
	267,000	241,000
Noncurrent Liabilities		
Long-term borrowings	99,000	125,000
Current Liabilities		
Creditors	72,000	35,000
Bank	43,000	–
Taxation due	40,000	10,000
	155,000	45,000
Total Equity and Liabilities	**521,000**	**411,000**

Additional information

1. The following depreciation charges are included in operating expenses:

Machinery	$25,000
Motor vehicles	$ 2,000

2. Fully depreciated machinery with an original cost price of $15,000 was sold for $5,000 during the year. The profit is included in operating expenses.

3. The financial manager mentions that the accountants allege the company is heading for a possible liquidity crisis. According to him, the company struggled to meet its short-term obligations during the current year.

EXPLANATION

The cash flow statement would be presented as follows if the **direct method** were used for its preparation:

LINCO INC. Cash Flow Statement for the Year Ending September 30, 20X4	$
Cash flows from operating activities	
Cash receipts from customers **(Calculation e)**	830,000
Cash payments to suppliers and employees **(Calculation f)**	(725,200)
Net cash generated by operations	104,800
Interest paid	(15,800)
Taxation paid **(Calculation d)**	(14,000)
Dividends paid	(25,000)
	50,000
Cash flows from investing activities	
Purchases of property, plant and equipment **(Calc. a, b, c)**	(54,000)
Proceeds on sale of machinery	5,000
Loans to directors	(4,000)
	(53,000)
Cash flows from financing activities	
Decrease in long-term loan (125 – 99)	(26,000)
Repayment of share capital	(20,000)
	(46,000)
Net decrease in bank balance for the period	(49,000)
Bank balance at beginning of the year	6,000
Overdraft at end of the year	**(43,000)**

Commentary

1. The total increase in creditors was used to partially finance the increase in working capital.

2. The rest of the increase in working capital as well as the interest paid, taxation paid, and dividends paid were financed by cash generated from operations.

3. The remaining balance of cash generated by operating activities and the proceeds on the sale of fixed assets were used to finance the purchase of fixed assets.

4. The overdrawn bank account was used for the repayment of share capital and the redemption of the long-term loan.

CALCULATIONS

		$
a.	**Office buildings**	
	Balance at beginning of year	220,000
	Revaluation	20,000
	Purchases (balancing figure)	10,000
	Balance at end of the year	250,000
b.	**Machinery**	
	Balance at beginning of year	20,000
	Depreciation	(25,000)
	Purchases (balancing figure)	40,000
	Balance at end of the year	35,000
c.	**Vehicles**	
	Balance at beginning of year	4,000
	Depreciation	(2,000)
	Purchases (balancing figure)	4,000
	Balance at end of the year	6,000
d.	**Taxation**	
	Amount due at beginning of year	10,000
	Charge in income statement	44,000
	Paid in cash (balancing figure)	(14,000)
	Amount due at end of the year	40,000
e.	**Cash receipts from customers**	
	Sales	850,000
	Increase in debtors (63 – 43)	(20,000)
		830,000
f.	**Cash payments to suppliers and employees**	
	Cost of sales	637,500
	Administrative expenses	28,100
	Operating expenses	73,600
	Adjusted for non-cash flow items:	
	Depreciation	(27,000)
	Profit on sale of machinery	5,000
	Increase in inventories (82 – 42)	40,000
	Increase in creditors (72 – 35)	(37,000)
	Increase in prepaid expenses (21 – 16)	5,000
		725,200

Chapter Five

Accounting Policies, Changes in Accounting Estimates, and Errors (IAS 8)

5.1   OBJECTIVE

This standard prescribes the criteria for selecting and changing accounting policies, changes in accounting estimates, and correction of errors. The standard aims at enhancing the relevance, reliability, and comparability of an entity's financial statements.

5.2   SCOPE OF THE STANDARD

IAS 8 covers situations where the entity

- is selecting and applying accounting policies,
- is accounting for changes in accounting policies,
- has changes in accounting estimates, and
- has corrections of prior-period errors.

5.3   KEY CONCEPTS

5.3.1   **Accounting policies** are specific principles, bases, conventions, rules, and practices applied by an entity in preparing and presenting financial statements.

5.3.2   **Changes in accounting estimates** result from new information or new developments and, accordingly, are not corrections of errors or changes in policy. Changes in accounting estimates result in adjustments of an asset's or liability's carrying amount or the amount of the periodic consumption of an asset that result from the assessment of the present status of, and expected future benefits and obligations associated with, assets and liabilities. For example, a change in the method of depreciation results from new information about the use of the related asset and is, therefore, a change in accounting estimate.

5.3.3   **Prior-period errors** are omissions from and misstatements in the entity's financial statements for one or more prior periods. Errors arise from a failure to use, or a misuse of, reliable information that

- was available when prior-period financial statements were authorized for issue, or

> could reasonably have been obtained and taken into account in the preparation and presentation of those financial statements.

Such errors include the effects of

- mathematical mistakes,
- mistakes in applying accounting policies,
- oversights or misinterpretations of facts, or
- fraud.

5.3.4 Omissions or misstatements are **material** if they could, individually or collectively, influence users' economic decisions that are made on the basis of the financial statements.

5.3.5 **Impracticable changes** are requirements that an entity cannot apply after making every **reasonable effort** to do so. The application of a change in accounting policy or retrospective correction of an error becomes impracticable when

- effects are not determinable,
- assumptions about management intent in a prior period are required, and
- it is impossible to distinguish information about circumstances in a prior period and information that was available in that period from other information.

5.4 ACCOUNTING TREATMENT

5.4.1 When a standard or an interpretation **specifically applies** to a transaction, other event, or condition, the **accounting policy** or policies applied to that item should be **determined (chosen)** by applying the standard or interpretation, considering any implementation guidance issued by the IASB for that standard or interpretation.

5.4.2 In the **absence of specific guidance on accounting policies** (that is, a standard or an interpretation that specifically applies to a transaction, other event, or condition), management should use its judgment in developing and applying an accounting policy that results in relevant and reliable information. In making the judgment, management should consider the applicability of the following factors in the following order:

- The requirements and guidance in standards and interpretations dealing with similar and related issues
- The definitions, recognition criteria, and measurement concepts for assets, liabilities, income, and expenses in the framework

To the extent that there is no conflict with the above, management may also consider the following:

- The most recent pronouncements of other standard-setting bodies that use a similar conceptual framework
- Other accounting literature and accepted industry practices

5.4.3 Accounting policies are **applied consistently** for similar transactions, other events, and conditions (unless a standard or interpretation requires or permits categorization, for which different policies may be appropriate).

5.4.4 A **change in accounting policy** is allowed only under one of the following conditions:

- ■ The change is required by a standard or interpretation.
- ■ The change will provide reliable and more relevant information about the effects of transactions, other events, and conditions.

5.4.5 When a change in accounting policy results from **application of a new standard** or interpretation, any specific transitional provisions in the standard or interpretation should be followed. If there are no specific transitional provisions, the change in accounting policy should be applied in the same way as a voluntary change.

5.4.6 A **voluntary change in accounting policies** is applied as follows:

- ■ Policies are applied retroactively as though the new policy had always applied, unless it is impracticable to do so.
- ■ Opening balances are adjusted at the earliest period presented.
- ■ Policies are applied prospectively if it is impracticable to restate prior periods or to adjust opening balances.

5.4.7 Carrying amounts of assets, liabilities, or equity should be adjusted when **changes in accounting estimates necessitate a change in assets, liabilities, or equity.**

5.4.8 **Other changes in accounting estimates** should be included in the profit or loss in the period of the change, or in the period of change and future periods if the change affects both.

5.4.9 Financial statements do not comply with IFRS if they contain **prior-period material errors**. In the first set of financial statements authorized for issue after the discovery of a material error, an entity should correct material prior-period errors **retroactively** by

- ■ restating the comparative amounts for the prior period or periods presented in which the error occurred, or
- ■ restating the opening balances of assets, liabilities, and equity for the earliest prior period presented.

5.5   PRESENTATION AND DISCLOSURE

5.5.1 If an entity makes a **voluntary change in accounting policies**, it should disclose

- ■ the nature of the change,
- ■ the reason or reasons why the new policy provides reliable and more relevant information,
- ■ the adjustment in the current and each prior period presented,
- ■ the adjustment to the basic and diluted earnings per share, and
- ■ the adjustments to periods prior to those presented.

5.5.2 When initial application of a standard or an interpretation has or could have an effect on the current period or any prior period, unless it is **impracticable** to determine the amount of the adjustment, an entity should disclose

- ■ the title of the standard or interpretation,

- that the change in accounting policy is made in accordance with the standard's or interpretation's transitional provisions (when applicable),
- the nature of the change in accounting policy,
- a description of the transitional provisions (when applicable), and
- the transitional provisions that might have an effect on future periods (when applicable).

5.5.3 In considering an **impending change in accounting policy**, an entity should disclose

- pending implementation of a new standard, and
- known or reasonably estimable information relevant to assessing the possible impact of new standards.

5.5.4 With reference to a **change in accounting estimates**, an entity should disclose

- the nature of the change in the estimate, and
- the amount of the change and its effect on the current and future periods.

If estimating the future effect is impracticable, that fact should be disclosed.

5.5.5 In considering **prior-period errors**, an entity should disclose

- the nature of the error,
- the amount of correction in each prior period presented and the line items affected,
- the correction to the basic and diluted earnings per share,
- the amount of correction at the beginning of the earliest period presented, and
- the correction relating to periods prior to those presented.

5.6   FINANCIAL ANALYSIS AND INTERPRETATION

5.6.1 Analysts find it useful to break reported earnings down into recurring and nonrecurring income or losses. Recurring income is similar to permanent or sustainable income, whereas nonrecurring income is considered to be random and unsustainable. Even so-called nonrecurring events tend to recur from time to time. Therefore, analysts often exclude the effects of **nonrecurring** items when performing a short-term analysis of an entity (such as estimating next year's earnings). They also might include them on some average (per year) basis for longer-term analyses.

5.6.2 The analyst should be aware that, when it comes to reporting nonrecurring income, IFRS does not distinguish between items that are and are not likely to recur. Furthermore, IFRS does not permit any items to be classified as extraordinary items.

5.6.3 However, IFRS does require the disclosure of all material information that is relevant to an understanding of an entity's performance. It is up to the analyst to use this information, together with information from outside sources and management interviews, to determine to what extent reported profit reflects sustainable income and to what extent it reflects nonrecurring items.

5.6.4 Analysts generally need to identify such items as

- changes in accounting policies,
- changes in estimates,

- errors,
- unusual or infrequent items, and
- discontinued operations (see chapter 18).

EXAMPLES: ACCOUNTING POLICIES, CHANGES IN ACCOUNTING ESTIMATES, AND ERRORS

EXAMPLE 5.1

Which of the following items is not included in an IFRS Statement of Comprehensive Income for the current period?

a. The effects of corrections of prior-period errors

b. Income gains or losses from discontinued operations

c. Income gains or losses arising from extraordinary items

d. Adjustments resulting from changes in accounting policies

EXPLANATION

Choice a. is incorrect. An entity should correct material prior-period errors retroactively in the first set of financial statements authorized for issue after their discovery by

- restating the comparative amounts for the prior period or periods presented in which the error occurred, or
- restating the opening balances of assets, liabilities, and equity for the earliest prior period presented.

Choice b. is correct. Income gains and losses from discontinued operations (net of taxes) are shown on a separate line of the Statement of Comprehensive Income, called Income (Loss) from Discontinued Operations (see IFRS 5).

Choice c. is incorrect. The items are included in the Statement of Comprehensive Income but they are not shown as extraordinary items. (Extraordinary items are not separately classified under IAS 1.)

Choice d. is incorrect. Adjustments from changes in accounting policies should be applied retroactively, as though the new policy had always applied. Opening balances are adjusted at the earliest period feasible, when amounts prior to that period cannot be restated.

EXAMPLE 5.2

Unicurio Inc. is a manufacturer of curios that are sold at international airports. The following transactions and events occurred during the year under review:

a. As of the beginning of the year, the remaining useful life of the plant and equipment was reassessed as four years rather than seven years.

b. Bonuses of $12 million, compared with $2.3 million in the previous year, had been paid to employees. The financial manager explained that a new incentive scheme was adopted whereby all employees shared in increased sales.

c. There was a $1.25 million profit on the nationalization of land.

d. During the year, the corporation was responsible for the formation of the ECA Foundation, which donates funds to welfare organizations. This foundation forms part of the corporation's social investment program. The company contributed $7 million to the fund.

How would each transaction and event be treated in the Statement of Comprehensive Income?

EXPLANATION

Each of the transactions and events mentioned above would be **treated** as follows **in the Statement of Comprehensive Income** for the current year:

1. A change in the useful life of plants and equipment is a change in accounting estimate and is applied prospectively. Therefore, the carrying amount of the plant and equipment is written off over four years rather than seven years. All the effects of the change are included in profit or loss. The nature and amount of the change should be disclosed.

2. The item is included in profit or loss. Given its nature and size, it may need to be disclosed separately.

3. The profit is included in profit or loss (that is, it is not an "extraordinary item").

4. The contribution is included in profit or loss. It is disclosed separately if it is material.

Part II

Group Statements

Chapter Six

Business Combinations (IFRS 3)

6.1 OBJECTIVE

Many business operations take place within the context of a group structure that involves many inter-related companies and entities. IFRS 3 prescribes the accounting treatment for business combinations where control is established. It is directed principally to a group of entities in which the acquirer is the parent entity and the acquiree is a subsidiary.

IFRS 3 aims to improve the relevance, reliability, and comparability of the information that a reporting entity provides in its financial statements about a business combination and its effects. To accomplish that, this standard establishes principles and requirements for how the acquirer recognizes and measures the identifiable assets and goodwill acquired in the business combination, or its gain from a bargain purchase, in its financial statements. The core principle established is that a business should recognize assets at their acquisition-date fair values and disclose information that enables users to evaluate the nature and financial effects of the acquisition.

The IFRS framework for dealing with equity and other securities investments is outlined in table 6.1.

Table 6.1 Accounting Treatment of Various Securities Acquisitions

Acquisition of Securities		
Percentage Ownership	Accounting Treatment	IFRS Reference
Less than 20%	Fair value	IAS 39
Between 20% and 50%	Equity accounting	IAS 28
More than 50%	Consolidation and business combinations	IAS 27
Other	Joint ventures	IAS 31
	Business combinations	IFRS 3

6.2 SCOPE OF THE STANDARD

IFRS 3 addresses the following points:

- The focus is on the accounting treatment at **date of acquisition**.
- All business combinations should be accounted for by applying the **purchase method of accounting**.
- The initial measurement of the identifiable assets acquired as well as liabilities and contingent liabilities assumed in a business should be at fair value.
- The liabilities for terminating or reducing the activities of the acquired entity should be recognized.
- The accounting issues related to goodwill and intangible assets acquired in a business combination.

IFRS 3 does not apply to the following:

- Business combinations in which separate entities or businesses are brought together to form a joint venture
- Business combinations involving entities or businesses under common control
- Business combinations involving two or more mutual entities
- Business combinations in which separate entities or businesses are brought together to form a reporting entity by contract alone without obtaining an ownership interest (for example, a dual-listed corporation)

6.3 KEY CONCEPTS

6.3.1 A **business** is an integrated set of activities and assets that can be conducted and managed to provide a return in the form of dividends, lower costs, or other economic benefits.

6.3.2 A **business combination** is the bringing together of separate entities into one economic entity as a result of one entity obtaining control over the net assets and operations of another entity.

6.3.3 The **purchase method** views a business combination from the perspective of the combining entity that is identified as the **acquirer**. The acquirer purchases net assets and recognizes the assets acquired and the liabilities and contingent liabilities assumed from the acquiree, including those not previously recognized by the acquiree.

6.3.4 **Noncontrolling interest** is that portion of a subsidiary attributable to equity interests that are not owned by the parent, either directly or indirectly through subsidiaries. Noncontrolling interest is disclosed as equity in consolidated financial statements.

6.3.5 A **subsidiary** is an entity—including an unincorporated entity such as a partnership—that is controlled by another entity, known as the parent.

6.3.6 **Control** is the power to govern the financial and operating policies of an entity or **business** to obtain benefits from its activities.

6.3.7 **Fair value** is the amount for which an asset could be exchanged, or a liability settled, between knowledgeable, willing parties in an arm's-length transaction.

6.3.8 **Goodwill** is the future economic benefits arising from assets that cannot be individually identified and separately recognized.

6.4 ACCOUNTING TREATMENT

6.4.1 This standard requires an **acquirer to be identified** for every business combination within its scope. The acquirer is the combining entity that obtains control of the other combining entities or businesses.

6.4.2 An **acquisition** should be accounted for by use of the **purchase method** of accounting. From the date of acquisition, an acquirer should incorporate into the Statement of Comprehensive Income the results of operations of the acquiree, and recognize in the Statement of Financial

Position the identifiable assets, liabilities, and contingent liabilities of the acquiree as well as any goodwill arising from the acquisition. Applying the purchase method involves the following steps:

- Identifying an acquirer
- Measuring the cost of the business combination
- Allocating, at the acquisition date, the cost of the business combination to the assets acquired and liabilities and contingent liabilities assumed

6.4.3 The **cost of acquisition** carried by the acquirer is the aggregate of the fair values of assets given, liabilities incurred or assumed, and equity instruments issued by the acquirer in exchange for control of the acquiree, at the date of exchange. It includes directly attributable costs but not professional fees or the costs of issuing debt or equity securities used to settle the consideration.

6.4.4 The identifiable assets, liabilities, and contingent liabilities acquired should be those of the acquiree that existed at the date of acquisition.

6.4.5 Intangible assets should be identified separately and recognized as acquired assets if they meet the definition of an intangible asset in IAS 38.

6.4.6 If the initial accounting for a business combination can be determined only provisionally because either the fair values to be assigned or the cost of the combination can be determined only provisionally, the acquirer should account for the combination using those **provisional values**. The acquirer should recognize any adjustments to the provisional values as a result of completing the accounting within 12 months of the acquisition date.

6.4.7 The identifiable assets, liabilities, and contingent liabilities acquired should be measured at their fair values at the date of acquisition. Any minority interest should be stated at the minority's proportion of their fair values.

6.4.8 The excess of the cost of acquisition by the acquirer and noncontrolling interest, in the fair value of the identifiable assets and liabilities acquired, is described as **goodwill** and is recognized as an asset.

6.4.9 **Goodwill** should be tested for impairment annually. Goodwill is not amortized.

6.4.10 The excess or shortfall of the acquirer's interest in the fair value of the identifiable assets and liabilities acquired, over the cost of acquisition is a gain and is recognized in profit or loss. It is not recognized on the Statement of Financial Position as negative goodwill. However, before any gain is recognized, the acquirer should reassess the cost of acquisition and the fair values attributed to the acquiree's identifiable assets, liabilities, and contingent liabilities.

6.5   PRESENTATION AND DISCLOSURE

6.5.1 The acquirer should disclose information that enables users of its financial statements to evaluate the nature and financial effect of business combinations that were concluded during the period and before the financial statements are authorized for issue (in aggregate where the individual effects are immaterial). The information that should be disclosed includes the following:

- Names and descriptions of the combining entities or businesses

- Acquisition date
- Percentage of voting equity instruments acquired
- Cost of the combination and a description of the components of that cost, such as the number of equity instruments issued or issuable, the fair value of those instruments, and the basis for determining that fair value
- Details of any operations the entity has decided to dispose of as a result of the combination
- Amounts recognized at the acquisition date for each class of the acquiree's assets, liabilities, and contingent liabilities
- Amount of any excess (negative goodwill) recognized in profit or loss, and the line item in the Statement of Comprehensive Income in which the excess is recognized
- A description of factors that contributed to goodwill
- A description of each intangible asset that was not recognized separately from goodwill
- The amount of the acquiree's profit or loss since the acquisition date included in the acquirer's profit or loss for the period
- The revenue and profit and loss of the combined entity for the period as though the acquisition date for all business combinations concluded during the period had been the beginning of that period

6.5.2   Information to enable users to evaluate the effects of adjustments that relate to prior business combinations should be disclosed.

6.5.3   All information necessary to evaluate changes in the carrying amount of goodwill during the period must be disclosed.

Business Combinations Concluded After the Date of the Statement of Financial Position

To the extent practicable, the disclosures mentioned above should be furnished for all business combinations concluded after the date of the Statement of Financial Position. If it is impracticable to disclose any of this information, this fact should be disclosed.

6.6   FINANCIAL ANALYSIS AND INTERPRETATION

6.6.1   When one entity seeks to obtain control over the net assets (assets less liabilities) of another, there are a number of ways that this control can be achieved from a legal perspective: merger, consolidation, tender offer, and so forth. Business combinations occur in one of two ways:

- In an **acquisition of net assets**, some (or all) of the assets and liabilities of one entity are directly acquired by another.
- With an **equity (stock) acquisition**, one entity (the parent) acquires control of more than 50 percent of the voting common stock of another entity (the subsidiary). Both entities can continue as separate legal entities, producing their own independent set of financial statements, or they can be merged in some way.

Under IFRS 3, the same accounting principles apply to both ways of carrying out the combination.

6.6.2 Under the purchase method, the acquisition price must be allocated to all of the acquired company's identifiable tangible and intangible assets, liabilities, and contingent liabilities. The assets and liabilities of the acquired entity are combined into the financial statements of the acquiring firm at their fair values on the acquisition date. Because the acquirer's assets and liabilities, measured at their historical costs, are combined with the acquired company's assets and liabilities, measured at their fair market value on the acquisition date, the acquirer's pre- and postmerger Statements of Financial Position might not be easily compared.

6.6.3 The fair value of long-term debt acquired in a business combination is the present value of the principal and interest payments over the remaining life of the debt, which is discounted using current market interest rates. Therefore, the fair value of the acquiree's debt that was issued at interest rates below current rates will be lower than the amount recognized on the acquiree's Statement of Financial Position. Conversely, the fair value of the acquiree's debt will be higher than the amount recognized on the acquiree's Statement of Financial Position if the interest rate on the debt is higher than current interest rates.

6.6.4 The cost of acquisition is compared with the fair values of the acquiree's assets, liabilities, and contingent liabilities, and any excess is recognized as goodwill. If the fair market value of the acquiree's assets, liabilities, and contingent liabilities is greater than the cost of acquisition (effectively resulting in negative goodwill), IFRS 3 requires that the excess be reported as a gain.

6.6.5 The purchase method of accounting can be summarized by the following steps:

1. The cost of acquisition is determined.

2. The fair value of the acquired firm's assets is determined.

3. The fair value of the acquired firm's liabilities and contingent liabilities is determined.

4. The fair value of the acquired firm's net assets equals the difference between the fair market values of the acquired firm's assets and liabilities.

5. Calculate the new goodwill arising from the purchase as follows:

Fair Market Value of Acquired Firm's Net Assets	=	Fair Market Value of Acquired Firm's Assets	−	Fair Market Value of Acquired Firm's Liabilities and Contingent Liabilities

6. The book value of the acquirer's assets and liabilities should be combined with the fair values of the acquiree's assets, liabilities, and contingent liabilities.

7. Any goodwill should be recognized as an asset in the combined entity's Statement of Financial Position.

8. The acquired firm's net assets should not be combined with the acquiring company's equity because the acquired firm ceases to exist (separately in the combined financial statements) after the acquisition. Therefore, the acquired firm's net worth is eliminated (replaced with the market value of the shares issued by the acquirer).

Goodwill	=	Purchase Price	−	Fair Market Value of Acquired Firm's Net Assets, Liabilities, and Contingent Liabilities

6.6.6 In applying the purchase method, the Statement of Comprehensive Income and the cash flow statements will include the operating performance of the acquiree from the date of the acquisition forward. Operating results prior to the acquisition are not restated and remain the same as historically reported by the acquirer. Consequently, the financial statements (Statement of Financial Position, Statement of Comprehensive Income, and cash flow statement) of the acquirer will not be comparable before and after the merger, but will reflect the reality of the merger.

6.6.7 Despite the sound principles incorporated in IFRS 3, many analysts believe that the determination of fair values involve considerable management discretion. Values for intangible assets such as computer software might not be easily validated when analyzing purchase acquisitions.

6.6.8 Management judgment can be particularly apparent in the allocation of excess purchase price (after all other allocations to assets and liabilities). If, for example, the remaining excess purchase price is allocated to goodwill, there will be no impact on the firm's net income, because goodwill is not amortized (but is tested for impairment). If the excess were to be allocated to fixed assets, depreciation would rise, thus reducing net income and producing incorrect financial statements.

6.6.9 Under the purchase method, the acquirer's gross margin usually decreases in the year of the combination (assuming the combination does not occur near the end of the year) because the write-up of the acquired firm's inventory will almost immediately increase the cost of goods sold. However, in the year following the combination, the gross margin might increase, reflecting the fact that the cost of goods sold decreases after the higher-cost inventory has been sold. Under some unique circumstances—for instance, when an entity purchases another for less than book value—the effect on the ratios can be the reverse of what is commonly found. Therefore, **there are no absolutes in using ratios, and analysts need to assess the calculated ratios carefully to determine the real effect.**

6.6.10 This points to an important analytical problem. Earnings, earnings per share, the growth rate of these variables, rates of return on equity, profit margins, debt-to-equity ratios, and other important financial ratios have no objective meaning. There is no rule of thumb that the ratios will always appear better under the purchase method or any other method that might be allowed in non-IASB jurisdictions. The financial ratios must be interpreted in light of the accounting principle that is employed to construct the financial statements, as well as the substance of the business combination.

6.6.11 One technique an analyst can use in reviewing a company is to examine cash flow. Cash flow, being an objective measure (in contrast to accounting measures such as earnings, which are subjectively related to the accounting methods used to determine them), is less affected by the accounting methods used. Therefore, it is often instructive to compare companies, and to examine the performance of the same company over time, in terms of cash flow.

6.6.12 Over the years, **goodwill** has become one of the most controversial topics in accounting. Goodwill cannot be measured directly. Its value is generally determined through appraisals, which are based on appraiser assumptions. As such, the value of goodwill is subjectively determined.

6.6.13 The subject of recognizing goodwill in financial statements has found both proponents and opponents among professionals. The proponents of goodwill recognition assert that goodwill is the "present value of excess returns that a company is able to earn." This group claims that determining the present value of these excess returns is analogous to determining the present value of future cash flows associated with other assets and projects. Opponents of goodwill recognition claim that the prices paid for acquisitions often turn out to be based on unrealistic expectations, thereby leading to future write-offs of goodwill.

6.6.14 Both arguments have merit. Many companies are able to earn excess returns on their investments. As such, the prices of the common shares of these companies should sell at a premium to the book value of their tangible assets. Consequently, investors who buy the common shares of such companies are paying for the intangible assets (reputation, brand name, and so forth).

6.6.15 There are companies that earn low returns on investment despite the anticipated excess returns indicated by the presence of a goodwill balance. The common share prices of these companies tend to fall below book value because their assets are overvalued. Therefore, it should be clear that simply paying a price in excess of the fair market value of the acquired firm's net assets does not guarantee that the acquiring company will continue earning excess returns.

6.6.16 In short, analysts should distinguish between accounting goodwill and economic goodwill. Economic goodwill is based on the economic performance of the entity, whereas accounting goodwill is based on accounting standards. Economic goodwill is what should concern analysts and investors. So, when analyzing a company's financial statements, it is imperative that the analysts remove goodwill from the Statement of Financial Position. Any excess returns that the company earns will be reflected in the price of its common shares.

6.6.17 Under IFRS 3, goodwill should be capitalized and tested for impairment annually. Goodwill is not amortized. Impairment of goodwill is a noncash expense. However, the impairment of goodwill does affect reported net income. When goodwill is charged against income in the current period, current reported income decreases, but future reported income should increase when the asset is written off or no longer impaired. This also leads to reduced net assets and reduced shareholders' equity on the one hand, but improved return on assets, asset turnover ratios, return on equity, and equity turnover ratios on the other hand.

6.6.18 Even when the marketplace reacts indifferently to these impairment write-offs, it is an analyst's responsibility to carefully review a company's goodwill to determine whether or not it has been impaired.

6.6.19 Goodwill can significantly affect the comparability of financial statements between companies using different accounting methods. As a result, an analyst should remove any distortion that goodwill, its recognition, amortization, and impairment might create by adjusting the company's financial statements. Adjustments should be made by

- computing financial ratios using Statement of Financial Position data that exclude goodwill,
- reviewing operating trends using data that exclude the amortization of goodwill or impairment to goodwill charges, and
- Evaluating future business acquisitions by taking into account the purchase price paid relative to the net assets and earnings prospects of the acquired firm.

EXAMPLES: BUSINESS COMBINATIONS

EXAMPLE 6.1

H Ltd. acquired a 70 percent interest in the equity shares of F Ltd. for $750,000 on January 1, 20X1. The abridged Statements of Financial Position of both companies at the date of acquisition were as follows:

	H Ltd. $'000	F Ltd. $'000
Identifiable assets	8,200	2,000
Investment in F Ltd.	750	–
	8,950	2,000
Equity	6,000	1,200
Identifiable liabilities	2,950	800
	8,950	2,000

The fair value of the identifiable assets of F Ltd. amounts to $2,800,000, and the fair value of its liabilities is $800,000. Demonstrate the results of the acquisition.

EXPLANATION

	H Ltd. $'000	Minority $'000
Fair value of assets less liabilities	2,000	360
Minority interest	600	240
Fair value of net acquisition	1,400	600
Cost of acquisition	(750)	
Gain	650	

The abridged consolidated Statement of Financial Position at the date of acquisition will appear as follows:

	$'000
Assets	11,000ᵃ
Shareholders' equity	6,650ᵇ
Minority interest	600
Liabilities	3,750ᶜ
	11,000

a = 8,200 + 2,800
b = 6,000 + 650 (gain included in profit or loss)
c = 2,950 + 800

EXAMPLE 6.2

Big Company is buying Small for $100,000 plus the assumption of all of Small's liabilities. Indicate what cash balance and goodwill amount would be shown on the consolidated Statement of Financial Position.

Assume that Big Company is planning to fund the acquisition using $10,000 in cash and new borrowings of $90,000 (long-term debt).

Postacquisition Statements of Financial Position			
	$	$	$
	Big	Small	Small (Fair Value)
Cash	20,000	3,000	3,000
Inventory	40,000	10,000	15,000
Accounts receivable	20,000	8,000	8,000
Current assets	80,000	21,000	26,000
Property, plant, and equipment	120,000	50,000	60,000
Goodwill	–	–	–
Total assets	200,000	71,000	86,000
Accounts payable	22,000	10,000	10,000
Accrued liabilities	3,000	1,000	1,000
Current liabilities	25,000	11,000	11,000
Long–term debt	25,000	10,000	10,000
Common stock	10,000	1,000	
Paid–in capital	40,000	9,000	
Retained earnings	100,000	40,000	65,000
Total equity	150,000	50,000	
Total	200,000	71,000	86,000
Common stock			
Par value	10	2	
Market value	80	8	

continued

Example 6.2 (continued)

Postacquisition Statements of Financial Position (Purchase Method)			
	$ **Big**	**$** **Small**	**$** **Small** **(Fair Value)**
Cash	10,000	3,000	3,000
Inventory	40,000	10,000	15,000
Accounts receivable	20,000	8,000	8,000
Current assets	80,000	21,000	26,000
Investment in subsidiary	100,000		
Property, plant, and equipment	120,000	50,000	60,000
Goodwill	–	–	–
Total assets	290,000	71,000	86,000
Accounts payable	22,000	10,000	10,000
Accrued liabilities	3,000	1,000	1,000
Current liabilities	25,000	11,000	11,000
Long–term debt	115,000	10,000	10,000
Common stock	10,000	1,000	
Paid–in capital	40,000	9,000	
Retained earnings	100,000	40,000	65,000
Total equity	150,000	50,000	
Total	290,000	71,000	86,000
Common stock			
Par value	10	2	
Market value	80	8	

EXAMPLE 6.2.A

Using the purchase method, Big's postacquisition consolidated Statement of Financial Position will reflect a cash balance of:

a. $13,000   b. $20,000   c. $23,000   d. $33,000

EXPLANATION

Choice a. is correct. In a purchase method business combination, add the cash balances of the two companies together and deduct any cash paid out as part of the purchase. Here the two companies have $20,000 + $3,000 = $23,000 less $10,000 paid as part of the purchase, leaving a balance of $13,000.

EXAMPLE 6.2.B

Using the information provided, complete the consolidated Statement of Financial Position.

EXPLANATION

Completed Postacquisition Statement of Financial Position (Purchase Method)					
	$	$	$ Small (Fair Value)	$	$
	Big	Small		Adjustments	Consolidated
Cash	10,000	3,000	3,000		13,000
Inventory	40,000	10,000	15,000		55,000
Accounts receivable	20,000	8,000	8,000		28,000
Current assets	80,000	21,000	26,000		96,000
Investment in subsidiary	100,000			−100,000	
Property, plant, and equipment	120,000	50,000	60,000		180,000
Goodwill	–	–	–	35,000 (b)	35,000
Total assets	290,000	71,000	86,000	25,000	311,000
Accounts payable	22,000	10,000	10,000		32,000
Accrued liabilities	3,000	1,000	1,000		4,000
Current liabilities	25,000	11,000	11,000		36,000
Long-term debt	115,000	10,000	10,000		125,000
Common stock	10,000	1,000			10,000
Paid-in capital	40,000	9,000			40,000
Retained earnings	100,000	40,000	65,000	(65,000) (c)	100,000
Total equity	150,000	50,000			150,000
Total	290,000	71,000	86,000	25,000	311,000
Common stock					
Par value	10	2			
Market value	80	8			

Note: The goodwill is the difference between the consideration, including debt assumed, and the fair market value of assets. In this case, the fair market value of Small's assets is $86,000. The consideration paid is $121,000 – $10,000 (cash) + $90,000 (debt issued) + $21,000 (liabilities assumed, including Small's accounts payable, accrued liabilities, and long-term debt). The net difference between the $121,000 paid and the fair market value of the assets of $86,000 is the goodwill of $35,000.

Chapter Seven

Consolidated and Separate Financial Statements (IAS 27)

7.1   OBJECTIVE

Users of the financial statements of a parent entity need information about the financial position, results of operations, and changes in financial position of the group as a whole. Hence, the main objective of IAS 27 is to ensure that parent entities provide consolidated financial statements incorporating all subsidiaries, jointly controlled entities, and associates.

7.2   SCOPE OF THE STANDARD

This standard's main provisions address

- the demonstration of actual control by the parent entity,
- the preparation and presentation of consolidated financial statements for a group of entities under the control of a parent, and
- separate financial statements accounting for investments in subsidiaries, jointly controlled entities, and associates when an entity elects to—or is required by local regulations to—present separate financial statements.

7.3   KEY CONCEPTS

7.3.1   Consolidated financial statements are the financial statements of a group presented as the financial statements of a single economic entity.

7.3.2   Control is the power to govern the financial and operating policies of an entity to obtain benefits from the entity's activities. Control is generally evidenced by one of the following:

- Ownership. The parent entity owns (directly or indirectly through subsidiaries) more than 50 percent of the voting power of another entity.
- Voting rights. The parent entity has power over more than 50 percent of the voting rights of another entity by virtue of an agreement with other investors.
- Policies. The parent entity has the power to govern the financial and operating policies of the other entity under a statute or agreement.
- Board of directors. The parent entity has the power to appoint or remove the majority of the members of the board of directors.
- Voting rights of directors. The parent entity has the power to cast the majority of votes at meetings of the board of directors.

7.3.3 A group is a parent and all of the parent's subsidiaries.

7.3.4 A parent is an entity that has one or more subsidiaries.

7.3.5 Minority interest is that portion of the profit or loss and net assets of a subsidiary attributable to equity interests that are not owned, directly or indirectly through subsidiaries, by the parent.

7.3.6 Separate financial statements are those presented by a parent, an investor in an associate, or a venturer in a jointly controlled entity in which the investments are accounted for on the basis of the direct equity interest rather than on the basis of the reported results and net assets of the investees.

7.3.7 A subsidiary is an entity—including an unincorporated entity such as a partnership—that is controlled by another entity (known as the parent).

7.3.8 Cost method of accounting is the recognition of the investment at cost and recognition of income only to the extent that the investor receives distributions from accumulated profits of the investee arising after the date of acquisition. Distributions received in excess of such profits are regarded as a recovery of investment and are recognized as a reduction of the cost of the investment.

7.4   ACCOUNTING TREATMENT

7.4.1 A parent should present consolidated financial statements as if the group were a single entity. Consolidated financial statements should include

- the parent and all its foreign and domestic subsidiaries (including those that have dissimilar activities);
- special-purpose entities if the substance of the relationship indicates control;
- subsidiaries that are classified as held for sale; and
- subsidiaries held by venture capital entities, mutual funds, unit trusts, and similar entities.

7.4.2 Consolidated financial statements combine the financial statements of the parent and its subsidiaries on a line-by-line basis by adding together like items of assets, liabilities, equity, income, and expenses. Other basic procedures include the following:

- The carrying amount of the parent's investment and its portion of equity of each subsidiary are eliminated in accordance with the procedures of IFRS 3.
- Minority interests in the net assets of consolidated subsidiaries are identified and presented separately as part of equity.
- Intragroup balances and intragroup transactions are eliminated in full.
- Minority interests in the profit or loss of subsidiaries for the period are identified but are not deducted from profit for the period.
- Consolidated profits are adjusted for the subsidiary's cumulative preferred dividends, whether or not dividends have been declared.
- An investment is accounted for in terms of IAS 39 from the date that the investee ceases to be a subsidiary and does not subsequently become an associate.

- If losses applicable to the minority interest exceed the minority investor's interest in the equity of the subsidiary, the excess is charged against the majority interest—except to the extent that the minority has a binding obligation to, and is able to, make good on the losses.

7.4.3 Consolidated financial statements should be prepared using uniform accounting policies for like transactions and events.

7.4.4 Investments in subsidiaries should be accounted for in a parent entity's separate financial statements (if any) either

- at cost, or
- as financial assets in accordance with IAS 39.

7.4.5 When the reporting dates of the parent and subsidiaries differ, adjustments are made for significant transactions or events that occur between those dates. The difference should be no more than three months.

7.4.6 Consolidated financial statements need not be presented in the case of a wholly owned subsidiary or a virtually wholly owned subsidiary (with unanimous approval of minority shareholders) if

- debt or equity instruments are not traded in a public market;
- the wholly owned subsidiary did not file—or is not filing—financial statements with a securities commission; and
- the parent publishes IFRS-compliant consolidated financial statements.

7.5 PRESENTATION AND DISCLOSURE

7.5.1 Consolidated financial statements should include

- the nature of the relationship when the parent does not own (directly or indirectly) more than 50 percent of the voting power; and
- the name of an entity in which more than 50 percent of the voting power is owned (directly or indirectly), but is not a subsidiary because of the absence of control.

7.5.2 If the parent does not present consolidated financial statements, the parent's financial statements should include

- the fact that the exemption from publishing consolidated financial statements has been exercised;
- the name and country of incorporation of the parent that publishes a consolidated financial statement;
- a list of subsidiaries, associates, and joint ventures; and
- the method used to account for subsidiaries, associates, and joint ventures.

7.5.3 In the parent's separate financial statements, the following should be stated:

- List of subsidiaries, associates, and joint ventures
- Method used to account for subsidiaries, associates and joint ventures

7.6 FINANCIAL ANALYSIS AND INTERPRETATION (See also chapter 6, paragraph 6)

7.6.1 IAS 27 requires that the financial statements of a parent company and the financial statements of the subsidiaries that it controls be consolidated. Control of a subsidiary is presumed when the parent company owns more than 50 percent of the voting stock of a subsidiary unless control demonstratively does not exist in spite of the parent's ownership of a majority of the voting stock of the subsidiary.

7.6.2 The process of consolidation begins with the Statement of Financial Positions and Statement of Comprehensive Income of the parent and the subsidiary constructed as separate entities. The parent's financial statements recognize the subsidiary as an asset (called an investment in subsidiary) and recognize any dividends received from the subsidiary as income from subsidiaries.

7.6.3 With the financial statements of the parent and subsidiary combined, the consolidated financial statements fully reflect the financial results and financial position of the parent and subsidiary. Consolidation does, however, pose problems:

- Combined financial statements of entities in totally different businesses limit analysis of operations and trends of both the parent and the subsidiary—a problem overcome somewhat by segment information.

- Regulatory or debt restrictions might not be easily discernible on the consolidated financial statements.

EXAMPLES: CONSOLIDATED FINANCIAL STATEMENTS AND ACCOUNTING FOR INVESTMENTS IN SUBSIDIARIES

EXAMPLE 7.1

The following amounts of profit after tax relate to the Alpha group of entities:

	$
Alpha Inc.	150,000
Beta Inc.	40,000
Charlie Inc.	25,000
Delta Inc.	60,000
Echo Inc.	80,000

Alpha Inc. owns 75 percent of the voting power in Beta Inc. and 30 percent of the voting power in Charlie Inc.

Beta Inc. also owns 30 percent of the voting power in Charlie Inc. and 25 percent of the voting power in Echo Inc.

Charlie Inc. owns 40 percent of the voting power in Delta Inc.

What is the status of each entity in the group, and how is the minority share in the group after-tax profit calculated?

EXPLANATION

Beta Inc. and Charlie Inc. are both subsidiaries of Alpha Inc., which owns, directly or indirectly through a subsidiary, more than 50 percent of the voting power in the entities.

Charlie Inc. and Echo Inc. are deemed to be associates of Beta Inc., whereas Delta Inc. is deemed to be an associate of Charlie Inc. unless it can be demonstrated that significant influence does not exist.

The minority interest in the group after-tax profit is calculated as follows:

	$	$
Profit after tax of Charlie Inc.		
Own	25,000	
Equity accounted Delta Inc. (40% x 60,000)	24,000	
	49,000	
Minority interest of 40%		19,600
Profit after tax of Beta Inc.		
Own	40,000	
Equity accounted:		
Charlie Inc. (30% x 49,000)	14,700	
Echo Inc. (25% x 8,000)	20,000	
	74,700	
Minority interest of 25%		18,675
		38,275

EXAMPLE 7.2

A European parent company, with subsidiaries in various countries, follows the accounting policy of FIFO costing for all inventories in the group. It has recently acquired a controlling interest in a foreign subsidiary that uses LIFO because of the tax benefits.

How is this aspect dealt with on consolidation?

EXPLANATION

IAS 27 requires consolidated financial statements to be prepared using uniform accounting policies However, it does not demand that an entity in the group change its method of accounting in its separate financial statements to that method which is adopted for the group.

Therefore, on consolidation appropriate adjustments must be made to the financial statements of the foreign subsidiary to convert the carrying amount of inventories to a FIFO-based amount.

EXAMPLE 7.3

Below are the balance sheet and income statements of a parent company and an 80 percent–owned subsidiary. The table depicts the method and adjustments required to construct the consolidated financial statements. All allocations that cannot be accounted for in any other way are attributed to goodwill.

	Parent Only ($)	Subsidiary Only ($)	Adjustments ($)	Consolidated ($)
Cash	50	120		170
Receivables				
From Others	320	20		340
From Subsidiary	30		(30) (1)	—
Inventories	600	100		700
Plant and Equipment	1,000	500		1,500
Investments				
In Others	800	40		840
In Subsidiary	360		(360) (2)(3)	—
Total Assets	3,160	780	(390)	3,550
Accounts Payable				
To Others	250	100		350
To Parent		30	(30) (1)	—
Long-Term Debt	1,350	200		1,550
Minority Interest			90 (2)(3)	90 (4)
Common Stock	100	40	(40) (2)(3)	100 (5)
Paid-in Capital	300	160	(160) (2)(3)	300 (5)
Retained Earnings	1,160	250	(250) (2)(3)	1,160 (5)
Total Liabilities and Capital	3,160	780	(390)	3,550

Notes to the balance sheet:

(1) The intercompany receivables or payables are eliminated against each other so they do not affect the consolidated group's assets and liabilities.

(2) Investment in subsidiary $360
Less 80% of subsidiary's equity = 0.80 ($40 + $160 + $250)   360
Goodwill from consolidation $ 0

(3) This represents the pro rata share of the book value of the subsidiary's equity (its common stock, paid-in capital, and retained earnings) that is not owned by the parent: 20% of $450 = $90.

(4) Note that the minority interest is an explicit item only on the consolidated balance sheet.

(5) Note that the equity of the consolidated group is the same as the equity of the parent, which is the public entity.

	Parent Only ($)	Subsidiary Only ($)	Adjustments ($)	Consolidated ($)
Sales to Outside Entities	2,800	1,000		3,800
Receipts from Subsidiary	500		(500) (2)	—
Total Revenues	3,300	1,000	(500)	3,800
Costs of Goods Sold	1,800	400		2,200
Other Expenses	200	50		250
Payments to Parent	—	500	(500) (2)	—
Minority Interest (1)			10 (3)	10
Pretax Income	1,300	50	(10)	1,340
Tax Expense (30%)	390	15	(3) (3)	402

Notes to the income statement:

(1) Sometimes minority interest ($10) is shown after taxes, in which case it would be reported as $7 and placed below the tax expense line.

(2) The receipts from or payable by the subsidiary ($500) are eliminated against each other and do not appear on the consolidated income statement.

(3) The pro forma share of the pretax income of the subsidiary that does not accrue to the parent is reported as a minority interest expense on the consolidated income statement. It is computed as follows:

   20% of $50 = $10

   Note that the calculation could have also been done on an after-tax basis:

   20% of $35 = $7

(4) The net income of the subsidiary is eliminated against the net minority interest expense and the net income from unconsolidated subsidiaries account on the parent-only income statement. This elimination is accounted for using the following journal entries:

	Dr	Cr
Minority Interest (net of taxes)	$7	
Parent's Net Income from Unconsolidated Subsidiaries	$28	
Subsidiary's Net Income		$35

(5) The consolidated net income of the parent (the public entity) equals the parent-only net income computed using the equity method. This is because the parent-only statement includes the parent's share of the net income from the (unconsolidated) subsidiary, just as for the consolidated income.

Chapter Eight

Investments in Associates (IAS 28)

8.1 OBJECTIVE

Associate entities are distinct from subsidiaries in that the influence and ownership of associates by the parent entity is not as extensive as for subsidiaries (IAS 27). The main issue is identifying the amount of influence needed for an entity to be classified as an associate. Conceptually, a parent entity has "significant" influence over an associate entity; in practical terms, this is measured by the degree of ownership. A conjunct issue of IAS 28 is the appropriate accounting treatment for the parent's investment in the associate.

8.2 SCOPE OF THE STANDARD

IAS 28 applies to each investment in an associate. The main requirements are

- identification and requirements for the significant-influence test, and
- use of the equity method of accounting for associates (which captures the parent's interest in the earnings and the underlying assets and liabilities of the associate).

IAS 28 does not apply to joint ventures or entities that are subsidiaries.

The following entities could account for investments in associates as (a) associates in accordance with IAS 28, or (b) held for trading financial assets in accordance with IAS 39:

- Venture capital organizations
- Mutual funds
- Unit trusts and similar entities
- Investment-linked insurance funds

8.3 KEY CONCEPTS

8.3.1 The equity method of accounting initially recognizes at cost the investor's share of the net assets acquired and thereafter adjusts for the postacquisition change in the investor's share of net assets of the investee. The profit or loss of the investor includes the investor's share of the profit or loss of the investee.

8.3.2 An associate is an entity (including an unincorporated entity such as a partnership) over which the investor has significant influence. An associate is neither a subsidiary nor an interest in a joint venture.

8.3.3 Significant influence is the power to participate in the financial and operating policy decisions of the investee, but is not control or joint control over those policies. If an investor holds, directly or indirectly through subsidiaries, 20 percent or more of the voting power of the investee, it is presumed to have significant influence, unless it can be clearly demonstrated that this is not the case. Significant influence is evidenced by, among other things, the following:

- Representation on the board of directors or governing body
- Participation in policy-making processes
- Material transactions between parties
- Interchange of managerial personnel
- Provision of essential technical information

8.3.4 Control is the power to govern the financial and operating policies of an entity to obtain benefits from its activities.

8.3.5 Joint control is the contractually agreed sharing of control over an economic activity.

8.3.6 A subsidiary is an entity—including an unincorporated entity such as a partnership—that is controlled by another entity (known as the parent).

8.3.7 Consolidated financial statements are the financial statements of a group presented as those of a single economic entity.

8.3.8 Separate financial statements are those presented by a parent, an investor in an associate, or a venturer in a jointly controlled entity, in which the investments are accounted for on the basis of the direct equity interest rather than on the basis of the reported results and net assets of the investees.

8.4   ACCOUNTING TREATMENT

8.4.1 An investment in an associate should be accounted for in the consolidated financial statements of the investor and in any separate financial statements, using the equity method.

8.4.2 Equity accounting should commence from the date that the investee meets the definition of an associate. Equity accounting should be discontinued when

- the investor ceases to have significant influence, but retains whole or part of the investment; and
- the associate operates under severe long-term restrictions that significantly impair its ability to transfer funds.

8.4.3 The equity method is applied as follows:

- Initial measurement is applied at cost (excluding borrowing costs, as per IAS 23).
- Subsequent measurement is adjusted for postacquisition change in the investor's share of the net assets of the associate share of profit or loss included in the Statement of Comprehensive Income, and the share of other changes included in equity.

8.4.4 Many procedures for the equity method are similar to consolidation procedures, such as the following:

- Eliminating intragroup profits and losses arising from transactions between the investor and the investee

- Identifying the goodwill portion of the purchase price
- Amortizing goodwill
- Adjusting for depreciation of depreciable assets, based on their fair values
- Adjusting for the effect of cross-holdings
- Using uniform accounting policies

8.4.5 The investor computes its share of profits or losses after adjusting for the cumulative preferred dividends, whether or not they have been declared. The investor recognizes losses of an associate until the investment is zero. Further losses are provided for only to the extent of guarantees given by the investor.

8.4.6 The same principles outlined for consolidating subsidiaries should be followed under equity accounting—namely, using the most recent financial statements and using uniform accounting policies for the investor and the investee. If reporting dates differ, make adjustments for significant events after the date of the Statement of Financial Position of the associate.

8.4.7 With regard to impairment of an investment, the investor applies IAS 39 to determine whether it is necessary to recognize any impairment loss. If the application of IAS 39 indicates that the investment may be impaired, the investor applies IAS 36 to determine the value in use of the associate.

8.5 PRESENTATION AND DISCLOSURE

8.5.1 **Statement of Financial Position and notes** should include the following:

- The investment in associates is shown as a separate item on the face of the statement and classified as noncurrent.

- The statement should contain a list and description of significant associates, including name, nature of the business, and the investor's proportion of ownership interest or voting power (if different from the ownership interest).

- If the investor does not present consolidated financial statements and does not equity account the investment, a description of what the effect would have been had the equity method been applied should be disclosed.

- If it is not practicable to calculate adjustments when associates use accounting policies other than those adopted by the investor, the fact should be mentioned.

- The investor's share of the contingent liabilities and capital commitments of an associate for which the investor is contingently liable should be disclosed.

8.5.2 **The Statement of Comprehensive Income and notes** should include the investor's share of the associate's profits or losses for the period and prior-period items. The investor's share of the profits or losses of such associates, and the carrying amount of those investments, should be separately disclosed. The investor's share of any discontinued operations of such associates should also be separately disclosed, as follows:

- The investor's share of the contingent liabilities of an associate incurred jointly with other investors

- Contingent liabilities that arise because the investor is severally liable for all or part of the liabilities of the associate

8.5.3 Disclose in the **accounting policy notes** the method used to account for

- associates,
- goodwill and negative goodwill, and
- the amortization period for goodwill.

8.5.4 The fair value of investments in associates for which there are published price quotations should be disclosed.

8.5.5 Summarize the financial information of associates, including the aggregated amounts of

- assets,
- liabilities,
- revenues, and
- profit or loss.

8.5.6 The following disclosures should also be made:

- The reasons for deviating from the significant-influence presumptions
- The reporting date of the financial statements of an associate, when such financial statements are used in applying the equity method and differ from the reporting date or period of the investor, and the reason for using a different reporting date or different period
- The nature and extent of any significant restrictions (for example, resulting from borrowing arrangements or regulatory requirements) on the ability of associates to transfer funds to the investor in the form of cash dividends or repayment of loans or advances
- The unrecognized share of losses of an associate, both for the period and cumulatively, if an investor has discontinued recognition of its share of losses of an associate

8.6 FINANCIAL ANALYSIS AND INTERPRETATION

8.6.1 Under the equity method, the investment in an associate is initially recognized at cost, and the carrying amount is increased or decreased to recognize the investor's share of the profit or loss of the associate after the date of acquisition. The investor's share of the profit or loss of the associate is recognized in the investor's profit or loss. Distributions received from an associate reduce the carrying amount of the investment.

8.6.2 Adjustments to the carrying amount might also be necessary for changes in the investor's proportionate interest in the associate arising from changes in the associate's equity that have not been recognized in the associate's profit or loss. Such changes may arise from the revaluation of property, plant, and equipment and from foreign exchange translation differences. The investor's share of those changes is recognized directly in equity of the investor.

EXAMPLE 8.1

Dolo Inc. acquired a 40 percent interest in the ordinary shares of Nutro Inc. on the date of incorporation, January 1, 20X0, for $220,000. This enabled Dolo to exercise significant influence over Nutro. On December 31, 20X3, the shareholders' equity of Nutro was as follows:

Ordinary issued share capital	$550,000
Reserves	180,000
Accumulated profit	650,000
Total	$1,380,000

The following abstracts were taken from the financial statements of Nutro for the year ending December 31, 20X4:

Statement of Comprehensive Income

Profit after tax	$228,000
Extraordinary item	(12,000)
Net profit for the period	$216,000

Statement of Changes in Equity

Accumulated profits at the beginning of the year	$650,000
Net profit for the period	216,000
Dividends paid	(80,000)
Accumulated profits at the end of the year	$786,000

In November 20X4, Dolo sold inventories to Nutro for the first time. The total sales amounted to $50,000, and Dolo earned a profit of $10,000 on the transaction. None of the inventories had been sold by Nutro by December 31. The income tax rate is 30 percent.

EXPLANATION

The application of the equity method would result in the carrying amount of the investment in Nutro Inc. being reflected as follows:

Original cost	$220,000
Postacquisition profits accounted for at beginning of the year (40% x [$180,000 + $650,000])	332,000
Carrying amount on January 1, 20X4	$552,000

Attributable portion of net profit for the period (calculation a)	83,600
Dividends received (40% x $80,000)	(32,000)
Total	$603,600

Calculation a – Attributable Portion of Net Profit

Net profit (40% x $216,000)	$86,400
After-tax effect of unrealized profit [40% x (70% x $10,000)]	(2,800)
All	$83,600

Chapter Nine

Interests in Joint Ventures (IAS 31)

9.1 OBJECTIVE

Joint ventures occur where there is an arrangement to undertake an activity where control is shared jointly by two or more business entities. This is different from arrangements where a parent has sole control over a subsidiary or a significant influence over an associate. The overall objective of IAS 31 is to provide users with information concerning the investing owners' (venturers') interest in the earnings and the underlying net assets of the joint venture.

9.2 SCOPE OF THE STANDARD

IAS 31 applies to all interests in joint ventures and the reporting of their assets, liabilities, income, and expenses, regardless of the joint ventures' structures or forms. The standard specifically outlines

- the characteristics necessary to be classified as a joint venture, and
- the distinction between jointly controlled operations, assets, and entities and the specific accounting requirements for each.

The following entities may account for investments in joint ventures either as joint ventures in accordance with IAS 31, or as held for trading financial assets in accordance with IAS 39:

- Venture capital organizations
- Mutual funds
- Unit trusts and similar entities
- Investment-linked insurance funds

9.3 KEY CONCEPTS

9.3.1 A joint venture is a contractual arrangement whereby two or more parties undertake an economic activity that is subject to joint control.

9.3.2 The following are **characteristics of all joint ventures:**

- Two or more venturers are bound by a contractual arrangement.
- A joint venture establishes joint control; that is, the contractually agreed sharing of control over a joint venture is such that no one party can exercise unilateral control.
- A **venturer** is a party to a joint venture and has joint control over that joint venture.

9.3.3 The existence of a **contractual arrangement** distinguishes joint ventures from associates. It is usually in writing and deals with such matters as

- activity, duration, and reporting;

- appointment of a board of directors or equivalent body and voting rights;
- capital contributions by venturers; and
- sharing by the venturers of the output, income, expenses, or results of the joint venture.

9.3.4 IAS 31 identifies three forms of joint ventures: jointly controlled operations, jointly controlled assets, and jointly controlled entities.

9.3.5 **Jointly controlled operations** involve the use of resources of the venturers; they do not establish separate structures. An example is when two or more parties combine resources and efforts to manufacture, market, and jointly sell a product.

9.3.6 **Jointly controlled assets** refers to joint ventures that involve the joint control and ownership of one or more assets acquired for and dedicated to the purpose of the joint venture (for example, factories sharing the same railway line). The establishment of a **separate entity** is unnecessary.

9.3.7 **Jointly controlled entities** are joint ventures that are conducted through **a separate entity** in which each venturer owns an interest. An example is when two entities combine their activities in a particular line of business by transferring assets and liabilities into a joint venture.

9.3.8 **Proportionate consolidation** is a method of accounting whereby a venturer's share of each of the assets, liabilities, income, and expenses of a jointly controlled entity is combined line by line with similar items in the venturer's financial statements or reported as separate line items in the venturer's financial statements.

9.3.9 **Separate financial statements** are those presented by a parent, an investor in an associate, or a venturer in a jointly controlled entity, in which the investments are accounted for on the basis of the direct equity interest rather than on the basis of the reported results and net assets of the investees.

9.4   ACCOUNTING TREATMENT

9.4.1 For interests in **jointly controlled operations**, a venturer should recognize in its separate and consolidated financial statements

- the assets that it controls,
- the liabilities that it incurs,
- the expenses that it incurs, and
- its share of the income that the joint venture earns.

9.4.2 For the **jointly controlled assets**, a venturer should recognize in its separate and consolidated financial statements

- its share of the assets,
- any liabilities that it has incurred,
- its share of any liabilities incurred jointly with the other venturers in relation to the joint venture,
- any income it receives from the joint venture,
- its share of any expenses incurred by the joint venture, and

- any expenses that it has incurred individually from its interest in the joint venture.

9.4.3 An entity should account for its interest as a venturer in jointly controlled entities using one of the following two treatments:

1. **Proportionate consolidation**, whereby a venturer's share of each of the assets, liabilities, income, expenses, and cash flows of a jointly controlled entity is combined with similar items of the venturer or reported separately. The following principles apply:
   - One of two formats could be used:
     - combining items line by line, or
     - listing separate line items.
   - The interests in the joint ventures are included in consolidated financial statements for the venturer, even if it has no subsidiaries.
   - Proportionate consolidation commences when the venturer acquires joint control.
   - Proportionate consolidation ceases when the venturer loses joint control.
   - Many procedures for proportionate consolidation are similar to **consolidation procedures**, described in IAS 27.
   - Assets and liabilities can be offset only if
     - a legal right to set-off exists, and
     - there is an expectation of realizing an asset or settling a liability on a net basis.

2. **The equity method** is an allowed alternative but is not recommended. The method should be discontinued when joint control or significant influence is lost by the venturer.

9.4.4 The following **general accounting considerations** apply:
- Transactions between a venturer and a joint venture are treated as follows:
- The venturer's share of unrealized profits on sales or contribution of assets to a joint venture is eliminated.
- Full unrealized loss on sale or contribution of assets to a joint venture is eliminated.
- The venturer's share of profits or losses on sales of assets by a joint venture to the venturer is eliminated.
- An investor in a joint venture that does not have joint control should report its interest in a joint venture in the **consolidated** financial statements in terms of IAS 39 or, if it has significant influence, in terms of IAS 28.
- Operators or managers of a joint venture should account for any fees as revenue in terms of IAS 18.

9.5   PRESENTATION AND DISCLOSURE

9.5.1 The following contingent liabilities (IAS 37) should be shown **separately** from others:
- Liabilities incurred jointly with other venturers
- Share of a joint venture's contingent liabilities
- Contingencies for liabilities of other venturers

9.5.2 Amount of commitments shown separately include the following:

- Commitments incurred jointly with other venturers
- Share of a joint venture's commitments

9.5.3 Present a list of significant joint ventures, including the names of the ventures, a description of the investor's interest in all joint ventures, and the investor's proportion of ownership.

9.5.4 A venturer that uses the line-by-line reporting format or the equity method should disclose aggregate amounts of each of the current assets, long-term assets, current liabilities, long-term liabilities, income, and expenses related to the joint ventures.

9.5.5 A venturer not issuing consolidated financial statements (because it has no subsidiaries) should nevertheless disclose the above information.

9.6   FINANCIAL ANALYSIS AND INTERPRETATION

9.6.1 Entities can form joint ventures in which none of the entities own more than 50 percent of the voting rights in the joint venture. This enables every member of the venturing group to use the equity method of accounting for unconsolidated affiliates to report their share of the activities of the joint ventures. They can also use proportionate consolidation—and each venturer need not use the same method.

9.6.2 If they use the equity method, joint ventures enable firms to report lower debt-to-equity ratios and higher interest-coverage ratios, although this does not affect the return on equity.

9.6.3 Forming joint ventures also affects the cash flow reported by the sponsoring group of firms. When the equity method of accounting for jointly controlled entities is used, monies exchanged between a parent and the jointly controlled entities are reported as income or expenses, whereas in consolidation accounting any cash flows that are internal to members of the consolidated group are not reported separately.

EXAMPLES: FINANCIAL REPORTING OF INTERESTS IN JOINT VENTURES

EXAMPLE 9.1

Techno Inc. was incorporated after three independent engineering corporations decided to pool their knowledge to implement and market new technology. The three corporations acquired the following interests in the equity capital of Techno on the date of its incorporation:

- Electro Inc.   30 percent
- Mechan Inc.   40 percent
- Civil Inc.   30 percent

The following information was taken from the financial statements of Techno as well as one of the owners, Mechan.

Abridged Statement of Comprehensive Income for the Year Ending June 30, 20X1		
	Mechan Inc. ($'000)	Techno Inc. ($'000)
Revenue	3,100	980
Cost of sales	(1,800)	(610)
Gross profit	1,300	370
Other operating income	150	–
Operating costs	(850)	(170)
Profit before tax	600	200
Income tax expense	(250)	(90)
Net profit for the period	350	110

Mechan sold inventories with an invoice value of $600,000 to Techno during the year. Included in Techno's inventories June 30, 20X1, is an amount of $240,000, which is inventory purchased from Mechan at a profit markup of 20 percent. The income tax rate is 30 percent.

Techno paid an administration fee of $120,000 to Mechan during the year. This amount is included under "Other operating income."

EXPLANATION

To combine the results of Techno Inc. with those of Mechan Inc., the following issues would need to be resolved:

- Is Techno an associate or joint venture for financial reporting purposes?
- Which method is appropriate for reporting the results of Techno in the financial statements of Mechan?
- How are the above transactions between the entities to be recorded and presented for financial reporting purposes in the consolidated Statement of Comprehensive Income?

First issue

The existence of a **contractual agreement**, whereby the parties involved undertake an economic activity subject to joint control, distinguishes a joint venture from an associate. No one of the venturers should be able to exercise unilateral control. However, if no contractual agreement exists, the investment would be regarded as an associate because the investor holds more than 20 percent of the voting power and is therefore presumed to have significant influence over the investee.

Second issue

If Techno is regarded as a joint venture, the proportionate consolidation method or the equity method must be used. However, if Techno is regarded as an associate, the equity method would be used.

Third issue

It is assumed that Techno is a joint venture for purposes of the following illustration.

Consolidated Statement of Comprehensive Income for the Year Ending June 30, 20X1	
	$'000
Revenue **(Calculation a)**	3,252
Cost of sales **(Calculation b)**	(1,820)
Gross profit	1,432
Other operating income **(Calculation c)**	102
Operating costs **(Calculation d)**	(870)
Profit before tax	664
Income tax expense **(Calculation e)**	(281)
Net profit for the period	383

Remarks

- The proportionate consolidation method is applied by adding 40 percent of the Statement of Comprehensive Income items of Techno to those of Mechan.

- The transactions between the corporations are then dealt with by recording the following consolidation journal entries:

	Dr ($'000)	Cr ($'000)
Sales (40% x 600)	240	
Cost of sales		240
(Eliminating intragroup sales)		
Cost of sales (40% x 20/120 x 240)	16	
Inventories		16
(Eliminating unrealized profit in inventory)		
Deferred taxation (Statement of Financial Position) (30% x 16)	4.8	
Income tax expense (Statement of Comprehensive Income)		4.8
(Taxation effect on elimination of unrealized profit)		

Note: The administration fee is eliminated by reducing other operating income with Mechan's portion of the total fee, namely $48,000, and reducing operating expenses accordingly. The net effect on the consolidated profit is nil.

Calculations	
	$'000
a. **Sales**	
Mechan	3,100
Intragroup sales (40% x 600)	(240)
Techno (40% x 980)	392
	3,252
b. **Cost of sales**	
Mechan	1,800
Intragroup sales	(240)
Unrealized profit (40% x 20/120 x 240)	16
Techno (40% x 610)	244
	1,820
c. **Other operating income**	
Mechan	150
Intragroup fee (40% x 120)	(48)
	102
d. **Operating costs**	
Mechan	850
Techno (40% x 170)	68
Intra-group fee (40% x 120)	(48)
	870
e. **Income tax expense**	
Mechan	250
Unrealized profit (30% x 16 rounded-up)	(5)
Techno (40% x 90)	36
	281

Part III

Statement of Financial Position

Balance Sheet

Chapter Ten

Property, Plant, and Equipment (IAS 16)

10.1 OBJECTIVE

This objective of IAS 16 is to prescribe the accounting treatment for property, plant, and equipment (PPE), including

- timing of the recognition of assets,
- determination of asset carrying amounts using both the cost model and the revaluation model,
- depreciation charges and impairment losses to be recognized in relation to these values, and
- disclosure requirements.

10.2 SCOPE OF THE STANDARD

This standard deals with all property, plant, and equipment, including that which is held as a lessee under a finance lease (IAS 17) and property that is being constructed or developed for future use as investment property (IAS 40). The standard prescribes that the initial amount of the asset be recognized at cost, but after that an election between the cost model or the revaluation model must be made.

This standard does not apply to

- property, plant, and equipment that is classified as held for sale (see IFRS 5);
- biological assets related to agricultural activity (see IAS 41 Agriculture);
- mineral rights and mineral reserves, such as oil or natural gas; or
- similar nonregenerative resources.

10.3 KEY CONCEPTS

10.3.1 Property, plant, and equipment are tangible items that are

- held for use in the production or supply of goods or services, for rental to others, or for administrative purposes; and
- expected to be used during more than one period.

10.3.2 Cost is the amount of cash or cash equivalents paid and the fair value of any other consideration given to acquire an asset at the time of its acquisition or construction.

10.3.3 Fair value is the amount for which an asset could be exchanged between knowledgeable, willing parties in an arm's-length transaction.

10.3.4 **Carrying amount** is the amount at which an asset is recognized after deducting any accumulated depreciation and accumulated impairment losses.

10.3.5 **Depreciable amount** is the cost of an asset, or other amount substituted for cost (such as a revaluation amount), less its residual value.

10.3.6 **Depreciation** is the systematic allocation of the depreciable amount of an asset over its useful life.

10.3.7 An **impairment loss** is the amount by which the carrying amount of an asset exceeds its recoverable amount. **Recoverable amount** is the higher of an asset's net selling price and its value in use.

10.3.8 The **residual value** of an asset is the estimated amount that an entity would currently obtain from disposal of the asset, after deducting the estimated costs of disposal (assuming the asset is already of the age and in the condition expected at the end of its useful life). If the intent is to scrap an asset, it will have no residual value.

10.3.9 Useful life is not the theoretical life span of an asset but

- the intended period over which an asset is expected to be available for use by an entity, or

- the number of production or similar units expected to be obtained from the asset by an entity.

10.4 ACCOUNTING TREATMENT

Initial Measurement

10.4.1 The **cost** of an item of property, plant, and equipment should be **recognized** as an asset only if

- it is probable that future economic benefits associated with the item will flow to the entity, and

- the cost of the item can be measured reliably.

10.4.2 The above principle is applied to both costs incurred to acquire an item of property, plant, or equipment, and to any subsequent expenditure incurred to add to, replace part of, or service the item. Therefore, an entity should

- **capitalize** replacement or renewal components and major inspection costs,

- **write off** replaced or renewed components related to a previous inspection (whether or not identified on acquisition or construction), and

- **expense** day-to-day servicing costs.

10.4.3 Safety and environmental assets qualify as property, plant, and equipment if they enable the entity to increase future economic benefits from related assets in excess of what it could derive if they had not been acquired (for example, chemical protection equipment). Following are examples:

- Insignificant items (for example, molds and dies) could be aggregated as single asset items.

- Specialized spares and servicing equipment are accounted for as property, plant, and equipment.

10.4.4 The **cost** of an item of property, plant and equipment **includes**

- its **purchase price** and duties paid;
- any costs directly attributable to bringing the asset to the location and condition necessary for it to be capable of operating in its intended manner;
- the initial estimate of the costs of dismantling and removing the asset and restoring the site (see IAS 37); and
- materials, labor, and other inputs for **self-constructed assets**.

10.4.5 The **cost** of an item of property, plant and equipment **excludes**

- general and administrative expenses, and
- start-up costs.

10.4.6 The **cost** of an item of property, plant, and equipment **might** include the effects of **government grants** (IAS 20) deducted from cost or set-up as deferred income.

10.4.7 When assets are exchanged and the transaction has commercial substance, items are recorded at the fair value of the asset(s) received. In other cases, items are recorded at the carrying amount of the asset(s) given up.

10.4.8 The amount expected to be recovered from the future use (or sale) of an asset, including its residual value on disposal, is referred to as the **recoverable amount**. The carrying amount should be compared with the recoverable amount whenever there is an indication of impairment. If the recoverable amount is lower, the difference is recognized as an expense (IAS 36).

Subsequent Measurement

10.4.9 **Choice of cost or fair value.** Subsequent to initial recognition, an entity should choose either the **cost model** or the **revaluation model** as its accounting policy for items of property, plant, and equipment and should apply that policy to an entire class of property, plant, and equipment.

10.4.10 **Cost model.** The **carrying amount** of an item of property, plant, and equipment is its cost less accumulated depreciation and impairment losses. Assets classified as held for sale are shown at the lower of fair value less costs to sell and carrying value.

10.4.10 **Revaluation model.** The **carrying amount** of an item of property, plant, and equipment is its fair value less subsequent accumulated depreciation and impairment losses. Assets classified as held for sale are shown at the lower of fair value less costs to sell and carrying value.

10.4.12 Property, plant, and equipment is measured at **fair value** at date of revaluation as follows:

- If an item of property, plant, and equipment is revalued, the entire class of property, plant, and equipment to which that asset belongs should be revalued.
- Assets should be regularly revalued so that carrying value does not differ materially from fair value.

Income and Expenses

10.4.13 Revaluation profits and losses. Adjustments to the carrying value are treated as follows:

- Increases should be **credited** directly to **equity** under the heading of revaluation surplus. A reversal of a previous loss for the same asset is reported in the Statement of Comprehensive Income.

- Decreases should be recognized (debited) in profit or loss. A reversal of a profit previously taken to equity can be debited to equity.

10.4.14 Depreciation of an asset is recognized as an expense unless it is included in the carrying amount of a self-constructed asset. The following principles apply:

- The depreciable amount is allocated on a systematic basis over the useful life.

- The method reflects the pattern of expected consumption.

- Each part of an item of property, plant, and equipment with a cost that is significant in relation to the total cost of the item should be depreciated separately at appropriately different rates.

- Component parts are treated as separate items if the related assets have different useful lives or provide economic benefits in a different pattern (for example, an aircraft and its engines or land and buildings).

10.4.15 The **depreciation method** applied to an asset should be reviewed at least at each financial year-end. If there has been a significant change in the expected pattern of consumption of the future economic benefits embodied in the asset, the method should be changed to reflect the changed pattern. Such a change should be accounted for as a change in an **accounting estimate** in accordance with IAS 8.

10.4.16 Depreciation starts when the asset is ready for use and ends when the asset is derecognized or classified as held for sale. When depreciation is based on hourly usage (for example, depreciation of a machine), such assets are not depreciated when not in use.

10.5 PRESENTATION AND DISCLOSURE

10.5.1 For **each class** of property, plant, and equipment, the following must be presented:

- The measurement **bases** used for determining the gross carrying amount

- The depreciation **methods** used

- The useful lives or the depreciation **rates** used

- The **gross** carrying amount and the **accumulated** depreciation (together with accumulated impairment losses) at the beginning and end of the period

- A **reconciliation** of the carrying amount at the beginning and end of the period, showing
  - additions, disposals, or depreciation;
  - acquisitions through business combinations;
  - increases or decreases resulting from revaluations and impairment losses recognized or reversed directly in equity;
  - impairment losses recognized in profit or loss;
  - impairment losses reversed in profit or loss;
  - net exchange differences arising on the translation of the financial statements; and
  - other changes.

10.5.2 The financial statements should also disclose

- restrictions on title and pledges as security for liabilities;
- expenditures recognized in the carrying amount in the course of construction;
- contractual commitments for the acquisition of property, plant, and equipment; and
- compensation for impairments included in profit or loss.

10.5.3 The depreciation methods adopted and the estimated **useful lives or depreciation rates** must be disclosed and should include

- depreciation, whether recognized in profit or loss or as a part of the cost of other assets, during a period; and
- accumulated depreciation at the end of the period.

10.5.4 Disclose the nature and effect of a **change in an accounting estimate** with respect to

- residual values;
- the estimated costs of dismantling, removing, or restoring items;
- useful lives; and
- depreciation methods.

10.5.5 If items of property, plant, and equipment are stated at **revalued amounts**, the following must be disclosed:

- Effective date of revaluation
- Independent valuator involvement
- Methods and significant assumptions applied
- Reference to observable prices in an active market or recent arm's-length transactions
- Carrying amount that would have been recognized had the assets been carried under the cost model
- Revaluation surplus

10.5.6 Users of financial statements can also find the following information relevant to their needs and **disclosure is therefore encouraged**:

- Carrying amount of temporarily idle property, plant, and equipment
- Gross carrying amount of fully depreciated items still in use
- The carrying amount of items retired from active use and held for disposal
- Fair value of property, plant, and equipment when this is materially different from the carrying amount per the cost model in use

10.6.1 The original costs of acquired fixed assets are usually recognized over time by systematically writing down the asset's book value on the Statement of Financial Position and reporting a commensurate expense on the Statement of Comprehensive Income. The systematic expensing of the original cost of physical assets over time is called **depreciation**. The systematic expensing of the original cost of natural resources over time is called **depletion**. The systematic expensing of the original cost of intangible assets over time is called **amortization**. Essentially, all three of these concepts are the same. The cost of acquiring land is never depleted because land does not get used up over time. However, if the land has a limited useful life, the cost of acquiring it can be depreciated.

10.6.2 **Depreciation** is a method of expensing the original purchase cost of physical assets over their useful lives. It is neither a means of adjusting the asset to its fair market value nor a means to provide funds for the replacement of the asset being depreciated.

10.6.3 There are several methods of determining **depreciation expense** for fixed assets on the financial statements. In some countries, these depreciation methods include straight-line, sum-of-the-years' digits, double-declining balance, and units-of-production (service hours). Regardless of the terminology used, the principles that should be applied in IFRS financial statements are

- the depreciable amount is allocated on a systematic basis over the asset's useful life; and
- the method used must reflect the pattern of expected consumption.

10.6.4 The straight-line depreciation method is generally used worldwide to determine IFRS depreciation. Both sum-of-the-years' digits and the double-declining balance methods are classified as **accelerated depreciation** (or rather, accelerated consumption-pattern methods; they are often used for tax purposes and do not comply with IFRS if they do not reflect the pattern of the expected consumption of the assets).

10.6.5 In some countries, management has more flexibility than is permitted by IFRS when deciding whether to expense or capitalize certain expenditures. Capitalizing could result in the recognition of an asset that does not qualify for recognition under IFRS. Expensing a transaction that would otherwise qualify as an asset under IFRS means avoiding depreciating it over time. This flexibility will impact the Statement of Financial Position, Statement of Comprehensive Income, a number of key financial ratios, and the classification of cash flows in the statement of cash flows. Consequently, the analyst must understand the financial data effects of the capitalization or expensing choices made by management.

10.6.6 Table 10.1 summarizes the effects of expensing versus capitalizing costs on the financial statements and related key ratios.

Table 10.1 Effects of Capitalizing vs. Expensing Costs

Variable	Expensing	Capitalizing
Shareholders' Equity	**Lower** because earnings are lower	**Higher** because earnings are higher
Earnings	**Lower** because expenses are higher	**Higher** because expenses are lower
Pretax Cash Generated from Operating Activities	**Lower** because expenses are higher	**Higher** because expenses are lower
Cash Generated from Investing Activities	**None** because no long-term asset is put on the Statement of Financial Position	**Lower** because a long-term asset is acquired (invested in) for cash
Pretax Total Cash Flow	**Same** because amortization is not a cash expense	**Same** because amortization is not a cash expense
Profit Margin	**Lower** because earnings are lower	**Higher** because earnings are higher
Asset Turnover	**Higher** because assets are lower	**Lower** because assets are higher
Current Ratio	**Same** on a pretax basis because only long-term assets are affected	**Same** on a pretax basis because only long-term assets are affected
Debt-to-Equity	**Higher** because shareholders' equity is lower	**Lower** because shareholders' equity is higher
Return on Assets	**Lower** because the earnings are lower percentage-wise than the reduced assets	**Higher** because the earnings are higher percentage-wise than the increased assets
Return on Equity	**Lower** because the earnings are lower percentage-wise than the reduced shareholders' equity	**Higher** because the earnings are higher percentage-wise than the increased shareholders' equity
Stability over Time	**Less stable** earnings and ratios because large expenses may be sporadic	**More stable** earnings and ratios because amortization smooths earnings over time

10.6.7 Management must make three choices when deciding how to depreciate assets:

- The method of depreciation that will be used (straight-line, accelerated consumption, or depletion in early years)
- The useful life of the asset, which is the time period over which the depreciation will occur
- The residual value of the asset

In IFRS financial statements, these choices are determined by the application of the principles in IAS 16.

10.6.8 The easiest way to understand the impact of using **straight-line versus accelerated depreciation** is as follows: An accelerated consumption method will increase the depreciation expense in the early years of an asset's useful life relative to what it would be if the straight-line method were used. This lowers reported income and also causes the book value of the long-term assets reported on the Statement of Financial Position to decline more quickly relative to what would be reported under the straight-line method. As a result, the shareholders' equity will be lower in the early years of an asset's life under accelerated depreciation. Furthermore, the percentage impact falls more heavily on the smaller income value than on the larger asset and shareholders' equity values. Many of the key financial ratios that are based on income, asset values, or equity values will also be affected by the choice of depreciation method.

10.6.9 No matter which depreciation method is chosen, the total accumulated depreciation will be the same over the entire useful life of an asset. Thus, the effects shown in table 10.2 for the early year or years of an asset's life tend to reverse over time. However, these reversals apply to the depreciation effects associated with an **individual asset**. If a company's asset base is growing, the depreciation applicable to the most-recently acquired assets tends to dominate the overall depreciation expense of the entity. The effects described in the table will normally apply over time because the reversal process is overwhelmed by the depreciation charges applied to newer assets. Only if an entity is in decline and its capital expenditures are low will the reversal effects be noticeable in the aggregate.

10.6.10 The determination of the **useful life** of an asset also affects financial statement values and key financial ratios. The intended usage period—not the actual life—should determine the useful life. All other factors being held constant, the shorter the useful life of an asset, the larger its depreciation will be over its depreciable life. This will raise the depreciation expense, lower reported income, reduce asset values, and reduce shareholders' equity relative to what they would be if a longer useful life were chosen.

Reported cash flow will not be affected, because depreciation is not a cash expense. However, key financial ratios that contain income, asset values, and shareholders' equity will be affected. A shorter useful life tends to lower profit margins and return on equity, while at the same time raising asset turnover and debt-to-equity ratios.

10.6.11 Choosing a large **residual value** has the opposite effect of choosing a short useful life. All other factors being constant, a high salvage (residual) value will lower the depreciation expense, raise reported income, and raise the book values of assets and shareholders' equity relative to what they would be if a lower salvage value had been chosen. Cash flow, however, is unaffected because depreciation is a noncash expense. As a result of a high salvage value, an entity's profit margin and return on equity increase, whereas its asset turnover and debt-to-equity ratios decrease.

10.6.12 When depreciation is based on the historical cost of assets, it presents a problem during periods of inflation. When the prices of capital goods increase over time, the depreciation accumulated over the life of such assets will fall short of the amount needed to replace them when they wear out.

To understand this concept, consider equipment that costs $10,000, has a five-year useful life, and has no salvage value. If straight-line depreciation is used, this asset will be depreciated at a rate of $2,000 per year for its five-year life. Over the life of the equipment, this depreciation will accumulate to $10,000. If there had been no inflation in the intervening period, the original equipment could then be replaced with a new $10,000 piece of equipment. Historical-cost depreciation makes sense in a zero-inflation environment, because the amount of depreciation expensed matches the cost to replace the asset.

However, suppose the inflation rate over the equipment's depreciable life had been 10 percent per year, instead of zero. When it is time to replace the asset, its replacement will cost $16,105 ($10,000 ¥ 1.105). The accumulated depreciation is $6,105 less than what is required to physically restore the entity to its original asset position. In other words, the real cost of the equipment is higher, and the reported financial statements are distorted.

This analysis illustrates that, during periods of inflation, depreciating physical assets on the basis of historical cost, in accordance with the financial capital maintenance theory of income, tends to understate the true depreciation expense. As such, it overstates the true earnings of an entity from the point of view of the physical capital maintenance (replacement cost) theory of income.

10.6.13 Table 10.2 provides an overview of the impact of changes in consumption patterns, depreciable asset lives (duration of consumption), and salvage values on financial statements and ratios. Comparisons of a company's financial performance with industry competitors would be similar to the effects of changes in table 10.2's variables if competitors use different depreciation methods, higher (or lower) depreciable asset lives, and relatively higher (or lower) salvage values.

Table 10.2 Impact of Changes on Financial Statements and Ratios

Variable	Change from Straight-Line to Depreciation Based on Accelerated Consumption Pattern in Early Years	Change from Accelerated Consumption Pattern in Early Years to Straight-Line Depreciation	Increase (Decrease) in Asset Depreciable Life (Duration of Consumption)	Increase (Decrease) in Salvage Value
Earnings	**Lower** due to higher depreciation expense	**Higher** due to lower depreciation expense	**Higher (lower)** due to lower (higher) depreciation expense	**Higher (lower)** due to lower (higher) depreciation expense
Net Worth	**Lower** due to higher asset write-down	**Higher** due to lower asset write-down	**Higher (lower)** due to lower (higher) asset write-down	**Higher (lower)** due to lower (higher) asset write-down
Cash Flow	No effect	No effect	No effect	No effect
Profit Margin	**Lower** due to lower earnings	Higher due to lower earnings	**Higher (lower)** due to higher (lower) earnings	**Higher (lower)** due to higher (lower) earnings
Current Ratio	**None**; only affects long-term assets	**None**; only affects long-term assets	**None**; only affects long-term assets	**None**; only affects long-term assets
Asset Turnover	**Higher** due to lower assets	**Lower** due to higher assets	**Lower (higher)** due to higher (lower) assets	**Lower (higher)** due to higher (lower) assets
Debt-to-Equity	**Higher** due to lower net worth	**Lower** due to higher net worth	**Lower (higher)** due to higher (lower) net worth	**Lower (higher)** due to higher (lower) net worth
Return on Assets	**Lower** due to a larger percentage decline in earnings versus asset decline	**Higher** due to a larger percentage rise in earnings versus asset rise	**Higher (lower)** due to a larger (smaller) percentage rise in earnings versus asset rise	**Higher (lower)** due to a larger (smaller) percentage rise in earnings versus asset rise
Return on Equity	**Lower** due to a larger percentage decline in earnings versus equity decline	**Higher** due to a larger percentage rise in earnings versus equity rise	**Higher (lower)** due to a larger (smaller) percentage rise in earnings versus equity rise	**Higher (lower)** due to a larger (smaller) percentage rise in earnings versus equity rise

EXAMPLE 10.1

An entity begins the year with assets of $8,500, consisting of $500 in cash and $8,000 in plant and equipment. These assets are financed with $200 of current liabilities, $2,000 of 7 percent long-term debt, and $6,300 of common stock. During the year, the entity has sales of $10,000 and incurs $7,000 of operating expenses (excluding depreciation), $1,000 of construction costs for new plant and equipment, and $140 of interest expense. The entity depreciates its plant and equipment over 10 years (no residual [salvage] value). Ignoring the effect of income taxes, develop **pro forma** Statements of Comprehensive Income and Statements of Financial Position for the company's operations for the year if it expenses the $1,000 of construction costs and if it capitalizes these costs.

The effect of the expense-or-capitalize-cost decision on the company's shareholders' equity, pretax income, pretax operating and investing cash flows, and key financial ratios should be analyzed.

It is assumed that construction costs will be depreciated over four years and that the resulting asset will be ready for use on the first day of Year 1.

The results of the expense-or-capitalize-cost decision should be summarized.

EXPLANATION

	Expense construction costs		Capitalize construction costs		
	Year 0 ($)	Year 1 ($)	Year 0 ($)	Year 1 ($)	
Sales		10,000		10,000	
Operating expenses		7,000		7,000	
Construction costs		1,000		–	
Depreciation expense		800		800	(8000-0/10)
Amortization expense		–		250	(1000/4)
Interest expense		140		140	
Pretax Income		1,060		1,810	
Cash	500	2,360	500	2,360	
Plant and equipment	8,000	7,200	8,000	7,200	($8,000 − $800)
Construction costs	–	–	–	750	($1,000 − $250)
Total Assets	8,500	9,560	8,500	10,310	
Current Liabilities	200	200	200	200	
Long-term debt	2,000	2,000	2,000	2,000	
Common stock	6,300	6,300	6,300	6,300	
Retained earnings	–	1,060	–	1,810	
Total Liabilities and Capital	8,500	9,560	8,500	10,310	
Shareholders' equity		7,360		8,110	
Pretax earnings		1,060		1,810	
Operating cash flow (pretax + depreciation and amortization)		1,860		2,860	
Investing cash flow		–		(1,000)	(construction cost)
Net Cash Flow		1,860		1,860	
Pretax Profit Margin		10.6%		18.1%	
Asset Turnover (Sales/Average Assets)		1.11x		1.06x	
Current Ratio		11.8x		11.8x	
Long-Term Debt-to-Equity		27.2%		24.7x	
Pretax ROE (Income/Average Equity)		15.5%		25.1%	

EXAMPLE 10.2

On January 1, 20X1, Zakharetz Inc. acquired production equipment in the amount of $250,000. The following further costs were incurred:

	$
Delivery	18,000
Installation	24,500
General administration costs of an indirect nature	3,000

The installation and setting-up period took three months, and an additional $21,000 was spent on costs directly related to bringing the asset to its working condition. The equipment was ready for use on April 1, 20X1.

Monthly managerial reports indicated that for the first five months, the production quantities from this equipment resulted in an initial operating loss of $15,000 because of small quantities produced. The months thereafter showed much more positive results.

The equipment has an estimated useful life of 14 years and a residual value of $18,000. Estimated dismantling costs are $12,500.

What is the cost of the asset and what are the annual charges in the Statement of Comprehensive Income related to the consumption of the economic benefits embodied in the assets?

EXPLANATION

Historical cost of equipment	
	$
Invoice price	250,000
Delivery	18,000
Installation	24,500
Other costs directly related to bringing the asset to its working condition	21,000
Initial estimate of dismantling costs	12,500
	326,000

Annual charges related to equipment	
	$
Historical cost	326,000
Estimated residual value	(18,000)
Depreciable amount	308,000

The annual charge to the Statement of Comprehensive Income is $22,000 ($308,000 ÷ 14 years). However, note that in the year ending December 31, 20X1, the charge will be $16,500 (9/12 ¥ $22,000) because the equipment was ready for use on April 1, 20X1, after the installation and setting-up period.

EXAMPLE 10.3

Delta Printers Inc. acquired its buildings and printing machinery on January 1, 20X1, for the amount of $2 million and recorded it at the historical acquisition cost. During 20X3, the directors made a decision to account for the machinery at fair value in the future, to provide for the maintenance of capital of the business in total.

Will measurement at fair value achieve the objective of capital maintenance? How is fair value determined? What are the deferred tax implications?

EXPLANATION

Maintenance of capital

The suggested method of accounting treatment will not be completely successful for the maintenance of capital due to the following:

- No provision is made for maintaining the current cost of inventory, work-in-process, and other nonmonetary assets.
- No provision is made for the cost of holding monetary assets.
- No provision is made for backlog depreciation.

Fair value

The fair value of plant and equipment items is usually their market value determined by appraisal. When there is no proof of market value, due to the specialized nature of plant and equipment and because these items are rarely sold (except as part of a going concern), then the items are to be valued at net replacement cost.

Deferred tax implication of revaluation

Deferred taxation is provided for on the revaluation amount for the following reasons:

- The revalued carrying amount is recovered through use, and taxable economic benefits are obtained against which no depreciation deductions for tax purposes are allowed. Therefore, the taxation payable on these economic benefits should be provided.
- Deferred taxation, as a result of revaluation, is charged directly against the revaluation surplus (equity).

Chapter Eleven

Investment Property (IAS 40)

11.1   OBJECTIVE

The objective of IAS 40 is to prescribe the accounting treatment for investment property and related disclosure requirements. The main issue arises when entities decide whether to adopt the fair value or the cost model for investment property for recordkeeping purposes. Whichever choice is exercised, the standard specifies that the fair value amount of investment property should be disclosed.

11.2   SCOPE OF THE STANDARD

IAS 40 applies to all investment property. This standard permits entities to choose either

- a **fair value model,** under which an investment property, after initial measurement, is measured at fair value, with changes in fair value recognized in profit or loss; or

- a **cost model,** under which investment property, after initial measurement, is measured at depreciated cost (less any accumulated impairment losses).

The following major aspects of accounting for investment property are prescribed:

- Classification of a property as investment property
- Recognition as an asset
- Determination of the carrying amount at
  - initial measurement, and
  - subsequent measurement
- Disclosure requirements

11.3   KEY CONCEPTS

11.3.1 Investment property is property that is held by the owner or the lessee under a finance lease to earn rentals, or for capital appreciation, or both. An investment property should generate cash flows that are largely independent of the other assets held by the entity.

11.3.2 Investments property includes land and buildings or part of a building or both. It **excludes**

- owner-occupied property (PPE—IAS 16),
- property held for sale (Inventory—IAS 2),
- property being constructed or developed (Construction Contracts—IAS 11),
- property held by a lessee under an operating lease (see section 11.4.2),
- biological assets (IAS 41), and

■ mining rights and mineral resources (ED 6).

11.4   ACCOUNTING TREATMENT

Recognition

11.4.1 An investment property is recognized as an asset if

■ it is **probable** that the future economic benefits attributable to the asset will flow to the entity, and

■ the cost of the asset can be **reliably measured**.

11.4.2 A **property interest that is held by a lessee under an operating lease** does not meet the definition of an investment property, but could be classified and accounted for as investment property provided that

■ the rest of the definition of investment property is met,

■ the operating lease is accounted for as if it were a finance lease in accordance with IAS 17, and

■ the lessee uses the fair value model set out in this standard for the asset recognized.

Initial Measurement

11.4.3 On **initial measurement**, investment property is recognized at its cost, comprising the purchase price and directly attributable transaction costs (for example, legal services, transfer taxes, and other transaction costs). However, general administrative expenses as well as start-up costs are excluded. Cost is determined the same way as for other property (see IAS 16, chapter 10).

Subsequent Measurement

11.4.4 An entity might choose to **subsequently** measure all of its investment property, using either of the following:

■ **Cost model**. Measures investment property at cost less accumulated depreciation and impairment losses.

■ **Fair value model**. Measures investment properties at fair value. Gains and losses from changes in the fair value are recognized in the Statement of Comprehensive Income as they arise. (**Fair value** is the amount at which an asset could be exchanged between knowledgeable, willing parties in an arm's-length transaction.)

11.4.5 The following principles are applied to determine the **fair value** for investment property:

■ Where an active market on similar property exists, this might be a reliable indicator of fair value, provided the differences in the nature, condition, and location of the properties are considered and amended, where necessary.

■ Other more pragmatic valuation approaches are also allowed when an active market is not available. (See also International Valuation Standards at www.ivsc.org.)

- In exceptional circumstances, where it is clear when the investment property is first acquired that the entity will not be able to determine its fair value, the property is measured using the benchmark treatment in IAS 16 until its disposal date. The entity measures all of its other investment property at fair value.

11.4.6 Transfers to or from investment property should be made when there is a change in use. Special provisions apply for determining the carrying value at the date of such transfers.

11.4.7 Subsequent expenditures on investment property are recognized as expenses if they restore the performance standard. These expenditures are capitalized when it is probable that economic benefits **in excess** of the original standard of performance will flow to the entity.

11.5 PRESENTATION AND DISCLOSURE

11.5.1 Accounting policies should specify the following:

- Criteria to distinguish investment property from owner-occupied property
- Methods and significant assumptions applied in determining **fair value**
- Extent to which fair value has been determined by an external independent valuer
- Measurement bases, depreciation methods, and rates for investment property valued according to the **cost model**
- The existence and amounts of restrictions on the investment property
- Material contractual obligations to purchase, construct, or develop investment property or for repairs or enhancement to the property

11.5.2 Statement of Comprehensive Income and notes should include the following:

- Rental income
- Direct operating expenses arising from an investment property that generated rental income
- Direct operating expenses from an investment property that did not generate rental income

11.5.3 Statement of Financial Position and notes should include the following:

- When an entity applies the **fair value model**—
  - A detailed reconciliation of movements in the carrying amount during the period should be provided.
  - In exceptional cases when an investment property cannot be measured at fair value (because of a lack of fair value), the reconciliation above should be separately disclosed from other investment property shown at fair value.
- When an entity applies the **cost model**—
  - All the disclosure requirements of IAS 16 should be furnished.
  - The fair value of investment property is disclosed by way of a note.

Decision Tree

Figure 11.1 summarizes the classification, recognition, and measurement issues of an investment property. The diagram is based on a decision tree adapted from IAS 40.

Figure 11.1 Decision Tree

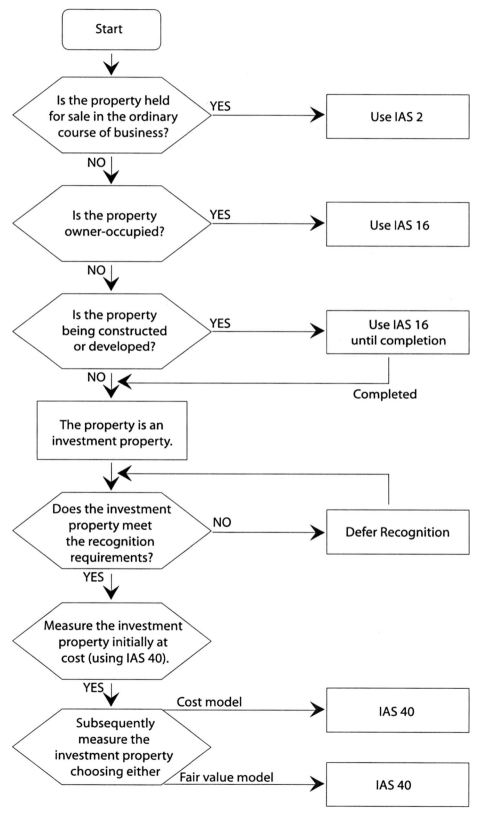

EXAMPLE 11.1

Matchbox Inc. manufactures toys for boys. The following information relates to fixed property owned by the company:

	$'000
Land - Plot 181 Hatfield	800
Buildings thereon (acquired June 30, 20X0)	2,100
Improvements to the building to extend rented floor capacity	400
Repairs and maintenance to investment property for the year	50
Rentals received for the year	160

Approximately 6 percent of the property's floor space is used as the administrative head office of the company. The property can be sold only as a complete unit. The remainder of the building is leased out under operating leases. The company provides lessees with security services.

The company values investment property using the fair value model. On December 31, 20X0, the Statement of Financial Position date, Mr. Proper (an independent valuer) valued the property at $3.6 million.

EXPLANATION

To account for the property in the financial statements of Matchbox Inc. as of December 31, 20X0, the property should first be classified as either investment property or owner-occupied property. It is classified as an **investment property** and is accounted for in terms of the fair value model in IAS 40. The motivation is that the portion occupied by the company for administrative purposes (6 percent) is deemed to be insignificant, and the portions of the property cannot be sold separately. In addition, the majority of the floor space of the property is used to generate rental income, and the security services rendered to lessees are insignificant.

The accounting treatment and disclosure of the property in the financial statements of Matchbox Inc. are as follows:

Statement of Financial Position at December 31, 20X0		
	Note	$'000
Noncurrent Assets		
Property, plant, and equipment		Xxx
Investment property **(Calculation a)**	4	3,600

Accounting policies

Investment property is property held to earn rentals. Investment property is stated at fair value, determined at the Statement of Financial Position date by an independent valuer based on market evidence of the most recent prices achieved in arm's-length transactions of similar properties in the same area.

Notes to the Financial Statements

Investment Property	$'000
Opening balance	–
Additions	2,900
Improvements from subsequent expenditure	400
Net gain in fair value adjustments	300
Closing balance at fair value	3,600

Calculation a

Carrying Amount of Investment Property	$'000
Land	800
Building	2,100
Improvements to building	400
	3,300
Fair value	(3,600)
Increase in value shown in Statement of Comprehensive Income	(300)

Chapter Twelve

Agriculture (IAS 41)

12.1 OBJECTIVE

IAS 41 prescribes the accounting treatment, financial statement presentation, and disclosures related to biological assets and agricultural produce at the point of harvest insofar as they relate to agricultural activity.

The accounting treatment of related government grants is also prescribed in IAS 41 (see also chapter 27, IAS 20).

12.2 SCOPE OF THE STANDARD

This standard should be applied to account for the following when they relate to agricultural activity:

- Biological assets
- Agricultural produce at the point of harvest
- Government grants

This standard does **not** apply to

- land related to agricultural activity (IAS 16), or
- intangible assets related to agricultural activity (IAS 38).

IAS 41 does not deal with processing agricultural produce after harvest; for example, it does not deal with processing grapes into wine or wool into yarn. Such processing is accounted for as inventory in accordance with IAS 2.

12.3 KEY CONCEPTS

12.3.1 Agricultural activity is the management by an entity of the biological transformation of biological assets for sale, into agricultural produce, or into additional biological assets. For example, a fish farm would qualify as agricultural activity, but not fishing on its own.

12.3.2 Agricultural produce is the harvested product of the entity's biological assets.

12.3.3 A **biological asset** is a living animal or plant.

12.3.4 Harvest is the detachment of produce from a biological asset or the cessation of a biological asset's life processes.

12.3.5 An **active market** is a market where all the following conditions exist:

- The items traded within the market are homogeneous.
- Willing buyers and sellers can normally be found at any time.
- Prices are available to the public.

12.4   ACCOUNTING TREATMENT

Recognition

12.4.1 An entity should **recognize** a biological asset or agricultural produce when, and only when

- the entity controls the asset as a result of past events,
- it is probable that future economic benefits associated with the asset will flow to the entity, and
- the fair value or cost of the asset can be measured reliably.

Initial Measurement

12.4.2 A biological asset should be **measured on initial recognition** and at each Statement of Financial Position date at its fair value less estimated point-of-sale costs. However, if on initial recognition it is determined that fair value cannot be measured reliably, a biological asset should be measured at cost less accumulated depreciation and any accumulated impairment losses. Once the fair value of such an asset becomes reliably measurable, it should be measured at fair value less estimated point-of-sale costs.

12.4.3 Agricultural produce **harvested** from an entity's biological assets should be measured at its fair value less estimated point-of-sale costs at the point of harvest. Such measurement is the cost at that date when applying IAS 2 or any other applicable IFRS.

12.4.4 If an **active market** exists for a biological asset or harvested produce, the quoted price in that market is the appropriate basis for determining the fair value of that asset. If an active market does not exist, an entity uses one or more of the following in determining fair value:

- The most recent market transaction price
- Market prices for similar assets
- Sector benchmarks such as the value of an orchard expressed per export tray, bushel, or hectare, and the value of cattle expressed per kilogram of meat

12.4.5 A **gain or loss** on the **initial recognition** of a biological asset or agricultural produce at **fair value** (less estimated point-of-sale costs) and from a **change in fair value** (less estimated point-of-sale costs) of a biological asset should be included in net profit or loss for the period in which the gain or loss arises.

12.4.6 An unconditional **government grant** related to a biological asset measured at its fair value (less estimated point-of-sale costs) should be recognized as income only when the grant becomes receivable.

12.5   PRESENTATION AND DISCLOSURE

12.5.1 An entity should present the **carrying amount** of its biological assets **separately** on the face of its Statement of Financial Position.

12.5.2 An entity should disclose the **aggregate gain or loss** arising during the current period on initial recognition of biological assets and agricultural produce and from the change in fair value less estimated point-of-sale costs of biological assets.

12.5.3 An entity should provide a **description** of each group of biological assets.

12.5.4 An entity should **describe**

- the nature of its activities involving each group of biological assets, and
- nonfinancial measures or estimates of the physical quantities of
    - each group of biological assets at the end of the period, and
    - output of agricultural produce during the period.

12.5.5 An entity should **disclose**

- the methods and significant assumptions applied in determining the fair value of each group of agricultural produce and biological assets;
- fair value less estimated point-of-sale costs of agricultural produce harvested during the period, determined at the point of harvest;
- the existence and carrying amounts of biological assets whose title is restricted, and the carrying amounts of biological assets pledged as security for liabilities;
- the amount of commitments for the development or acquisition of biological assets and the financial risk-management strategies related to its agricultural activity;
- the nature and extent of government grants recognized in the financial statements;
- unfulfilled conditions and other contingencies attaching to government grants; and
- significant decreases expected in the level of government grants.

12.5.6 An entity should present a **reconciliation** of changes in the carrying amount of biological assets between the beginning and the end of the current period, including

- decreases due to sales,
- decreases due to harvest,
- increases resulting from business combinations,
- net exchange differences arising on the translation of financial statements of a foreign entity, and
- other changes.

12.6 FINANCIAL ANALYSIS AND INTERPRETATION

12.6.1 As with any fair value standard, users should pay particular attention to the disclosure of key assumptions used to determine fair value and the consistency of those assumptions from year to year.

12.6.2 In particular, the discount rate estimation and estimation techniques used to determine volumes of agricultural assets are likely to have a significant impact on the fair value numbers.

EXAMPLE 12.1

12.1.A Statement of Financial Position

XYZ Dairy Ltd. Statement of Financial Position	Notes	December 31, 20X1	December 31, 20X0
ASSETS			
Noncurrent Assets			
Dairy livestock—immature		52,060	47,730
Dairy livestock—mature		372,990	411,840
Subtotal Biological Assets	3	425,050	459,570
Property, plant, and equipment		1,462,650	1,409,800
Total Noncurrent Assets		1,887,700	1,869,370
Current Assets			
Inventories		82,950	70,650
Trade and other receivables		88,000	65,000
Cash		10,000	10,000
Total Current Assets		180,950	145,650
TOTAL ASSETS		2,068,650	2,015,020
EQUITY AND LIABILITIES			
Equity			
Issued capital		1,000,000	1,000,000
Accumulated profits		902,828	865,000
Total Equity		1,902,828	1,865,000
Current Liabilities			
Trade and other payables		165,822	150,020
Total Current Liabilities		165,822	150,020
TOTAL EQUITY AND LIABILITIES		2,068,650	2,015,020

An enterprise is encouraged but not required to provide a quantified description of each group of biological assets, distinguishing between consumable and bearer biological assets or between mature and immature biological assets, as appropriate. An enterprise discloses the basis for making any such distinctions.

Source: International Accounting Standards Board, IAS 41: Agriculture, pp. 2297–2300. Used with permission.

12.1.B Statement of Comprehensive Income

XYZ Dairy Ltd. Statement of Comprehensive Income	Notes	Year Ended December 31, 20X1
Fair value of milk produced		518,240
Gains arising from changes in fair value less estimated point-of-sale costs of dairy livestock	3	39,930
Total Income		**558,170**
Inventories used		(137,523)
Staff costs		(127,283)
Depreciation expense		(15,250)
Other operating expenses		(197,092)
		(477,148)
Profit from Operations		**81,022**
Income tax expense		(43,194)
Net Profit for the Period		37,828

12.1.C Statement of Changes in Equity

XYZ Dairy Ltd. Statement of Changes in Equity	Year Ended December 31, 20X1		
	Share Capital	Accumulated Profits	Total
Balance at January 1, 20X1	1,000,000	865,000	1,865,000
Net profit for the period		37,828	37,828
Balance at December 31, 20X1	1,000,000	902,828	1,902,828

12.1.D Statement of Cash Flows

XYZ Dairy Ltd. Cash Flow Statement	Notes	Year Ended December 31, 20X1
Cash Flows from Operating Activities		
Cash receipts from sales of milk		498,027
Cash receipts from sales of livestock		97,913
Cash paid for supplies and to employees		(460,831)
Cash paid for purchases of livestock		(23,815)
		111,294
Income taxes paid		(43,194)
Net Cash from Operating Activities		68,100
Cash Flows from Investing Activities		
Purchase of property, plant, and equipment		(68,100)
Net Cash Used in Investing Activities		(68,100)
Net Increase in Cash		0
Cash at Beginning of Period		10,000
Cash at End of Period		10,000

12.1.E Notes to the Financial Statements

Note 1. Operations and Principal Activities

XYZ Dairy Ltd. ("the Company") is engaged in milk production for supply to various customers. At December 31, 20X1, the Company held 419 cows able to produce milk (mature assets) and 137 heifers being raised to produce milk in the future (immature assets). The Company produced 157,584 kg of milk with a fair value less estimated point-of-sale costs of 518,240 (determined at the time of milking) in the year ended December 31,20X1.

Note 2. Accounting Policies

Livestock and milk

Livestock are measured at their fair value less estimated point-of-sale costs. The fair value of livestock is determined based on market prices of livestock of similar age, breed, and genetic merit. Milk is initially measured at its fair value less estimated point-of-sale costs at the time of milking. The fair value of milk is determined based on market prices in the local area.

Note 3. Biological Assets

Reconciliation of Carrying Amounts of Dairy Livestock	20X1
Carrying Amount at January 1, 20X1	459,570
Increases due to purchases	26,250
Gain arising from changes in fair value less estimated point-of-sale costs attributable to physical changes	15,350
Gain arising from changes in fair value less estimated point-of-sale costs attributable to price changes	24,580
Decreases due to sales	(100,700)
Carrying Amount at December 31, 20X1	425,050

Note 4. Financial Risk-Management Strategies

The Company is exposed to financial risks arising from changes in milk prices. The Company does not anticipate that milk prices will decline significantly in the foreseeable future and, therefore, has not entered into derivative or other contracts to manage the risk of a decline in milk prices. The Company reviews its outlook for milk prices regularly in considering the need for active financial risk management.

EXAMPLE 12.2: PHYSICAL CHANGE AND PRICE CHANGE

Background

The following example illustrates how to separate physical change and price change. Separating the change in fair value less estimated point-of-sale costs between the portion attributable to physical changes and the portion attributable to price changes is encouraged but not required by this standard.

Example

A herd of 10 two-year old animals was held at January 1, 20X1. One animal 2.5 years of age was purchased on July 1, 20X1, for $108, and one animal was born on July 1, 20X1. No animals were sold or disposed of during the period. Per-unit fair values less estimated point-of-sale costs were as follows:

Animal Details	$	$
2-year-old animal at January 1, 20X1	100	
Newborn animal at July 1, 20X1	70	
2.5-year-old animal at July 1, 20X1	108	
Newborn animal at December 31, 20X1	72	
0.5-year-old animal at December 31, 20X1	80	
2-year-old animal at December 31, 20X1	105	
2.5-year-old animal at December 31, 20X1	111	
3-year-old animal at December 31, 20X1	120	
Fair value less estimated point-of-sale costs of herd on January 1, 20X1 (10 x 100)		1,000
Purchase on July 1, 20X1 (1 x 108)	108	
Increase in fair value less estimated point-of-sale costs due to price change:		
10 x (105 − 100)	50	
1 x (111 − 108)	3	
1 x (72 − 70)	2	55
Increase in fair value less estimated point-of-sale costs due to physical change:		
10 x (120 − 105)	150	
1 x (120 − 111)	9	
1 x (80 − 72)		8
1 x 70	70	237
Fair value less estimated point-of-sale costs of herd on December 31, 20X1		
11 x 120	1,320	
1 x 80	80	1,400

Source: International Accounting Standards Board, IAS 41: Agriculture, p. 2301. Used with permission.

EXAMPLE 12.3

In year 20X0, a farmer plants an apple orchard that costs him $250,000. At the end of year 20X1, the following facts regarding the orchard are available:

Disease. There has been widespread disease in the apple tree population. As a result there is no active market for the orchard, but the situation is expected to clear in six months. After the six months, it should also be clear which types of trees are susceptible to infection and which ones are not. Until that time, nobody is willing to risk an infected orchard.

Precedent. The last sale by the farmer of an orchard was six months ago at a price of $150,000. He is not sure which way the market has gone since then.

Local values. The farmers in the region have an average value of $195,000 for their orchards of a similar size.

National values. The farmer recently read in a local agricultural magazine that the average price of an apple tree orchard is $225,000.

What is the correct valuation of the apple tree orchard?

EXPLANATION

The valuation would be the fair value less estimated point-of-sales costs. Fair value is determined as follows:

- Use active market prices—there are none, due to the disease.
- Use other relevant information, such as
  - The most recent market transaction $150,000
  - Market prices for similar assets $195,000
  - Sector benchmarks $225,000

If the fair value **cannot** be determined, then the valuation would be determined at cost, less accumulated depreciation and accumulated impairment losses: $250,000.

However, there are other reliable sources available for the determination of fair value. Such sources should be used. The mean value of all the available indicators above would be used (in the range of $150,000 to $225,000).

In addition, the farmer would consider the reasons for the differences between the various sources of other information, prior to arriving at the most reliable estimate of fair value.

In the absence of recent prices, sector benchmarks, and other information, the farmer should calculate the fair value as comprising the cost price, less impairments, less depreciation—resulting in a valuation of $250,000.

Source: Deloitte Touche Tohmatsu.

Chapter Thirteen

Intangible Assets (IAS 38)

13.1 OBJECTIVE

An intangible asset is one that has no physical form, although it exists from contractual and legal rights and has an economic value. The objective of IAS 38 is to allow entities to identify and recognize separately the value of intangible assets on the Statement of Financial Position, providing certain conditions are satisfied. IAS 38 enables users to more accurately assess the value as well as the makeup of assets of the entity.

13.2 SCOPE OF THE STANDARD

IAS 38 applies to all intangible assets that are not specifically dealt with in another standard. Examples include brand names, computer software, licenses, franchises, and intangibles under development. This standard prescribes the accounting treatment of intangible assets, including

- the definition of an intangible asset,
- recognition as an asset,
- determination of the carrying amount,
- determination and the treatment of impairment losses, and
- disclosure requirements.

13.3 KEY CONCEPTS

13.3.1 An intangible asset is an identifiable nonmonetary asset

- without physical substance;
- that is separable;
- that arises from contractual or other legal rights, regardless of whether those rights are transferable or separable from the entity or other rights and obligations;
- that is capable of being separated from the entity and sold, transferred, licensed, rented, or exchanged—either individually or together with a related contract, asset, or liability; and
- that is clearly distinguishable and controlled separately from an entity's goodwill.

13.4 ACCOUNTING TREATMENT

Recognition

13.4.1 An intangible asset is **recognized** as an asset (in terms of the framework) if

- it is **probable** that the future economic benefits attributable to the asset will flow to the entity, and

- the cost of the asset can be **measured reliably**.

13.4.2 **Development expenditure** is recognized as an intangible asset if *all* of the following can be demonstrated:

- The technical feasibility of completing the intangible asset so that it will be available for use or sale (the "Eureka" moment where one can state with certainty that a product will result from the efforts)

- The availability of adequate technical, financial, and other resources to complete the development and to use or sell the intangible asset

- The intention to complete the intangible asset and use or sell it

- The ability to use or sell the intangible asset

- The means by which the intangible asset will generate probable future economic benefits

- The ability to measure the expenditure

13.4.3 **Development expenditure** previously recognized as an expense cannot be subsequently capitalized as an asset.

13.4.4 Expenses related to the following categories are *not* recognized as intangible assets and are **expensed**:

- Internally generated brands (externally purchased brand names might qualify for capitalization if independently valued)

- Mastheads, publishing titles, customer lists, and so on

- Start-up costs

- Training costs

- Advertising and promotion

- Relocation and reorganization expenses

- Redundancy and other termination costs

Initial Measurement

13.4.5 On **initial** recognition, an intangible asset is measured at **cost**, whether it is acquired externally or developed internally.

13.4.6 For any internal project to create an intangible asset, the research phase and development phase should be distinguished from one another. **Research expenditure** is treated as an expense. **Development expenditure** qualifying for recognition is measured at **cost**.

Subsequent Measurement

13.4.7 Subsequent to initial recognition, an entity should choose either the **cost model** or the **revaluation model** as its accounting policy for intangible assets and should apply that policy to an entire class of intangible assets:

- **Cost model.** The **carrying amount** of an intangible asset is its cost less accumulated amortization. Assets classified as held for sale are shown at the lower of fair value less costs to sell and carrying amount.

- **Revaluation model.** The **carrying amount** of an item of intangible asset is its fair value less subsequent accumulated amortization and impairment losses. Assets classified as held for sale are shown at the lower of fair value less costs to sell and carrying amount.

13.4.8 An entity should assess whether the **useful life** of an intangible asset is **finite** or **infinite**. If finite, the entity should determine the length of its life or the number of production or similar units constituting its useful life. Amortization and impairment principles apply as follows:

- An intangible asset with a **finite** useful life is amortized on a systematic basis over the best estimate of its useful life.

- An intangible asset with an **infinite** useful life should be tested for impairment annually, but not amortized.

13.4.9 To assess whether an **intangible asset** might be **impaired**, an entity should apply IAS 36, Impairment of Assets. Also, that standard requires an entity to estimate, at least annually, the recoverable amount of an intangible asset that is not yet available for use.

13.4.10 In the case of a business combination, expenditure on an intangible item that does not meet both the definition and recognition criteria for an intangible asset should form part of the amount attributed to goodwill.

13.5   PRESENTATION AND DISCLOSURE

13.5.1 Each class of intangible assets should distinguish between **internally generated** and **other** intangibles.

13.5.2 Accounting policies should specify

- measurement bases,
- amortization methods, and
- useful lives or amortization rates.

13.5.3 Statement of Comprehensive Income and notes should disclose

- the amortization charge for each class of asset, indicating the line item in which it is included; and
- the total amount of research and development costs recognized as an expense.

13.5.4 Statement of Financial Position and notes should disclose the following:

- Gross carrying amount (book value) less accumulated depreciation for each class of asset at the beginning and the end of the period
- Detailed itemized reconciliation of movements in the carrying amount during the period; **comparatives are not required**
- If an intangible asset is amortized over more than 20 years, the evidence that rebuts the presumption that the useful life will not exceed 20 years

- Carrying amount of intangibles pledged as security
- Carrying amount of intangibles whose title is restricted
- Capital commitments for the acquisition of intangibles
- A description, the carrying amount, and remaining amortization period of any intangible that is material to the financial statements of the entity as a whole
- For intangible assets acquired by way of a government grant and initially recognized at fair value—
  - the fair value initially recognized for these assets,
  - their carrying amount, and
  - whether they are measured at the benchmark or allowed alternative treatment.

13.5.5 Additional disclosures required for revalued amounts are as follows:

- Effective date of the revaluation
- Carrying amount of *each* class of intangibles had it been carried in the financial statements on the historical cost basis
- Amount as well as a detailed reconciliation of the balance of the revaluation surplus
- Any restrictions on the distribution of the revaluation surplus

13.6   FINANCIAL ANALYSIS AND INTERPRETATION

13.6.1 This accounting standard determines that the intangible assets reported on a Statement of Financial Position are only those intangibles that have been purchased or manufactured (in limited instances). However, companies have intangible assets that are not recorded on their Statements of Financial Position; these intangible assets include management skill, valuable trademarks and name recognition, a good reputation, proprietary products, and so forth. Such assets are valuable and would fetch their worth if a company were to be sold.

13.6.2 Analysts should try to assess the value of such assets based on a company's ability to earn economic profits or rents from them, even though it is difficult to do so.

13.6.3 Financial analysts have traditionally viewed the values assigned to intangible assets with suspicion. Consequently, in adjusting financial statements, they often exclude the book value assigned to intangibles (reducing net equity by an equal amount and increasing pretax income by the amortization expense associated with the intangibles).

13.6.4 This arbitrary assignment of zero value to intangibles might also be inadvisable. The analyst should decide if there is any extra earning power attributable to goodwill or any other intangible asset. If there is, it is a valuable asset.

13.6.5 An issue to be considered when comparing the returns on equity or assets of various companies is the degree of recognized intangible assets. An entity that has acquired many of its intangible assets in mergers and acquisitions will typically have a significantly higher amount of such assets in its Statement of Financial Position (and hence lower returns on equity and assets) than an equivalent entity that has developed most of its intangible assets internally.

EXAMPLE: INTANGIBLE ASSETS

EXAMPLE 13.1

Alpha Inc., a motor vehicle manufacturer, has a research division that worked on the following projects during the year:

- **Project 1:** The design of a steering mechanism that does not operate like a conventional steering wheel, but reacts to the impulses from a driver's fingers
- **Project 2:** The design of a welding apparatus that is controlled electronically rather than mechanically

The following is a summary of the expenses of the particular department:

	General $'000	Project 1 $'000	Project 2 $'000
Material and services	128	935	620
Labor			
■ Direct labor	–	620	320
■ Department head salary	400	–	–
■ Administrative personnel	725	–	–
Overhead			
■ Direct	–	340	410
■ Indirect	270	110	60

The department head spent 15 percent of his time on Project 1 and 10 percent of his time on Project 2.

EXPLANATION

The capitalization of development costs for the year would be as follows:

	$'000
Project 1. The activity is classified as research, and all costs are recognized as expenses	–
Project 2. (620 + 320 + 10% x 400 + 410 + 60)	1,450
	1,450

Chapter Fourteen

Leases (IAS 17)

14.1   OBJECTIVE

Lease accounting is mostly concerned with the appropriate criteria for the recognition, as well as the measurement, of the leased asset and liability. Associated with this primary concern is the somewhat artificial distinction between a finance lease (which is recognized as an asset and depreciated) and an operating lease (which is expensed as the charges occur).

14.2   SCOPE OF THE STANDARD

IAS 17 applies to all lease agreements whereby the lessor conveys to the lessee in return for a payment or series of payments the right to use an asset for an agreed period of time.

The standard prescribes, for **lessees** and **lessors**, the appropriate accounting policies and disclosure that should be applied to various types of lease transactions. It specifies the criteria for distinguishing between finance leases and operating leases, the recognition and measurement of the resulting assets and liabilities, as well as disclosures.

This standard should be applied in accounting for all leases other than

- leases to explore for or use minerals, oil, natural gas, and similar nonregenerative resources; and
- licensing agreements for such items as motion picture films, video recordings, plays, manuscripts, patents, and copyrights.

However, this standard should *not* be applied as the basis of measurement for

- property held by lessees that is accounted for as investment property (see IAS 40),
- investment property provided by lessors under operating leases (see IAS 40),
- biological assets held by lessees under finance leases (see IAS 41), or
- biological assets provided by lessors under operating leases (see IAS 41).

14.3   KEY CONCEPTS

14.3.1 A **lease** is an agreement whereby the lessor conveys to the lessee in return for a payment or series of payments the right to use an asset for an agreed period of time.

14.3.2 **Finance leases** transfer substantially all the risks and rewards incident to ownership of an asset.

14.3.3 The characteristics of **finance leases** include the following:

- The lease transfers ownership of the asset to the lessee at the expiration of the lease.

- The lessee has an option to purchase the asset at less than fair value; the option will be exercised with reasonable certainty.
- The lease term is for a major part of the economic life of the asset.
- The present value of minimum lease payments approximates fair value of the leased asset.
- The leased assets is of a specialized nature and suitable only for the lessee.
- The lessee will bear cancellation losses.
- The fluctuation gains or losses of residual value are passed on to the lessee.
- The lease for a secondary period is possible at substantially lower-than-market rent.

14.3.4 **Operating leases** are leases other than finance leases. Many lease contracts are artificially structured to qualify as operating leases, causing standard setters to reconsider whether this category should exist at all.

14.3.5 **Minimum lease payments** are the payments over the lease term that the lessee is required to make to a third party. Certain contingent and other items are excluded. However, if the lessee has an option to purchase the asset at a price that is expected to be sufficiently less than fair value at the date the option becomes exercisable, the minimum lease payments comprise the minimum payments payable over the lease term to the expected date of exercise of this purchase option plus the payment required to exercise it.

14.3.6 **Fair value** is the amount for which an asset could be exchanged, or a liability settled, between knowledgeable, willing parties in an arm's-length transaction.

14.4   ACCOUNTING TREATMENT

Accounting by Lessees

14.4.1 The **classification** of leases is done at inception of the lease. The substance rather than the form of the lease contract is indicative of the classification. The classification is based on the extent to which risks and rewards incident to ownership of a leased asset lie with the lessor or the lessee:

- **Risks** include potential losses from idle capacity, technological obsolescence, and variations in return because of changing economic conditions.
- **Rewards** include the expectation of profitable operation over the asset's economic life and of gain from appreciation in value or the realization of a residual value.

14.4.2 An asset held under a **finance lease** and its corresponding obligation are recognized in terms of the principle of **substance over form**. The accounting treatment is as follows:

- At inception, the asset (recognized as property, plant, and equipment) and a corresponding liability for future lease payments are recognized at the same amounts.
- Initial direct costs in connection with lease activities are capitalized to the asset.
- Lease payments consist of the finance charge and the reduction of the outstanding liability.
- The finance charge is to be a constant periodic rate of interest on the remaining balance of the liability for each period.
- Depreciation and impairment of the leased asset is recognized in terms of IAS 16 and IAS 36.

14.4.3 Operating lease payments (excluding costs for services such as insurance) are recognized as an expense in the Statement of Comprehensive Income on a straight-line basis, or a systematic basis that is representative of the time pattern of the user's benefit, even if the payments are not on that basis.

Accounting by Lessors

14.4.4 An asset held under a **finance lease** is presented as a receivable. It is accounted for as follows:

- The receivable is recorded at the net investment amount.
- The recognition of finance income is based on a pattern reflecting a constant periodic rate of return on the net investment.
- Initial direct costs are deducted from receivables (except for manufacturer or dealer lessors).

14.4.5 An **operating leased** asset is classified according to its nature (per the agreement). It is accounted for as follows:

- Depreciation is recognized in terms of IAS 16 and IAS 38.
- Lease income is recognized on a straight-line basis over the lease term, unless another systematic basis is more representative.
- Initial direct costs are either recognized immediately or allocated against rent income over the lease term.

Sale and Leaseback Transactions

14.4.6 If the leaseback is a **finance lease**, any excess of sales proceeds over the carrying amount in the books of the lessee (vendor) should be deferred and amortized over the lease term. The transaction is a means whereby the lessor **provides finance** to the lessee and the lessor retains risks and rewards of ownership. It is therefore inappropriate to recognize the profit as income immediately.

14.4.7 If the leaseback is classified as an **operating lease** concluded at fair value, profit and loss is recognized immediately. Transactions below or above fair value are recorded as follows:

- If the fair value is less than the carrying amount of the asset, a loss equal to the difference is recognized immediately.
- If the sale price is above fair value, the excess over fair value should be deferred and amortized over the lease period.
- If the sale price is below fair value, any profit or loss is recognized immediately unless a loss is compensated by future lease payments at below market price; in this case, the loss should be deferred and amortized in proportion to the lease payments.

14.5   PRESENTATION AND DISCLOSURE

IAS 17 requires the presentation and disclosure as per paragraph 14.5.

14.5.1   Lessees—Finance Leases:

- Asset: Carrying amount of *each* class of asset
- Liability: Total of minimum lease payments reconciled to the present values of lease liabilities in **three periodic bands**, namely
  - not later than one year
  - not later than five years
  - later than five years
- IAS 16 requirements for leased property, plant, and equipment
- General description of significant leasing arrangements
- Distinction between current and noncurrent lease liabilities
- Future minimum sublease payments expected to be received under noncancellable subleases at Statement of Financial Position date
- Contingent rents recognized in income for the period

Lessees—Operating Leases:

- General description of significant leasing arrangements (same information as for finance leases above)
- Lease and sublease payments recognized in income of the current period, separating minimum lease payments, contingent rents, and sublease payments
- Future minimum noncancellable lease payments in the **three periodic bands**
- Future minimum sublease payments expected to be received under noncancellable subleases at Statement of Financial Position date

14.5.2   Lessors—Finance Leases:

- The total gross investment reconciled to the present value of minimum lease payments receivable in the **three periodic bands**
- Unearned finance income
- Accumulated allowance for uncollectible receivables
- Contingent rents recognized in income
- General description of significant leasing arrangements
- Unguaranteed residual values

Lessors—Operating Leases:

- All related disclosures under IAS 16, IAS 36, IAS 38, and IAS 40
- General description of significant leasing arrangements
- Total future minimum lease payments under noncancellable operating leases in the **three periodic bands**
- Total contingent rents recognized in income

14.5.3 Sale and leaseback transactions

Same disclosures for lessees and lessors apply. Some items might be separately disclosable in terms of IAS 8.

14.6 FINANCIAL ANALYSIS AND INTERPRETATION

14.6.1 The effects of accounting for a lease in the financial statements of the lessee as an operating lease versus a finance lease can be summarized as follows:

- **Operating lease** accounting reports the lease payments as rental expense on the Statement of Comprehensive Income.

- The Statement of Financial Position is impacted only indirectly when the rental expense flows through to retained earnings via net income.

- The rental expense is reported as an **operating cash outflow** (as a part of the entity's net income) on the statement of cash flows.

- The total reported expense over the lease term should normally be the same for a **finance lease** as the total reported expense over the lease term would be under the **operating lease** method. However, costs are higher in the early years under the finance lease method, which causes the earnings trend to rise over the lease term.

- The **finance lease** method places both an asset and a net amount of debt on the Statement of Financial Position, whereas no such asset or debt items are reported under the **operating lease** method.

- Under **finance lease** accounting, the total lease payment is divided into an interest component and the repayment of principal; a depreciation component also arises when the principal (capital portion) is depreciated in terms of IAS 16. Under the **operating lease** method, the payment is simply a rental expense.

- Under the **operating lease** method, lease payments are reported as **operating cash outflows** (interest can be classified as a financing cash flow as well), whereas under the **finance lease** method, the cash outflow is normally allocated between operating and financing.

- The interest portion of the **finance lease** payment is normally reported as an **operating cash outflow**, whereas the repayment of the lease obligation portion is treated as a **financing cash outflow**. However, the net effect on total cash is the same in both methods.

- That portion of the lease obligation that is paid or eliminated within one year or one operating cycle, whichever is longer, is classified as a current liability. The remainder is classified as a long-term liability.

14.6.2 Why do companies lease assets and under what conditions will they favor operating or finance leases? Several possible answers can be given to this question, but it must be considered within the context of a specific situation—in other words, circumstances could arise that would invalidate the assumptions on which answers are based:

- Companies with low marginal tax rates or low taxable capacity generally find leasing to be advantageous, because they do not need or cannot obtain the tax advantages (depreciation) that go with the ownership of assets. In this case, either type of lease is appropriate. Companies with high tax rates prefer finance leases, because expenses are normally higher in early periods.

- Operating leases are advantageous when management compensation depends on return on assets or invested capital.

- An operating lease is advantageous when an entity wants to keep debt off of its Statement of Financial Position. This can help them if they have indenture covenants requiring low debt-to-equity ratios or high interest-coverage ratios.

- Finance leases are favored if an entity wants to show a high cash flow from operations.

- Finance leases have advantages when there is a comparative advantage to reselling property.

Table 14.1 summarizes the different effects of operating and finance leases on lessees' accounting, and table 14.2 summarizes the effects on lessors.

Table 14.1 Effect of Operating and Finance Leases on Lessee Financial Statements and Key Financial Ratios

Item or Ratio	Operating Lease	Finance Lease
Statement of Financial Position	**No effects** because no assets or liabilities are created under the operating lease method.	A leased asset (equipment) and a lease obligation are created when the lease is recorded. Over the life of the lease, both are written off, but the asset is usually written down faster, creating a net liability during the life of the lease.
Statement of Comprehensive Income	The lease payment is recorded as an expense. These payments are often constant over the life of the lease.	Both interest expense and depreciation expense are created. In the early years of the lease, they combine to produce a **higher expense** than is reported under the operating method. However, over the life of the lease, the interest expense declines, causing the total expense trend to decline. This produces a positive trend in earnings. In the later years, **earnings are higher** under the finance lease method than under the operating lease method. Over the entire term of the lease, the total lease expenses are the same under both methods.
Statement of Cash Flows	The entire cash outflow paid on the lease is recorded as an operating cash outflow.	The cash outflow from the lease payments is allocated partly to an operating or financing cash outflow (interest expense) and partly to a financing cash outflow (repayment of the lease obligation principal). The depreciation of the leased asset is not a cash expense and, therefore, is not a cash flow item.
Profit Margin	**Higher** in the early years because the rental expense is normally less than the total expense reported under the finance lease method. However, in later years, it will be lower than under the finance lease method.	**Lower** in the early years because the total reported expense under the finance lease method is normally higher than the lease payment. However, the profit margin will trend upward over time, so in the later years it will exceed that of the operating lease method.
Asset Turnover	**Higher** because there are no leased assets recorded under the operating lease method.	**Lower** because of the leased asset (equipment) that is created under the finance lease method. The ratio **rises over time** as the asset is depreciated.
Current Ratio	**Higher** because no short-term debt is added to the Statement of Financial Position by the operating lease method.	**Lower** because the current portion of the lease obligation created under the finance lease method is a current liability. The current ratio **falls farther over time** as the current portion of the lease obligation rises.
Debt-to-Equity Ratio	**Lower** because the operating lease method creates no debt.	**Higher** because the finance lease method creates a lease obligation liability (which is higher than the leased asset in the early years). However, the debt-to equity ratio **decreases over time** as the lease obligation decreases.
Return on Assets	**Higher** in the early years because profits are higher and assets are lower.	**Lower** in the early years because earnings are lower and assets are higher. However, the return on asset ratio **rises over time** because the earnings trend is positive and the assets decline as they are depreciated.
Return on Equity	**Higher** in the early years because earnings are higher.	**Lower** in the early years because earnings are lower. However, the return on equity **rises over time** because of a positive earnings trend.
Interest Coverage	**Higher** because no interest expense occurs under the operating lease method.	**Lower** because interest expense is created by the finance lease method. However, the interest-coverage ratio **rises over time** because the interest expense declines over time.

Table 14.2 Effects of Leasing Methods Used by Lessors on Financial Statements and Ratios

Item/Ratio	Operating Lease	Sales-Type Financial Lease	Direct-Financing Lease
Size of Assets	**Lowest**, because no investment write-up occurs. Low asset values tend to raise asset turnover ratios.	**Highest**, largely because of the sale of the leased asset. High asset value tends to lower asset turnover.	**Middle**, because there is an investment write-up, but no sale of the leased asset.
Size of Shareholders' Equity	**Lowest**, because no asset write-up occurs. Low shareholders' equity tends to raise returns on equity and debt or equity ratios.	**Highest**, largely because of the gain on the sale of the leased asset. High shareholders' equity tends to lower returns on equity and debt or equity ratios.	**Middle**, because the investment write-up adds to equity, but there is no sale of the leased asset.
Size of Income in Year Lease Is Initiated (Year 0)	**No effect** on income when lease is initiated.	**Highest**, because of the gain on the sale of the leased asset. High income tends to raise profit margins and returns on assets and equity.	**No effect** on income when lease is initiated.
Size of Income during Life of Lease (Years 1–3)	**Middle**, based on terms of the lease and method of depreciation. Income tends to be **constant over time** if lease receipts are fixed and straight-line depreciation is used.	**Lowest**, because of the relatively low prevailing interest rate. Interest income tends to **decline over time**. Low income tends to lower profit margins and returns on assets and equity.	**Highest**, because of the high effective return on the lease. Interest income tends to **decline over time**. High income tends to raise profit margins and returns on assets and equity.
Operating Cash Flow at Time Lease Is Initiated (Year 0)	**No effect**, because no cash flow occurs when lease is initiated.	**Highest**, because of the gain on the sale of the leased asset.	**No effect**, because no cash flow occurs when lease is signed.
Operating Cash Flow over Term of the Lease (Years 1–3)	**Highest**, because of the terms of the lease and the method of depreciation.	**Lowest**, because interest income is low.	**Middle**, because interest income is high due to high effective return on the lease.

EXAMPLES: LEASES

EXAMPLE 14.1

A manufacturing machine that costs $330,000 is acquired by a finance lease agreement under the following terms:

- The effective date is January 1, 20X2.
- The lease term is three years.
- Installments of $72,500 are payable half-yearly in arrears.
- The effective rate of interest is 23.5468 percent per annum.
- A deposit of $30,000 is immediately payable.

EXPLANATION

The amortization table for this transaction would be as follows:

	Installment $	Interest $	Capital $	Balance $
Cash Price	330,000			
Deposit	30,000	–	30,000	300,000
Installment 1	72,500	35,320	37,180	262,820
Installment 2	72,500	30,943	41,557	221,263
Subtotal	175,000	66,263	108,737	
Installment 3	72,500	26,050	46,450	174,813
Installment 4	72,500	20,581	51,919	122,894
Installment 5	72,500	14,469	58,031	64,863
Installment 6	72,500	7,637	64,863	–
TOTAL	465,000	135,000	330,000	

The finance lease would be recognized and presented in the financial statements as follows:

Books of the Lessee

An asset of $330,000 will be recorded and a corresponding liability will be raised on January 1, 20X2.

If it is assumed that the machine is depreciated on a straight-line basis over six years, the following expenses would be recognized in the **Statement of Comprehensive Income** for the first year:

Depreciation (330,000/6)	$55,000
Finance lease charges (35,320 + 30,943)	$66,263

The **Statement of Financial Position** at December 31, 20X2, would reflect the following balances:

Machine (330,000 – 55,000)	$275,000 (Asset)
Long-term finance lease liability	$221,263 (Liability)

Books of the Lessor

The gross amount of $465,000 due by the lessee would be recorded as a debtor at inception of the contract, that is, the deposit of $30,000 plus six installments of $72,500 each. The unearned finance income of $135,000 is recorded as a deferred income (credit balance). The net amount presented would then be $330,000 ($465,000 – $135,000).

The deposit and the first two installments are credited to the debtor account, which will then reflect a debit balance of $290,000 at December 31, 20X2.

A total of $66,263 ($35,320 + $30,943) of the unearned finance income has been earned in the first year, which brings the balance of this account to $68,737 at December 31, 20X2.

The **Statement of Comprehensive Income** for the year ending December 31, 20X2, will reflect finance income earned in the first year in the amount of $66,263.

The **Statement of Financial Position** at December 31, 20X2, will reflect the net investment as a long-term receivable at $221,263 ($290,000 – $68,737), which agrees with the liability in the books of the lessor at that stage.

EXAMPLE 14.2

What is the entry at the time of lease signing to record the assets being leased using the following information?

Asset 1. Lease payment of $15,000 per year for 8 years, $20,000 fair market value purchase option at the end of Year 8 (guaranteed by the lessee to be the minimum value of the equipment), estimated economic life is 10 years, fair market value of the leased asset is $105,000, and the interest rate implied in the lease is 10 percent.

Asset 2. Lease payment of $15,000 per year for 8 years, $35,000 fair market value purchase option at the end of Year 8 (guaranteed by the lessee to be the minimum value of the equipment), estimated economic life is 12 years, fair market value of the leased asset is $105,000, and the interest rate implied in the lease is 10 percent. The company's incremental borrowing rate is 11 percent.

Options:

a.   No entry

b. $89,354 increase in assets and liabilities

c. $192,703 increase in assets and liabilities

d.   None of the above

EXPLANATION

Issue 1:   Determine whether the leases are finance or operating.

Issue 2:   Determine the accounting entries needed.

Asset 1

The lease term is for a major part of the asset's life, 80 percent (8 out of 10 years). No further work is needed with respect to the criteria, because only one criterion (or a combination of criteria) has to be met to result in the lease being recorded as a finance lease (see IAS 17, paragraph 10). The amount to record is the present value of the 8 years of $15,000 lease payments, plus the present value of the $20,000 purchase option. The discount rate to use is 10 percent, which is the lower of the incremental borrowing rate and the lease's implicit rate. The present value is $89,354. This amount will be recorded as an asset and as a liability on the Statement of Financial Position.

Choice b. is correct. The entry required is to record an asset and liability in the amount of $89,354.

Asset 2

The lease term is less than a major part of the asset's life, defined as 67 percent (8 out of 12 years). There is no indication of a bargain purchase option, and the property does not go the lessee at the end of the lease (unless the lessee opts to pay $35,000). The present value of the lease payments, including the purchase option, is $96,351. The present value of the minimum lease payments does not approximate the fair market value of $105,000. Asset 2 does not meet any of the finance lease conditions and is accounted for using the operating lease method.

Choice d. is correct. No entries are required under the operating lease method when the lease is entered into.

EXAMPLE 14.3

Which of the following assets would have a higher cash flow from operations in the first year of the lease? (Assume straight-line depreciation, if applicable.)

Asset 1. Lease payment of $15,000 per year for 8 years, $20,000 fair market value purchase option at the end of Year 8 (guaranteed by the lessee to be the minimum value of the equipment), estimated economic life is 10 years, fair market value of the leased asset is $105,000, and the interest rate implied in the lease is 10 percent.

Asset 2. Lease payment of $15,000 per year for 8 years, $35,000 fair market value purchase option at the end of Year 8 (guaranteed by the lessee to be the minimum value of the equipment), estimated economic life is 12 years, fair market value of the leased asset is $105,000, and the interest rate implied in the lease is 10 percent. The company's incremental borrowing rate is 11 percent.

Options

a. Asset 1.

b. Asset 2.

c. Both assets would have the same total cash flow from operations.

d. Insufficient information given.

EXPLANATION

Asset 1

The lease term is for a major part of the asset's life, 80 percent (8 out of 10 years). No further work is needed with respect to the criteria, because only one criterion (or a combination of criteria has to be met to result in the lease being recorded as a finance lease (see IAS 17, paragraph 10). The amount to record is present value of the 8 years of $15,000 lease payments, plus the present value of the $20,000 purchase option. The discount rate to use is 10 percent, which is the lower of the incremental borrowing rate and the lease's implicit rate. The present value is $89,354. This amount will be recorded as an asset and as a liability on the Statement of Financial Position. The cash flows in the first year will consist of the $15,000 payment, which is allocated between operating cash flow (an outflow for the interest portion of the payment) and financing cash flow (an outflow for the principal portion of the payment):

Total payment	=	$15,000
Interest portion = 10 percent x $89,354	=	8,935
Principal portion	=	$6,065

Asset 2

The lease term at 67 percent (8 out of 12 years) is less than a major part of the asset's life. There is no indication of a bargain purchase option, and the property does not go to the lessee at the end of the lease (unless the lessee opts to pay $35,000). The present value of the lease payments is $96,351. Therefore, the present value of the minimum lease payments does not approximate the fair market value of $105,000. Asset 2 does not meet any of the finance lease conditions and is accounted for using the operating lease method. The annual lease payment of $15,000 is an operating cash outflow.

Choice a. is correct. There is the issue of whether the leases are finance or operating. Once this issue is resolved, then the amount and classification of the cash flows can be determined. As the explanation above shows, the total cash flows are the same—a negative $15,000. Asset 1, being a finance lease, results in a portion of this outflow being considered a financing cash flow. Thus it shows a lower operating cash outflow, meaning a higher cash flow from operations.

Choice b. is incorrect. Assuming the leases are of similar size, the finance lease will reflect a higher operating cash flow than the operating lease. This is true for every year of the lease term, because a portion of the lease payment is shifted under a finance lease to being a financing cash outflow.

Choice c. is incorrect. The only way for each to have the same operating cash flows in this scenario would be if both were treated as operating leases. But Asset 1 is required to be accounted for as a finance lease.

Choice d. is incorrect. Sufficient information has been provided.

EXAMPLE 14.4

The "capitalization" of a finance lease by a lessee will increase which of the following:

a. Debt-to-equity ratio

b. Rate of return on assets

c. Current ratio

d. Asset turnover

EXPLANATION

Choice a. is correct. Because the capitalization of a finance lease by a lessee increases the debt obligation and lowers net income (equity), the entity will be more leveraged as the debt-to-equity ratio will increase.

Choice b. is incorrect. Given that net income declines and total assets increase under a finance lease, the rate of return on assets would decrease.

Choice c. is incorrect. Because the current obligation of the finance lease increases current liabilities while current assets are unaffected, the current ratio declines.

Choice d. is incorrect. Finance leases increase a company's asset base, which lowers the asset turnover ratio.

EXAMPLE 14.5

All of the following are true statements regarding the impact of a lease on the statement of cash flows regardless of whether the finance lease or operating lease method is used— **except** for:

a. The total cash flow impact for the life of the lease is the same under both methods.

b. The interest portion of the payment under a finance lease will affect operating activities, whereas the principal reduction portion of the finance lease payment will affect financing activities.

c. Over time, a cash payment under the finance lease method will cause operating cash flow to decline, whereas financing cash flows will tend to increase.

d. Cash payments made under an operating lease will affect operating activities only.

EXPLANATION

Choice c. is false. When finance leases are used, operating cash flow will **increase** over time as the level of interest expense declines and more of the payment is allocated to principal repayment, which will result in a **decline** in financing cash flows over time.

Choice a. is true. Total cash flows over the life of the lease are the same under the operating and finance lease methods.

Choice b. is true. A finance lease payment affects operating cash flows and financing cash flows.

Choice d. is true. The operating lease payment is made up of the rent expense, which affects operating cash flow only.

EXAMPLE 14.6

On January 1, 20X1, ABC Company, lessee, enters into an operating lease for new equipment valued at $1.5 million. Terms of the lease agreement include five annual lease payments of $125,000 to be made by ABC Company to the leasing company.

During the first year of the lease, ABC Company will record which of the following?

a. Initially, an increase (debit) of leased equipment of $625,000 and an increase (credit) in equipment payables of $625,000. At year-end, a decrease (debit) in equipment payable of $125,000 and a decrease (credit) to cash of $125,000.

b. An increase (debit) in rent expense of $125,000 and a decrease (credit) in cash of $125,000.

c. No entry is recorded on the financial statements.

d. An increase (debit) in leased equipment of $125,000 and a decrease (credit) in cash of $125,000; no Statement of Comprehensive Income entry.

EXPLANATION

Choice b. is correct. Because the above transaction is an operating lease, only rent expense is recorded on the Statement of Comprehensive Income, with a corresponding reduction to cash on the Statement of Financial Position to reflect the payment.

Choice a. is incorrect. Operating leases do not include the present value of the asset on the Statement of Financial Position.

Choice c. is incorrect. Rent expense is recorded on the Statement of Comprehensive Income for operating leases.

Choice d. is incorrect. The leased asset is not recorded on the Statement of Financial Position for operating leases.

Chapter Fifteen

Income Taxes (IAS 12)

15.1   OBJECTIVE

The key objective of IAS 12, Accounting for Income Tax, is to address the problem of reconciling the tax liability (actual tax payable) with that of tax expense (accounting disclosure). Other issues are

- the distinction between permanent and timing differences,
- the future recovery or settlement of the carrying amount of deferred tax assets or liabilities in the Statement of Financial Position, and
- recognizing and dealing with income tax losses.

15.2   SCOPE OF THE STANDARD

This standard deals with all income taxes, including **domestic, foreign, and withholding taxes**, as well as income tax consequences of dividend payments. Following are the specific aspects that IAS 12 captures:

- Outlining the difference between the key concepts of accounting and taxable profit
- Criteria for recognizing and measuring deferred tax assets or liabilities
- Accounting for tax losses

15.3   KEY CONCEPTS

15.3.1 Accounting profit is net profit or loss for a period before deducting tax expense.

15.3.2 Taxable profit (or tax loss) is the profit (or loss) for a period, determined in accordance with the rules established by the taxation authorities, based on which income taxes are payable (or recoverable).

15.3.3 Tax expense (or tax income) is the aggregate amount included in the determination of net profit or loss for the period in respect of current tax and deferred tax.

15.3.4 Current tax is the amount of income taxes payable (or recoverable) on the taxable profit (or tax loss) for a period.

15.3.5 Deferred tax liabilities are the amounts of income taxes payable in future periods for taxable temporary differences.

15.3.6 Deferred tax assets are the amounts of income taxes recoverable in future periods for

- deductible temporary differences,
- the carry-forward of unused tax losses, and

■ the carry-forward of unused tax credits.

15.3.7 **Temporary differences** are differences between the carrying amount of an asset or liability in the Statement of Financial Position and its tax base. Temporary differences can be either

■ **taxable temporary differences**, which are temporary differences that will result in taxable amounts in determining taxable profit (or tax loss) of future periods when the carrying amount of the asset or liability is recovered or settled, or

■ **deductible temporary differences**, which are temporary differences that will result in amounts that are deductible in determining taxable profit (or tax loss) of future periods when the carrying amount of the asset or liability is recovered or settled.

15.3.8 The tax base of an asset or liability is the amount attributed to that asset or liability for tax purposes.

15.4 ACCOUNTING TREATMENT

15.4.1 **Current tax** should be recognized as a liability and expense in the period to which it relates:

■ A liability (asset) for unpaid (overpaid) current taxes should be raised.

■ The benefit of a tax loss carried back to recover tax paid with respect to a prior period should be recognized as an asset.

15.4.2 A **deferred tax liability** is recognized for all taxable temporary differences, except when those differences arise from

■ goodwill for which amortization is not deductible for tax purposes; or

■ the initial recognition of an asset or liability in a transaction that is not a business combination, and at the time of the transaction affects neither accounting nor taxable profit.

15.4.3 A **deferred tax asset** is recognized for all deductible temporary differences to the extent that it is probable that they are recoverable from future taxable profits. A recent loss is considered evidence that a deferred tax asset should not be recognized. A deferred tax asset is not recognized when it arises from the initial recognition of an asset or liability in a transaction that is not a business combination, and at the time of the transaction affects neither accounting nor taxable profit.

15.4.4 Current and deferred tax balances are **measured** using the following:

■ Tax rates and tax laws that have been substantively enacted by the Statement of Financial Position date

■ Tax rates that reflect how the asset will be recovered or liability will be settled (liability method)

■ The tax rate applicable to undistributed profits when there are different rates

15.4.5 Current and deferred tax should be recognized as income or expense and **included in the Statement of Comprehensive Income**. Exceptions are tax arising from

■ a transaction or event that is recognized directly in equity, or

■ a business combination that is an acquisition.

15.4.6 The income tax consequences of **dividends** are recognized when a liability to pay the dividend is recognized.

15.4.7 The entity should reassess the recoverability of recognized and unrecognized deferred tax assets at each Statement of Financial Position date. **Discounting** of tax balances is prohibited.

15.5 PRESENTATION AND DISCLOSURE

15.5.1 Taxation balances should be presented as follows:

- Tax balances are shown separately from other assets and liabilities in the Statement of Financial Position.
- Deferred tax balances are distinguished from current tax balances.
- Deferred tax balances are noncurrent.
- Taxation expense (income) should be shown for ordinary activities on the face of the Statement of Comprehensive Income.
- Current tax balances can be **offset** when
  - there is a legal enforceable right to offset, and
  - there is an intention to settle on a net basis.
- Deferred tax balances can be **offset** when
  - there is a legal enforceable right to offset, and
  - debits and credits relate to the same tax authority
    - for the same taxable entity, or
    - for different taxable entities that intend to settle on a net basis.

15.5.2 **Accounting policy**: The method used for deferred tax should be disclosed.

15.5.3 The **Statement of Comprehensive Income and notes** should contain

- major components of tax expense (income)—shown separately—including
  - current tax expense (income),
  - deferred tax expense (income),
  - deferred tax arising from the write-down (or reversal of a previous write-down) of a deferred tax asset, and
  - tax amount relating to changes in accounting policies and fundamental errors treated in accordance with IAS 8–allowed alternative;
- reconciliation between tax amount and accounting profit or loss in monetary terms, or a numerical reconciliation of the rate;
- explanation of changes in applicable tax rate (rates) compared to previous period (periods); and
- for each type of temporary difference, and in respect of each type of unused tax loss and credit, the amounts of the deferred tax recognized in the Statement of Comprehensive Income.

15.5.4 The **Statement of Financial Position and notes** should include

- aggregate amount of **current** and **deferred** tax charged or credited to equity;

- amount (and expiration date) of deductible temporary differences, unused tax losses, and unused tax credits for which no deferred tax asset is recognized;

- aggregate amount of temporary differences associated with investments in subsidiaries, branches, associates, and joint ventures for which deferred tax liabilities have not been recognized;

- for each type of temporary difference, and in respect of each type of unused tax loss and credit, the amount of the deferred tax assets and liabilities;

- amount of a deferred tax asset and nature of the evidence supporting its recognition, when

    - the utilization of the deferred tax asset is dependent on future taxable profits, or

    - the enterprise has suffered a loss in either the current or preceding period;

- amount of income tax consequences of dividends to shareholders that were proposed or declared before the Statement of Financial Position date, but are not recognized as a liability in the financial statements; and

- the nature of the potential income tax consequences that would result from the payment of dividends to the enterprises' shareholders, that is, the important features of the income tax systems and the factors that will affect the amount of the potential tax consequences of dividends.

15.6 FINANCIAL ANALYSIS AND INTERPRETATION

15.6.1 The first step in understanding how income taxes are accounted for in IFRS financial statements is to realize that **taxable profit** and **accounting profit** have very different meanings. Taxable profit is computed using procedures that comply with the tax code and is the basis upon which income taxes are paid. Accounting profit is computed using accounting policies that comply with IFRS.

15.6.2 When determining taxable profit, an entity might be allowed or required by the tax code to use accounting methods that are different from those that comply with IFRS. The resulting differences might increase or decrease profits. For example, an entity might be allowed to use accelerated depreciation to compute taxable profit and so reduce its tax liability, while at the same time it might be required to use straight-line depreciation in the determination of IFRS accounting profit.

15.6.3 The second step is to understand the difference between current taxes, deferred tax assets and liabilities, and income tax expense. **Current taxes** represent the income tax owed to the government in accordance with the tax code. **Deferred taxes** represent the other tax consequences of the recovery of assets and settlement of liabilities. **Income tax expense** is an expense reported in the Statement of Comprehensive Income, and it includes both current tax expense and deferred tax expense. This means that the income tax paid or payable to the government in an accounting period usually differs significantly from the income tax expense that is recognized in the Statement of Comprehensive Income.

15.6.4 Are deferred taxes a liability or equity for analysis purposes? An entity's deferred tax liability meets the definition of a liability. However, deferred tax liabilities are not current legal liabilities, because they do not represent taxes that are currently owed or payable to the government. Taxes that are owed to the government but which have not been paid are called current tax liabilities. They are classified as current liabilities on a Statement of Financial Position, whereas deferred tax liabilities are classified as noncurrent liabilities.

15.6.5 If an entity is growing, new deferred tax liabilities may be created on an ongoing basis (depending on the source of potential timing differences). Thus, the deferred tax liability balance will probably never decrease. Furthermore, changes in the tax laws or a company's operations could result in deferred taxes never being paid. For these reasons, many analysts treat deferred tax liabilities as if they are part of a company's **equity capital**.

15.6.6 Technically, treating deferred tax liabilities as if they were part of a company's equity capital should be done only if the analyst is convinced that the deferred tax liabilities will increase or remain stable in the foreseeable future. This will be the case when a company is expected to acquire new (or more expensive) assets on a regular basis so that the aggregate timing differences will increase (or remain stable) over time. Under such circumstances, which are normal for most entities, deferred tax liabilities could be viewed as being zero-interest loans from the government that will, in the aggregate, always increase without ever being repaid. The rationale for treating perpetually stable or growing deferred tax liabilities as equity for analytical purposes is that a perpetual loan that requires no interest or principal payments takes on the characteristics of permanent equity capital.

15.6.7 If an entity's deferred tax liabilities are expected to decline over time, however, they should be treated as liabilities for analytical purposes. One consideration is that the liabilities should be discounted for the time value of money; the taxes are not paid until future periods. An analyst should also consider the reasons that have caused deferred taxes to arise and how likely these causes are to reverse.

15.6.8 In some cases, analysts ignore the deferred tax liabilities for analytical purposes when it is difficult to determine whether they will take on the characteristics of a true liability or equity capital over time. Ultimately, the analyst has to decide whether deferred tax liabilities should be characterized as liabilities, equity, or neither based on the situation's unique circumstances.

15.6.9 Entities must include income tax information in their footnotes, which analysts should use to

- understand why the entity's effective income tax rate is different from the statutory tax rate;
- forecast future effective income tax rates, thereby improving earnings forecasts;
- determine the actual income taxes paid by an entity and compare them with the reported income tax expense to better assess operating cash flow; and
- estimate the taxable income reported to the government and compare it with the reported pretax income reported in the financial statements.

EXAMPLE 15.1

Difir Inc. owns the following property, plant, and equipment at December 31, 20X4:

	Cost $'000	Accumulated depreciation $'000	Carrying amount $'000	Tax base $'000
Machinery	900	180	720	450
Land	500	–	500	–
Buildings	1,500	300	1,200	–

In addition,

- Machinery is depreciated on the straight-line basis over 5 years. It was acquired on January 1, 20X4.

- Land is not depreciated.

- Buildings are depreciated on the straight-line basis over 25 years.

- Depreciation of land and office buildings is not deductible for tax purposes. For machinery, tax depreciation is granted over a period of 3 years in the ratio of 50/30/20 (percent) of cost, consecutively.

- The accounting profit before tax amounted to $300,000 for the 20X5 financial year and $400,000 for 20X6. These figures include nontaxable revenue of $80,000 in 20X5 and $100,000 in 20X6.

- Difir had a tax loss on December 31, 20X4, of $250,000. The tax rate for 20X4 was 35 percent, and for 20X5 and 20X6 it was 30 percent.

EXPLANATION

The movements on the deferred tax balance for 20X5 and 20X6 will be reflected as follows in the accounting records of the enterprise:

Deferred tax liability	$'000 Dr/(Cr)
January 1, 20X5, balance	
Machinery (Calculation a: 270 x 35%)	(94.5)
Tax loss carried forward (250 x 35%)	87.5
	(7.0)
Rate change (7 x 5/35)	1.0
Temporary differences: – Machinery (Calculation a)	(27.0)
–Loss utilized (Calculation b: 190 x 30%)	(57.0)
December 31, 20X5, balance	(90.0)
Temporary difference: – Machinery (Calculation a)	–
December 31, 20X6, loss utilized (Calculation b: 60 x 30%)	(18.0)
December 31, 20X6, balance	(108.0)

Calculations				
a. Machinery	Carrying amount $'000	Tax base $'000	Temporary difference $'000	Deferred tax $'000
January 1, 20X4, purchase	900	900		
Depreciation	(180)	(450)	270	94.5
December 31, 20X4	720	450	270	94.5
Rate change (5/35 x 94.5)				(13.5)
Depreciation	(180)	(270)	90	27.0
December 31, 20X5	540	180	360	108.0
Depreciation	(180)	(180)	–	–
December 31, 20X6	360	–	360	108.0

b. Income tax expense	20X6 $'000	20X5 $'000
Accounting profit before tax	400	300
Tax effect of items not deductible/taxable for tax purposes:		
Nontaxable revenue	(100)	(80)
Depreciation on buildings (1500/25)	60	60
	360	280
Temporary differences	–	(90)
Depreciation: accounting	180	180
Depreciation: tax	(180)	(270)
Taxable profit	360	190
Assessed loss brought forward	(60)	(250)
Taxable profit/(tax loss)	300	(60)
Tax loss carried forward	–	(60)
Tax payable/(benefit) @ 30%	90	(18)

EXAMPLE 15.2

Lipreaders Company has net taxable temporary differences of $90 million, resulting in a deferred tax liability of $30.6 million. An increase in the tax rate would have the following impact on deferred taxes and net income:

Deferred Taxes	Net Income
a. Increase	No effect
b. Increase	Decrease
c. No effect	No effect
d. No effect	Decrease

EXPLANATION

Choice b. is correct. Deferred tax is a liability that results when tax expense on the Statement of Comprehensive Income exceeds taxes payable. The amount of deferred tax liability will rise if tax rates are expected to rise. In effect, more taxes will be paid in the future as the timing differences reverse. This increase in the deferred tax liability will flow through the Statement of Comprehensive Income by raising income tax expense. Thus, net income will decrease.

Choice a. is incorrect. When deferred taxes increase, net income will be lower.

Choice c. is incorrect. The above scenario affects both deferred taxes and net income.

Choice d is incorrect. Although net income would decrease, deferred taxes would increase because tax rates in the future will be higher.

EXAMPLE 15.3

There are varying accounting rules throughout the world that govern how the income tax expense is reported on the Statement of Comprehensive Income. IFRS requires the use of the **liability method**. To illustrate the essential accounting problem posed when different accounting methods are used to develop financial information for tax and financial reporting purposes, consider the Engine Works Corporation. In the year just ended, Engine Works generated earnings from operations before depreciation and income taxes of $6,000. In addition, the company earned $100 of tax-free municipal bond interest income. Engine Works's only assets subject to depreciation are two machines, one that was purchased at the beginning of last year for $5,000, and one that was purchased at the beginning of this year for $10,000. Both machines are being depreciated over five-year periods. The company uses an accelerated-consumption method to compute depreciation for income tax purposes (worth $5,200 this year) and the straight-line method to calculate depreciation for financial reporting (book) purposes.

EXPLANATION

1. Based on this information, Engine Works's income tax filing and Statement of Comprehensive Income for the **current** year would be as follows:

Income Tax Filing ($)		Statement of Comprehensive Income ($)	
Income from operations before depreciation and income taxes	6,000	Income from operations before depreciation and income taxes	6,000
Tax-free interest income	—a	Tax-free interest income	100
Depreciation—tax allowance	5,200	Depreciation	3,000b
Taxable income	800	Pretax income	3,100
Income taxes payable (35%)	280	Income tax expense	?

a. Tax-free interest income is excluded from taxable income.

b. 1/5 x $5,000 + 1/5 x $10,000 = $3,000.

2. Based on the income tax filing, the income tax that is owed to the government is $280. The question is what income tax expense should be reported in Engine Works's Statement of Comprehensive Income? There are two reasons why accounting profit and taxable profit can be different: **temporary** and **permanent differences** (not a term specifically used in IFRS 12).

3. **Temporary differences** are those differences between accounting profit and taxable profit for an accounting period that arise whenever the measurement of assets and liabilities for income tax purposes differs from the measurement of assets and liabilities for IFRS purposes. For example, if an entity uses straight-line depreciation of its assets for IFRS purposes and accelerated depreciation for income tax purposes, the IFRS carrying amount of the assets will differ from the tax carrying amount of those assets. For income tax purposes, tax depreciation will be greater than IFRS depreciation in the early years and lower than IFRS depreciation in the later years.

4. **Permanent differences** are those differences between IFRS accounting profit and taxable profit that arise when income is not taxed or expenses are not tax deductible. For example, tax-free interest income is not included in taxable income, even though it is part of IFRS accounting profit.

Figure 15.1 Income Difference before Taxes—Engine Works

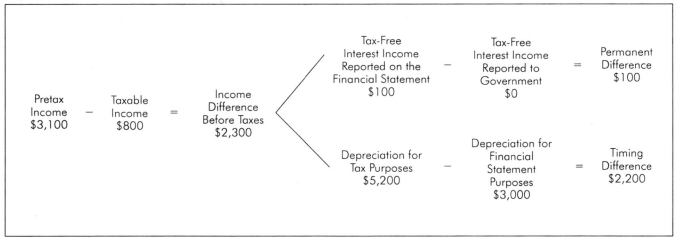

5. Permanent differences affect the current accounting period's **effective income tax rate** (the ratio of the reported income tax expense to pretax income), but do not have any impact on future income taxes. Temporary differences, on the other hand, affect the income taxes that will be paid in future years because they represent a deferral of taxable income from the current to subsequent accounting periods (or an acceleration of taxable income from the future into the current accounting period).

6. The $2,300 difference between pretax income and taxable income is attributable in part to the $100 of tax-free interest income that will never be taxed, but is included in the Statement of Comprehensive Income. This is a **permanent difference** because this income is permanently excluded from taxation; the amount of tax on it that has to be paid now or in the future is zero.

7. The $2,200 difference between the $5,200 accelerated consumption depreciation and the $3,000 straight-line depreciation is a **timing (temporary) difference** because the taxes that are saved in the current year are only deferred to the future when the timing differences **reverse**. Over the life of the equipment, the total depreciation expense will be the same for income tax and book purposes. The $2,200 is a reflection of the difference in the amount of the total cost of the equipment that is **allocated** to this period by the two methods of accounting for depreciation. The Statement of Comprehensive Income has a lower depreciation cost than the tax filing, which results in higher reported income. These differences will reverse over time when the straight-line depreciation rises above the double-declining balance depreciation.

Chapter Sixteen

Inventories (IAS 2)

16.1 OBJECTIVE

The objective of IAS 2 is to prescribe the accounting treatment of inventories. This standard deals with the calculation of the cost of inventory, the type of inventory method adopted, the allocation of cost to assets and expenses, and valuation aspects associated with any write-downs to net realizable value.

16.2 SCOPE OF THE STANDARD

This standard deals with all inventories of assets that are

- held for sale in the ordinary course of business,
- in the process of production for sale,
- in the form of materials or supplies to be consumed in the production process, and
- used in the rendering of services.

In the case of a service provider, inventories include the costs of the service for which the related revenue has not yet been recognized (for example, the work in progress of auditors, architects, and lawyers).

IAS 2 does not apply to the measurement of inventories held by producers of agricultural and forest products, agricultural produce after harvest, or minerals and mineral products to the extent that they are measured at net realizable value in accordance with well-established practices in those industries. Living plants, animals, and harvested agricultural produce derived from those plants and animals are also excluded (see IAS 41, chapter 12).

Although IAS 2 excludes construction contracts (IAS 11) and financial instruments (IAS 39), the principles in IAS 2 are still applied when deciding how to implement certain features of the excluded standards (see example 16.5).

16.3 KEY CONCEPTS

16.3.1 Inventories should be **measured** at the lower of cost and net realizable value.

16.3.2 **Cost of inventories** comprises all costs of purchase, costs of conversion, and other costs incurred in bringing the inventories to their **present location and condition**.

16.3.3 The **net realizable value (NRV)** is the estimated selling price less the estimated costs of completion and costs necessary to make the sale.

16.3.4 When inventories are sold, the carrying amount of the **expenses should be recognized** as an expense in the period in which the related revenue is recognized (see chapter 22).

16.3.5 The **amount of any write-down** of inventories to NRV and all losses of inventories should be recognized as an expense in the period of the write-down or loss.

16.4   ACCOUNTING TREATMENT

Measurement Techniques

16.4.1 The cost of inventories that are not ordinarily interchangeable and those produced and segregated for specific projects are assigned by **specific identification** of their individual costs.

16.4.2 The cost of other inventories is assigned by using either of the following **cost formulas**:

- Weighted average cost
- First in, first out (FIFO)

16.4.3 The following **techniques** can be used to measure the cost of inventories if the results approximate cost:

- **Standard cost:**
  - Normal levels of materials, labor, and actual capacity should be taken into account.
  - The standard cost should be reviewed regularly to ensure that it approximates actual costs.
- **Retail method:**
  - Sales value should be reduced by gross margin to calculate cost.
  - Average percentage should be used for each homogeneous group of items.
  - Marked-down prices should be taken into consideration.

Cost and NRV

16.4.4 Cost of inventories consists of

- purchase costs, such as the purchase price and import charges;
- costs of conversion
  - direct labor; and
  - production overheads, including variable overheads and fixed overheads allocated at normal production capacity;
- other costs, such as design and borrowing costs.

16.4.5 Cost of inventories excludes

- abnormal amounts of wasted materials, labor, and overheads;
- storage costs, unless they are necessary prior to a further production process;
- administrative overheads; and
- selling costs.

16.4.6 **NRV** is the estimated selling price less the estimated costs of completion and costs necessary to make the sale. These estimates are based on the most reliable evidence at the time the estimates are made. The purpose for which the inventory is held should be taken into account at the time of the estimate. Inventories are usually written down to NRV based on the following principles:

- Items are treated on an item-by-item basis.
- Similar items are normally grouped together.
- Each service is treated as a separate item.

16.5 PRESENTATION AND DISCLOSURE

The financial statements should disclose the following:

- Accounting policies, including the cost formulas used
- Total carrying amount of inventories and amount per category
- The amount of inventories recognized as an expense during the period, that is, cost of sales
- Amount of inventories carried at fair value less costs to sell
- Amount of any write-downs and reversals of any write-downs
- Circumstances or events that led to the reversal of a write-down
- Inventories pledged as security for liabilities
- Amount of inventories recognized as an expense

16.6 FINANCIAL ANALYSIS AND INTERPRETATION

16.6.1 The **accounting method** used to value inventories should be selected based on the order in which products are sold, relative to when they are put into inventory. Therefore, whenever possible, the costs of inventories are assigned by specific identification of their individual costs. In many cases, however, it is necessary to use a cost formula—for example, first-in, first-out (FIFO)—that represents fairly the inventory flows. IAS 2 does not allow the use of last-in, first-out (LIFO) because it does not faithfully represent inventory flows. The IASB has noted that the use of LIFO is often tax driven and concluded that tax considerations do not provide a conceptual basis for selecting an accounting treatment. IASB does not permit the use of an inferior accounting treatment purely because of tax considerations.

16.6.2 Analysts and managers often use **ratio analysis** to assess company performance and condition. The valuation of inventories can influence performance and cash flow through the events or manipulations in the presentation of data in table 16.1.

Table 16.1 Impact of Inventory Valuation on Financial Analysis

Valuation Element or Manipulation	Effect on Company
Beginning inventory overstated by $5,000	Profit will be understated by $5,000
Ending inventory understated by $2,000	Profit will be understated by $2,000
Inventory accounting method effect on cash flows	Taxes will be affected by the choice of accounting method
	Understatement of inventory
	Overstatement of receivables
Early recognition of revenue on a sale	Overstatement of profit

16.6.3 Although **LIFO is no longer allowed in IFRS financial statements**, some jurisdictions continue to allow the use of LIFO. When comparing entities in the same industry, inventories should be adjusted to FIFO to ensure comparability. (In a similar manner, analysts should adjust the statements of non-IFRS entities prior to comparing them with IFRS entities.)

16.6.4 **FIFO inventory balances** constitute a closer reflection of economic value because FIFO inventory is valued at the most recent purchase prices. Table 16.2 summarizes the effects of using FIFO and LIFO on some of the elements in financial statements.

Table 16.2 The Impact of LIFO vs. FIFO on Financial Statement Variables

Financial Statement Variable	LIFO	FIFO
Cost of goods sold (COGS)	Higher—more recent prices are used	Lower
Income	Lower—COGS is higher	Higher
Cash flow	Higher—taxes are lower	Lower
Working capital	Lower—current assets are lower	Higher

Table 16.3 Equivalent FIFO and LIFO Financial Statements and the Key Financial Ratios They Produce

	FIFO ($)	LIFO ($)
Cash	34	70
Accounts receivable	100	100
Inventories	200	110
Plant and equipment	300	300
Total Assets	634	580
Short-term debt	40	40
Long-term debt	200	200
Common stock	50	50
Paid-in capital	100	100
Retained earnings	244	190
Total Liabilities and Capital	634	580
Sales	600	600
Cost of goods sold	410	430
Interest expense	15	15
Pretax Income	175	155
Income tax expense	70	62
Net Income	105	93

	FIFO	LIFO
Net profit margin	17.5%	15.5%
Current ratio	8.4x	7.0x
Inventory turnover	2.1x	3.9x
Long-term debt or equity	50.8%	58.8%
Return on assets	16.6%	16.0%
Return on equity	26.6%	27.4%

EXAMPLE 16.1

Slingshot Corporation purchased inventory on January 1, 20X1, for $600,000. On December 31, 20X1, the inventory had an NRV of $550,000. During 20X2, Slingshot sold the inventory for $620,000. Based on the above, which of the following statements is true?

a. The December 31, 20X1, Statement of Financial Position reported the inventory at $600,000.

b. The December 31, 20X1, Statement of Financial Position reported the inventory at $620,000.

c. When the inventory was sold in 20X2, Slingshot reported a $20,000 gain on its income statement.

d. For the year ending December 31, 20X1, Slingshot recognized a $50,000 loss on its Statement of Comprehensive Income.

EXPLANATION

Choice d. is correct. Because IFRS requires the lower of cost or NRV reporting on inventory, the company must recognize a $50,000 loss ($550,000 – $600,000) on the Statement of Comprehensive Income for 20X1. When the inventory is sold in 20X2, a profit of $70,000 ($620,000 – $550,000) is recognized on the Statement of Comprehensive Income.

Choice a. is incorrect. The inventory must be written down to market value at year-end 20X1.

Choice b. is incorrect. The fact that the inventory was sold for $620,000 in 20X2 has no impact on the inventory balance at December 31, 20X1.

Choice c. is incorrect. The sale of the inventory at $620,000 must recognize the inventory market value of $550,000, resulting in a gain of $70,000.

EXAMPLE 16.2

The financial statements of Parra Imports for 20X0 and 20X1 had the following errors:

	20X0	20X1
Ending inventory	$4,000 overstated	$8,000 understated
Rent expense	$2,400 understated	$1,300 overstated

By what amount will the 20X0 and 20X1 pretax profits be overstated or understated if these errors are not corrected?

EXPLANATION

20X0. Because the ending inventory is overstated for 20X0, the COGS will be understated, resulting in pretax profits being overstated by $4,000. In addition, because rent expense is understated by $2,400, pretax profits will be overstated by an additional $2,400, for a total overstatement of $6,400.

20X1. The beginning inventory was overstated by $4,000 for 20X1, so COGS will be overstated by $4,000, resulting in a profit understatement of $4,000. Because ending inventory is also understated by $8,000, the impact of this error will be an additional COGS overstatement of $8,000 and additional profit understatement of $8,000. The overstatement of $1,300 for the rent will result in an additional understatement of profit, for a total pretax profit understatement of $13,300 (see below).

20X1			
	Correct ($)	Wrong ($)	Misstatement ($)
Beginning inventory	6,000	10,000	4,000
Purchases	20,000	20,000	0
Total	26,000	30,000	4,000
Ending inventory	−18,000	−10,000	8,000
COGS	8,000	20,000	12,000
Sales	30,000	30,000	0
Rent			1,300
Profit	22,000	10,000	13,300

EXAMPLE 16.3

The following information applies to the Grady Company for the current year:

Purchases of merchandise for resale	$300,000
Merchandise returned to vendor	3,000
Interest on notes payable to vendors	6,000
Freight-in on merchandise	7,500

Grady's inventory costs for the year would be

a. $297,000   b. $300,000   c. $304,500   d. $316,500

EXPLANATION

Choice c. is correct. The answer was derived from the following calculation:

Purchase	$300,000
+ Freight-in	7,500
− Returns	(3,000)
	$304,500

Choice a. is incorrect. Freight-in must also be included as part of the inventory costs.

Choice b. is incorrect. In addition to purchases of merchandise, the merchandise returned to the vendor and the freight-in must be included in the inventory calculation.

Choice d. is incorrect. Interest costs on financing are not part of inventory cost (exceptions are in IAS 23).

EXAMPLE 16.4

An entity has a current ratio greater than 1.0. If the entity's ending inventory is understated by $3,000 and beginning inventory is overstated by $5,000, the entity's net income and the current ratio would be

Net Income	Current Ratio
a. Understated by $2,000	Lower
b. Overstated by $2,000	Lower
c. Understated by $8,000	Lower
d. Overstated $8,000	Higher

EXPLANATION

Choice c. is correct. The answer was derived from the following calculations:

$$\Delta \text{ COGS} = \Delta \text{ Beginning Inventory} + \Delta \text{ Purchases} - \Delta \text{ Ending Inventory}$$
$$= \$5,000 + P - (- \$3,000)$$

Assuming $\Delta P = 0$

$$\Delta \text{ COGS} = \$5,000 + \$3,000 = \$8,000$$

If COGS is overstated by $8,000, then net income is understated by $8,000 (assuming taxes are zero). If the ending inventory is understated, then the current ratio is also lower because inventory is part of current assets.

EXAMPLE 16.5 (READ TOGETHER WITH IAS 39)

A portfolio manager purchases and sells the following securities over a four-day period. On day 5, the manager sells five securities at $4 each. Although IFRS does not allow LIFO as a cost formula, determine

> i) the cost price of the securities, using the FIFO, LIFO, and weighted average cost (WAC) formulae, and
>
> ii) the profit that will be disclosed under each of the three alternatives.

EXPLANATION

Determining the "Buy" Cost Related to the Sell

Day	Buy Par	Sell Par	FIFO	LIFO	WAC
1	10 at $1		5 at $1		
2	15 at $2				
3	20 at $3			5 at $3	
4		5 at $4			
Average	45 at $2.22				5 at $2.22
(a) Cost price			5	15	11
Selling price			(20)	(20)	(20)
(b) Profit			(15)	(5)	(9)

EXAMPLE 16.6

Arco Inc. is a manufacturing company in the food industry. The following matters relate to the company's inventories:

A. In recent years the company utilized a standard costing system as an aid to management. The standard cost variances had been insignificant to date and were written off directly in the published annual financial statements. However, the following two problems were experienced during the year ending March 31, 20X3:

- Variances were far greater as a result of a sharp increase in material and labor costs as well as a decrease in production.

- A large number of the units produced were unsold at year-end. This was partially attributable to the products of the company being considered overpriced.

The management of the company intends, as in the past, to write off these variances directly as term costs, and to also write off a portion of the cost of surplus unsold inventories.

B. Chocolate raw material inventories on hand at the end of the year represent eight months of usage. Inventory levels normally represent only two months' usage. The current replacement value of the inventories is less than the initial cost.

EXPLANATION

A. Both writing off the variances in labor and material as term costs and writing off a portion of the unsold inventories are unacceptable for the following reasons:

- The write-offs of the large variances result in the standard values not approximating cost according to IAS 2.

- Standard costs should be reviewed regularly and revised in light of the current conditions. The labor and material variances should be allocated to the standard cost of inventories. The production overhead variance resulting from idle capacity should be recognized as an expense in the current period.

- The term "overpriced" is arbitrary, and any write-down of inventory should be done only if the NRV of the inventory is lower than its cost.

B. The abnormal portion of raw material on hand (representing six months of production) might need to be written down to NRV. The other raw materials (representing two months of production) should be written down to NRV only if the estimated cost of the finished products will be more than the NRV.

Chapter Seventeen

Financial Instruments: Recognition and Measurement (IAS 39)

IAS 32 and 39 and IFRS 7 were issued as separate standards. However, in practice they are applied as a unit because they deal with the same accounting and financial risk issues. IAS 39 deals with the recognition and measurement issues of financial instruments. IAS 32 (chapter 32) deals with presentation issues, and IFRS 7 deals with disclosure issues (see chapter 33).

17.1   OBJECTIVE

IAS 39 establishes principles for recognizing, measuring, and disclosing information about financial instruments in the financial statements. IAS 39 significantly increases the use of fair value in accounting for financial instruments, particularly on the asset side of the Statement of Financial Position.

17.2   SCOPE OF THE STANDARD

The standard distinguishes between four classes of financial assets: assets held at fair value through profit and loss (for example, trading and other elected securities); assets available for sale; assets held to maturity; and loans and receivables. In addition, IAS 39 identifies two classes of financial liabilities: those at fair value, and liabilities shown at amortized cost. The standard outlines the accounting approach in each case. It also categorizes and sets out the accounting treatment for three types of hedging: (a) fair value, (b) cash flow, and (c) net investment in a foreign subsidiary.

IAS 39 should be applied to all financial instruments identified in table 17.1. The following elements are excluded from the requirements of IAS 39:

- Subsidiaries, associates, and joint ventures
- Rights and obligations under leases
- Employee benefit plan assets and liabilities
- Rights and obligations under insurance contracts
- Equity instruments issued by the reporting entity
- Financial guarantee contracts related to failure by a debtor to make payments when due
- Contracts for contingent consideration in a business combination
- Contracts based on physical variables, for example, climate

Financial Instruments

17.3.1 **Financial instruments** are contracts that give rise to both

- a financial asset of one entity, and
- a financial liability of another entity.

17.3.2 A **derivative** is a financial instrument or other contract for which

- the value changes in response to changes in an underlying interest rate, exchange rate, commodity price, security price, credit rating, and so on;
- little or no initial investment is required; and
- settlement takes place at a future date.

17.3.3 An **embedded derivative** is a component of a hybrid instrument that includes a nonderivative host contract—with the effect that some of the cash flows of the combined instrument vary in a way similar to a stand-alone derivative. A derivative that is attached to a financial instrument but is contractually transferable independently of that instrument, or has a different counterparty from that instrument, is not an embedded derivative, but a separate financial instrument.

Valuation and Market Practice

17.3.4 **Fair value** is the amount at which an asset could be exchanged, or a liability settled, between knowledgeable, willing parties in an arm's-length transaction.

17.3.5 **Mark-to-market (MTM: fair value adjustments to financial assets and liabilities)** is the process whereby the value of most trading assets (for example, those held for trading and that are available for sale) and trading liabilities are adjusted to reflect current fair value. Such adjustments are often made on a daily basis, and cumulative balances reversed on the subsequent day, prior to recalculating a fresh cumulative mark-to-market adjustment.

17.3.6 **Amortized cost** is the amount at which the financial asset or financial liability is measured at initial recognition

- minus any principal repayments,
- plus or minus the cumulative amortization of the premiums or discounts on the instrument, and
- minus any reduction for impairment or lack of collectability.

The amortization calculation should use the effective interest rate (not the nominal rate of interest).

17.3.7 **Trade or settlement date accounting** arises when an entity chooses to recognize the purchase of an instrument in its financial statements on either (a) the date when the commitment arises from the transaction (trade date), or (b) the date that the liability is settled (settlement date). Most treasury accountants prefer trade date accounting, because that is when the risks and rewards of ownership transfer—and when marking to market commences in any case (regardless of whether the asset has already been recognized in the balance sheet).

17.3.8 **Total return** is the actual return achieved on financial assets and the amount used to assess the performance of a portfolio; it includes income and expenses recorded in the profit and loss account (for example, interest earned, realized gains and losses) and **unrealized** gains and losses recorded in profit and loss or equity (for example, fair value adjustments to available-for-sale securities).

Hedging

17.3.9 A **fair value hedge** hedges the exposure to changes in fair value of a recognized asset or liability (for example, changes in the fair value of fixed-rate bonds as a result of changes in market interest rates).

17.3.10 A **cash flow hedge** hedges the exposure of cash flows related to a recognized asset or liability (for example, future interest payments on a variable-rate bond); a highly probable transaction (for example, an anticipated purchase or sale of inventories); or the foreign currency risk effect of a firm commitment (for example, a contract entered into to buy or sell an asset at a fixed price in the entity's reporting currency).

17.3.11 The **hedge of a net investment in a foreign entity** hedges the exposure related to changes in foreign exchange rates.

17.4   ACCOUNTING TREATMENT

Recognition and Classification

17.4.1 All financial assets and financial liabilities (including derivatives) should be **recognized when** the entity becomes a party to the contractual provisions of an instrument.

17.4.2 For the purchase or sale of **financial assets** where market convention determines a fixed period between trade and settlement dates, either the trade or settlement date can be used for recognition. As stated above, IAS 39 allows the use of either date, but trade date accounting is preferred by most treasury accountants.

17.4.3 Management should establish policies for the classification of portfolios into various asset and liability classes (see table 17.1).

Table 17.1 Financial Asset and Liability Categories

Category	Measurement	Financial Assets Classes	Financial Liabilities Classes	Comments
1	Fair value through profit and loss	Trading securities	Trading liabilities	Short sales or issued debt with intention to repurchase shortly
		Derivatives	Derivatives	Unless designated as qualifying hedging instruments
		Other elected assets	Other elected liabilities	Fair value option (elected)—inconsistencies reduced where part of a documented group risk management strategy, or liabilities contain embedded derivatives
2	Amortized cost	Held-to-maturity securities	Accounts payable Issued debt securities Deposits from customers	
3	Amortized cost	Loans and receivables	N/A	
4	Fair value through equity	Available-for-sale securities	N/A	

Initial Measurement

17.4.4 Financial assets and financial liabilities are **recognized initially at their cost**—which is the fair value of the consideration given or received. Transaction costs as well as certain hedging gains or losses are also included.

17.4.5 Interest is *not* normally **accrued** between trade and settlement dates, but mark-to-market adjustments are made regardless of whether the entity uses **trade date** or **settlement date** accounting.

Subsequent Measurement

17.4.6 **Unrealized gains or losses** on remeasurement to fair value of financial assets and financial liabilities are **included in net profit or loss for the period**. However there are **two exceptions to this rule**:

■ Unrealized gains or losses on an available-for-sale financial asset must be recognized in equity until it is sold or impaired, at which time the cumulative amount is transferred to net profit or loss for the period. (See also chapter 21 and example 17.1 at the end of this chapter.)

■ When financial assets and financial liabilities (carried at amortized cost) are being hedged, special hedging rules apply.

17.4.7 **Impairment losses** are included in net profit or loss for the period irrespective of the category of financial assets. An entity should **assess**, at each Statement of Financial Position date, whether financial assets could be impaired.

■ When impairment losses occur for **available-for-sale financial assets** (where fair value remeasurements are recognized in equity), an amount should be transferred from equity to net profit or loss for the period.

- A **financial asset** or a group of financial assets (for example, **loans and receivables**) is impaired if there is objective evidence (which includes observable data) as a result of one or more events that have already occurred after the initial recognition of the asset.

  - When performing a collective assessment of impairment, assets must be grouped according to similar credit risk characteristics, indicative of the debtors' ability to pay all amounts due according to the contractual terms.

  - Loss events must have an impact that can be reliably estimated on future cash flows.

  - Losses expected as a result of future events, no matter how likely, are not recognized. (This conditionality appears to create a conflict with bank supervisory approaches that require a general percentage provision for loan losses, based on empirical evidence that such losses have actually occurred somewhere in the portfolio. The differences in approach need not be insurmountable if one considers historical realities related to loan portfolios.)

  - Objective evidence includes

    - significant financial difficulty of the issuer or obligor;

    - a breach of contract, such as a default or delinquency in interest or principal payments; and

    - granting the borrower a concession that the lender would not otherwise consider.

An impairment loss could be **reversed** in future periods, but the reversal may not exceed the amortized cost for those assets that are not remeasured at fair value (for example, held-to-maturity assets).

17.4.8 **Subsequent measurement** of financial securities can be summarized, as shown in tables 17.1 and 17.2.

Table 17.2 Financial Impact of Various Portfolio Classification Choices under IAS 39

IAS 39 Portfolio Classification	Realized and Unrealized Coupon and Gains and Losses	Realized and Unrealized Discount/Premium Amortization	Changes in Clean Market Value
Trading	Income	Income	Income
Available for Sale (AFS)	Income	Income	Equity
Held to Maturity (HTM)	Income	Income	–

Note: Foreign exchange gains and losses (realized and unrealized) are accounted through profit and loss, per IAS 21 (except for the **mark-to-market** portion of AFS securities which will have been recorded in equity).

Derecognition

17.4.9 A **financial asset**, or portion thereof, is **derecognized** when the entity loses control of the contractual rights to the cash flows that compose the financial asset—through realization, expiration, or surrender of those rights.

17.4.10 When a financial asset is derecognized, the difference between the proceeds and the carrying amount is included in the profit or loss for the period. Any prior cumulative revaluation surplus or shortfall that had been recognized directly in equity is also included in the profit or loss for the period. When a part of a financial asset is derecognized, the carrying amount is allocated proportionally to the part sold using fair value at date of sale, and the resulting gain or loss is included in the profit or loss for the period.

17.4.11 A **financial liability is derecognized** when it is extinguished, that is, when the obligation is discharged, cancelled, or expires.

Reclassification

17.4.12 Assets originally classified or designated as **fair value** through the income statement may not be reclassified unless, *in rare circumstances (such as market turmoil)*, a financial asset is no longer held for the purpose of selling or repurchasing it in the near term. Such assets are reclassified at current fair value and differences between the fair values prior to and post reclassification may be amortized over the remaining life of the asset.

17.4.13 Entities are permitted to reclassify assets classified as **available for sale** to loans and receivables provided:

■ they would have met the definition of a loan or receivable at the date of reclassification, and

■ the entity has the intent and ability to hold the asset for the foreseeable future or to maturity.

* Additional disclosures and factors must be considered for items reclassified out of fair value and available-for-sale categories, as follows:

■ differences between the previous fair values and the new carrying values which are being amortized over the remaining life of the asset, via other comprehensive income

■ the amount reclassified into and out of each category

■ the carrying amounts and fair values of all financial assets that have been reclassified in the current and previous reporting periods

17.4.14 An entity may not classify any financial assets as **held to maturity**

■ if during the current year or preceding two years it sold or reclassified more than an insignificant amount of held-to-maturity investments before maturity

■ unless the action is as a result of an unanticipated, nonrecurring, isolated event beyond its control.

Misuse of the category will result in nonavailability of the category for a period of three years.

17.4.15 If the **held-to-maturity** category is discontinued, the assets in that category can be reclassified only as available for sale.

Hedging

17.4.16 Hedging contrasts with **hedge accounting** as follows:

■ Hedging changes risks, whereas hedge accounting changes the accounting for gains and losses.

■ Hedging and hedge accounting are both **optional activities**. (Even when a position is hedged, the entity does not have to use hedge accounting to account for the transaction.)

■ Hedging is a **business decision**; hedge accounting is an **accounting decision**.

■ Hedge accounting is allowed only when a hedging instrument is a

■ derivative (other than a written option),

- written option when used to hedge a purchased option, or
- nonderivative financial asset or liability when used to hedge foreign currency risks.

- A hedging instrument may not be designated for only a **portion** of the time period over which the instrument is outstanding.

17.4.17 Hedging means designating a derivative or nonderivative financial instrument as an offset to the change in fair value or cash flows of a hedged item. A hedging relationship qualifies for special hedge accounting if the following criteria apply:

- At the inception of the hedge, there is formal **documentation** setting out the hedge details.
- The hedge is expected to be highly effective.
- In the case of a forecasted transaction, the transaction must be highly probable.
- The effectiveness of the hedge is reliably measured.
- The hedge was effective *throughout* the period (as described in table 17.3).

17.4.18 Hedge accounting (see table 17.3) recognizes symmetrically the offsetting effects on net profit or loss of changes in the fair values of the hedging instrument and the related item being hedged. Hedging relationships are of three types:

1. **Fair value hedge**—hedges the exposure of a recognized asset or liability (for example, changes in the fair value of fixed-rate bonds as a result of changes in market interest rates).

2. **Cash flow hedge**—hedges the exposure to variability in cash flows related to a recognized asset or liability (for example, future interest payments on a bond); or a forecasted transaction (for example, an anticipated purchase or sale of inventories).

3. **Hedge of a net investment in a foreign entity**—hedges the exposure related to changes in foreign exchange rates.

17.4.19 Gain or loss on a fair value hedge should be recognized in net profit or loss, and the loss or the gain from adjusting the carrying amount of the hedged item should be recognized in net profit or loss. This applies even if the hedged item is accounted for at cost.

17.4.20 Profits and losses on cash flow hedges are treated as follows:

- The portion of the gain or loss on the hedging instrument deemed to be an **effective** hedge is recognized directly in equity through the changes in equity statement. The ineffective portion is reported in net profit or loss.

- If the hedged firm commitment or forecasted transaction results in the recognition of a financial asset or liability, the associated gain or loss previously recognized in equity should be removed and entered into the initial measurement of the acquisition cost of the asset or liability.

- For cash flow hedges that do not result in an asset or liability, the gain or loss in equity should be taken to profit or loss when the transaction occurs.

17.4.21 The portion of the **profits and losses on hedges of a net investment in a foreign entity** on the hedging instrument deemed to be an effective hedge is recognized directly in equity through the changes in equity statement. The ineffective portion is reported in net profit or loss.

Table 17.3 Hedge Accounting Rules

	Recognize in Statement of Comprehensive Income	Recognize directly in equity	Recognize in initial measurement of asset/liability
Fair value hedge	All adjustments on hedging instrument and hedged item		
Cash flow hedge	Gain/loss on ineffective[2] portion of hedging instrument		
	Gain/loss previously recognized in equity when hedge does not result in asset/liability	Gain/loss on the effective[1] portion of hedging instrument	Gain/loss previously recognized in equity
Hedge of net investment in foreign entity	Gain/loss on ineffective[2] portion of hedging instrument	Gain/loss on the effective[1] portion of hedging instrument	

1. A hedge is normally regarded to be highly effective if, at inception and throughout the life of the hedge, the entity can expect changes in the fair values or cash flows of the hedged item to be almost fully offset by the changes in the hedging instrument, and actual results are in the range of 80 percent to 125 percent. For example, if the loss on a financial liability is 56 and the profit on the hedging instrument is 63, the hedge is regarded to be effective: $63 \div 56 = 112.5$ percent.

2. An ineffective hedge would be one where actual results of offset are outside the range mentioned above. Furthermore, a hedge would not be fully effective if the hedging instrument and the hedged item are denominated in different currencies, and the two do not move in tandem. Also, a hedge of interest-rate risk using a derivative would not be fully effective if part of the change in the fair value of the derivative is due to the counterparty's credit risk.

17.5 PRESENTATION AND DISCLOSURE

17.5.1 Presentation issues are dealt with in IAS 32 (chapter 32).

17.5.2 Disclosure issues are dealt with in IFRS 7 (chapter 33).

17.6 FINANCIAL ANALYSIS AND INTERPRETATION

17.6.1 The analyst should obtain an understanding of management's policies for classifying securities.

17.6.2 **Securities held for trading** and available-for-sale securities are both valued at fair value. However, the unrealized profits and losses on available-for-sale securities do not flow directly through the Statement of Comprehensive Income. Therefore, total return calculations need to reflect this.

17.6.3 Available-for-sale securities must also be marked-to-market (fair valued) and **unrealized** profits and losses taken directly to equity (and not to the Statement of Comprehensive Income). Securities that are not held to maturity, but are also not held for trading, are classified as available for sale. These securities are valued in a similar way as trading securities: they are carried at fair value. However, only realized (actual sales) gains and losses arising from the sale or reclassification of investments are recorded on the Statement of Comprehensive Income. Unrealized (not sold, but with a changed value) gains and losses are shown as a separate component of stockholders' equity on the Statement of Financial Position.

17.6.4 If management decides to treat securities as available for sale and not as trading securities, the decision could potentially have a negative impact on the transparency of total return calculations. There is an added potential for letting losses accumulate in equity if information technology systems are not sophisticated enough to link securities to their respective accumulated profits and losses.

17.6.5 There are sound reasons why it might be preferable to take **unrealized gains and losses** through the income statement portion of the Statement of Comprehensive Income. The total return on the portfolio—including both coupon income and changes in price—is an accurate reflection of the portfolio performance. When there is an asymmetrical treatment of capital gains or losses and coupon income, it can lead to unsophisticated observers regarding trading income in a manner incompatible with the total return maximization objectives of modern portfolio management. By taking unrealized gains and losses through the Statement of Comprehensive Income, portfolio management will correctly focus on making portfolio decisions to maximize returns based on anticipated future relative returns, rather than on making decisions for income manipulation.

17.6.6 Available-for-sale securities require sophisticated systems and accounting capacity. As stated in chapter 21, the treatment of foreign currency translation gains and losses adds to this complexity.

17.6.7 **Held-to-maturity securities** are most often debt securities that management intends and is able to hold to maturity. These securities are recorded initially at cost and are valued on the Statement of Financial Position at amortized value. The book value of the marketable security is reported on the Statement of Financial Position, and the interest income as well as any amortization profits or losses and impairments losses are reported in the Statement of Comprehensive Income. The coupon receipt is recorded as an operating cash flow.

17.6.8 A key purpose of derivatives is to modify future cash flows by minimizing the entity's exposure to risks, by increasing risk exposure, or by deriving benefits from these instruments. An entity can readily adjust its positions in financial instruments to align its financing activities with operating activities and, thereby, improve its allocation of capital to accommodate changes in the business environment. All such activities, or their possible occurrence, should be transparent to financial statements' users. For example, not reporting significant interest rate or foreign currency swap transactions would be as inappropriate as not consolidating a significant subsidiary.

17.6.9 **Sensitivity analysis** is an essential element needed for estimating an entity's future expected cash flows; these estimates are needed in calculating the entity's valuation. Therefore, sensitivity analysis is an integral and essential component of fair value accounting and reporting. For example, many derivative instruments have significant statistical deviation from the expected norm, which affects future cash flows. Unless those potential effects are transparent in disclosures and analyses (for example, in sensitivity analyses or stress tests), the Statement of Financial Position representation of fair values for financial instruments is incomplete and cannot be used properly to assess risk-return relationships and to analyze management's performance.

EXAMPLE 17.1

An entity receives $100 million equity in cash on July 1, 20X5.

It invests in a bond of $100 million par at a clean price of 97 with a 5-percent fixed coupon on July 1, 20X5.

Coupons are paid annually, and the bond has a maturity date of June 30, 20X7.

The yield to maturity is calculated as 6.6513 percent.

On June 30, 20X6, the entity receives the first coupon payment of $5 million.

The clean market value of the security has increased to 99 at June 30, 20X6.

The security has not been impaired and no principal has been repaid.

Using the effective interest method, the $3 million discount is amortized 1.45 in year 1 and 1.55 in year 2.

17.1.A Illustrate how this situation will be portrayed in the entity's Statement of Financial Position assets and equity, as well as its Statement of Comprehensive Income—under each of the following three accounting policies for marketable securities: assets held for trading purposes, assets available for sale, assets held to maturity.

17.1.B Discuss the treatment of discounts or premiums on securities purchased in the financial statements of the entity.

17.1.C If these securities were denominated in a foreign currency, how would translation gains and losses be treated in the financial statements of the entity?

Source: Hamish Flett—Treasury Operations, World Bank.

EXPLANATIONS

17.1.A Financial Statements

Statement of Financial Position as of December 31, 20X6	Held-to-Maturity Portfolio	Trading Portfolio	Available-for-Sale Portfolio
Assets	8.00	8.00	8.00
Cash	98.45	99.00	99.00
Securities	106.45	107.00	107.00
Analysis of Securities			
Cost of securities	97.00	97.00	97.00
Amortization of discount/premium	1.45	–	1.45
Unrealized profit/loss	–	2.00	0.55
	98.45	99.00	99.00
Liabilities			
Equity	100.00	100.00	100.00
Unrealized profit/loss on securities	–	–	0.55
Net income	6.45	7.00	6.45
	106.45	107.00	107.00
Statement of Comprehensive Income for year ending December 31, 20X6			
Interest income	5.00	5.00	5.00
Amortization of discount/premium	1.45	–	1.45
Unrealized profit/loss on securities	–	2.00	–
Realized profit/loss net income	6.45	7.00	6.45

17.1.B

a. With the trading portfolio, the amortization of discount/premium is effectively accounted for in the mark-to-market adjustment. As the amortization of discount/premium, realized profit and loss (P&L), and unrealized P&L for a trading portfolio are all recorded in the Statement of Comprehensive Income, it is not necessary to separate the discount/premium amortization element from the mark-to-market adjustment. However, it may be desirable to record any discount/premium amortization separately, even for a trading portfolio, to provide additional management information on the performance of traders.

b. If the trading security were subsequently sold, the clean sale proceeds would be compared to its clean cost to determine the realized P&L.

c. If the available-for-sale security were subsequently sold, the clean sale proceeds would be compared to its amortized cost to determine the realized P&L, as amortization is already reflected.

d. Following is the interest amortization table:

	Amortized Cost	Effective Interest Rate	Effective Interest	Coupon Payment	Amortization Premium/ Discount
End of Period	97.000	6.651%	6.45	5.00	1.452
1	98.452	6.651%	6.55	5.00	1.548
2	100.00				3.00

17.1.C All foreign currency translations adjustments on the securities (see IAS 21) should be reflected in the Statement of Comprehensive Income. In the case of available-for-sale securities, the mark-to-market adjustment portion of the foreign currency translation should be reflected in equity— in line with the normal treatment of fair value adjustments for available-for-sale securities. It should be noted, however, that the foreign currency adjustment related to the principal amount of an available-for-sale security is taken directly to the Statement of Comprehensive Income.

EXAMPLE 17.2

The following example illustrates the accounting treatment of a hedge of the exposure to variability in cash flows (cash flow hedge) that is attributable to a forecast transaction.

The Milling Co. is reviewing its maize purchases for the coming season. It anticipates purchasing 1,000 tons of maize in two months. Currently, the two-month maize futures are selling at $600 per ton, and Milling will be satisfied with purchasing its maize inventory at this price by the end of May.

As renewed drought is staring the farmers in the face, Miller is afraid that the maize price might increase. It therefore hedges its anticipated purchase against this possible increase in the maize price by going long (buying) on two-month maize futures at $600 per ton for 1,000 tons. The transaction requires Milling to pay an initial margin of $30,000 into its margin account. Margin accounts are updated twice every month.

The following market prices are applicable:

Date	Futures Price (per Ton)
April 1	$600
April 15	$590
April 30	$585
May 15	$605
May 31	$620 (spot)

The maize price in fact increased because of the drought, and Milling purchases the projected 1,000 tons of maize at the market (spot) price of $620 per ton on May 31.

EXPLANATION

The calculation of variation margins is as follows:

April 15 (600 – 590) × 1,000 tons = $10,000 (payable)

April 30 (590 – 585) × 1,000 tons = $5,000 (payable)

May 15 (605 – 585) × 1,000 tons = $20,000 (receivable)

May 31 (620 – 605) × 1,000 tons = $15,000 (receivable)

The accounting entries will be as follows:

	Dr ($)	Cr ($)
April 1		
Initial Margin Account (B/S)	30,000	
Cash		30,000
(Settlement of initial margin)		
April 15		
Hedging Reserve (Equity)	10,000	
Cash Payable (variation margin)		10,000
(Account for the loss on the futures contract—cash flow hedge)		
April 30		
Hedging Reserve (Equity)	5,000	
Cash Payable (variation margin)		5,000
(Account for the loss on the futures contract—cash flow hedge)		
May 15		
Cash Receivable (variation margin)	20,000	
Hedging Reserve (Equity)		20,000
(Account for the profit on the futures contract—cash flow hedge)		
May 31		
Cash Receivable (variation margin)	15,000	
Hedging Reserve (Equity)		15,000
(Account for the profit on the futures contract—cash flow hedge)		
May 31		
Inventory	620,000	
Cash		620,000
(Purchase the inventory at spot—1,000 tons @ $620 per ton)		
May 31		
Cash	30,000	
Margin Account		30,000
(Receive initial margin deposited)		
May 31		
Hedging Reserve (Equity)	20,000	
Inventory		20,000

The gain or loss on the cash flow hedge should be removed from equity, and the value of the underlying asset recognized should be adjusted.

It is clear from this example that the value of the inventory is adjusted with the gain on the hedging instrument, resulting in the inventory being accounted for at the hedged price or futures price.

If the futures contract did not expire or was not closed out on May 31, the gains or losses calculated on the futures contract thereafter would be accounted for in the Statement of Comprehensive Income, because the cash flow hedge relationship no longer exists.

EXAMPLE 17.3

This example concerns short-term money market instruments not marked-to-market (held in a held-to-maturity portfolio).

A company buys a 120-day Treasury bill with a face value of $1 million for $996,742. When purchased, the recorded book value of the bill is this original cost.

EXPLANATION

Held-to-maturity instruments are normally recorded at cost and valued on the Statement of Financial Position at cost adjusted for the effects of interest (or discount earned). The book value of the marketable security is reported on the Statement of Financial Position, and the interest income is reported in the Statement of Comprehensive Income. The discount earned is recorded as an operating cash flow. Following is the entry to record the purchase of the bill:

	Dr ($)	Cr ($)
Short-term Investments	996,742	
Cash		996,742

If 60 days later the company is constructing its financial statements, the bill must be marked up to its amortized cost using the following adjusting entry:

	Dr ($)	Cr ($)
Short-term Investments	1,629	
Interest Income		1,629[1]

$$\text{Interest income} = (Pm - Po)\, t/tm$$
$$= \$1,000,000 - 996,742\,(60/120)$$
$$= \$1629$$

where P_m is the value of the bill at maturity.

P_o is the value of the bill when purchased.

t is the number of days the bill has been held.

t_m is the number of days until the bill matures from when purchased.

The Treasury bill will be recorded on the Statement of Financial Position as a short-term investment valued at its adjusted cost of $998,371 ($996,742 + $1,629), whereas the $1,629 discount earned will be reported as interest income on the Statement of Comprehensive Income.

When the Treasury bill matures, the entry is as follows:

	Dr ($)	Cr ($)
Cash	1,000,000	
Short-term Investments		998,371
Interest Income		1,629*

*Assumes 60 days of interest on a straight-line basis as an approximation of effective interest rate.

EXAMPLE 17.4

This is an example of accounting for trading securities—marked-to-market and unrealized profits taken through the income statement portion of the Statement of Comprehensive Income.

On November 30, 20X3, a company buys 100 shares of Amazon for $90 per share and 100 shares of IBM for $75 per share.

The securities are classified as trading securities (current assets) and are valued at fair value (market value).

EXPLANATION

Any increase or decrease in the value is included in net income in the year in which it occurs. Also, any income received from the security is recorded in net income.

To record the initial purchases, the entry is

	Dr ($)	Cr ($)
Traded Equities	16,500 (100 x $90 + 100 x $75)	
Cash		16,500

One month later, the company is preparing its year-end financial statements. On December 31, 20X3, Amazon's closing trade was at $70 per share, and IBM's was at $80 per share. Thus, the company's investment in these two firms has fallen to $15,000 (100 x $70 + 100 x $80). The traded securities account is adjusted as follows:

	Dr ($)	Cr ($)
Unrealized Gains/Loss on Investments	1,500	
Traded Equities		1,500

Notice that the loss on Amazon and gain on IBM are netted. Thus, a net loss is recorded, which reduces the firm's income. This is an unrealized loss, as the shares have not been sold, so the firm has not actually realized a loss, but this is still recorded in the Statement of Comprehensive Income.

In mid-January 20X4, the firm receives a dividend of $0.16 per share on its IBM stock. The entry is as follows:

	Dr ($)	Cr ($)
Cash	16 ($0.16 x 100)	
Investment Income		16

Finally, on January 23, 20X4, the firm sells both stocks. It receives $80 per share for Amazon and $85 per share for IBM. The entry is as follows:

	Dr ($)	Cr ($)
Cash	16,500 (100 x $80 + 100 x $85)	
Traded Equities		15,000
Unrealized Gains/Loss on Investments		1,500

By consistently recording fair value adjustments to an unrealized gain/loss account, that account is cleared when the security is sold.

Chapter Eighteen

Noncurrent Assets Held for Sale and Discontinued Operations (IFRS 5)

18.1 OBJECTIVE

The objective of IFRS 5 is to specify the accounting for assets held for sale, and the presentation and disclosure of discontinued operations. It is important to highlight the fact that some assets of an entity are held for sale or that operations are discontinued so that investors can appreciate that these assets and earnings will not be available to the firm in future periods.

18.2 SCOPE OF THE STANDARD

IFRS 5 and its measurement requirements apply to all recognized noncurrent assets and disposal groups.

It requires that such assets and intended operations

- be measured at the lower of carrying amount and fair value less costs to sell,
- cease to be depreciated,
- be presented separately on the face of the Statement of Financial Position, and
- have their results disclosed separately in the Statement of Comprehensive Income.

The measurement provisions of this IFRS do not apply to the following assets:

- Deferred tax assets (IAS 12)
- Assets arising from employee benefits (IAS 19)
- Financial assets within the scope of IAS 39
- Noncurrent assets that are accounted for in accordance with the fair value model in IAS 40
- Noncurrent assets that are measured at fair value less estimated point-of-sale costs (IAS 41)
- Contractual rights under insurance contracts as defined in IFRS 4

18.3 KEY CONCEPTS

18.3.1 An **operation** is **discontinued** at the date the operation meets the criteria to be classified as held for sale or when the entity has disposed of the operation.

18.3.2 A **disposal group** is a group of assets (and associated liabilities) to be disposed of, by sale or otherwise, together as a group in a single transaction.

18.3.3 An entity should classify a noncurrent asset or disposal group as **held for sale** if its carrying amount will be recovered principally through a sale transaction rather than through continuing use. For this to be the case, the asset or disposal group must be available for immediate sale in its present condition—subject only to terms that are usual and customary for sales of such assets or disposal groups—and its sale must be highly probable.

18.3.4 For a sale to be **highly probable,** the appropriate level of management must be committed to a plan to sell the asset or disposal group, and management must have initiated an active program to locate a buyer and complete the plan.

18.4   ACCOUNTING TREATMENT

Recognition

18.4.1 **An asset or disposal group** should be **classified** as held for sale in a period in which all the following criteria are met:

- Management commits to a plan to sell.
- The component is available for immediate sale in its present condition.
- An active program and other actions exist to locate a buyer.
- A sale is highly probable and expected to be completed within one year.
- The asset or disposal group is actively marketed at a reasonable price, and it is unlikely that there will be significant changes to the marketing plan or that management will consider withdrawing its plan to sell.

18.4.2 When an entity acquires a noncurrent asset (or disposal group) exclusively with a view to its subsequent disposal, it should **classify** the noncurrent asset (or disposal group) as **held for sale** at the acquisition date only if the one-year requirement in this IFRS is met (except in circumstances beyond the entity's control). If any other criteria are not met at that date, it must be highly probable that the other criteria will be met within a short period following the acquisition (usually within three months). If the entity's plans for sale change, classification as a discontinued operation must cease immediately due to the requirements of 18.3.1.

Initial Measurement

18.4.3 Noncurrent assets held for sale

- should be **measured** at the lower of carrying amount or fair value, less cost to sell; and
- are not depreciated.

Subsequent Measurement

18.4.4 An entity should recognize an **impairment loss** for any initial or subsequent write-down of the asset (or disposal group) to fair value less costs to sell.

18.4.5 An entity should recognize a **gain** for any subsequent increase in fair value less costs to sell of an asset, but not in excess of the cumulative impairment loss that has been previously recognized.

18.4.6 When a sale is expected to occur beyond one year, the entity should measure the costs to sell at their present value. Any increase in the present value of the costs to sell that arises from the passage of time should be presented in profit or loss as a financing cost.

Dercognition

18.4.7 An entity should not classify as held for sale a noncurrent asset (or disposal group) that is to be abandoned. This is because its carrying amount will be recovered principally through continuing use.

18.5   PRESENTATION AND DISCLOSURE

18.5.1 An entity should present and disclose information that enables users of the financial statements to evaluate the financial effects of discontinued operations and disposals of noncurrent assets or disposal groups.

18.5.2 Noncurrent assets held for sale and assets and liabilities (held for sale) of a disposal group should be presented separately from other assets and liabilities in the Statement of Financial Position.

18.5.3 **Statement of Comprehensive Income or notes** should disclose (after the net profit for the period)

- the amounts and analyses of revenue, expenses, and pretax profit or loss attributable to the discontinued operation; and

- the amount of any gain or loss that is recognized on the disposal of assets or settlement of liabilities attributable to the discontinued operation and the related income tax expense.

18.5.4 The **cash flow statement** should disclose the net cash flows attributable to the operating, investing, and financing activities of the discontinued operation.

18.5.5 An entity should disclose the following information in the notes **to the financial statements** in the period in which a noncurrent asset or disposal group has been either classified as held for sale or sold:

- A description of the noncurrent asset or disposal group

- A description of the facts and circumstances of the sale, or leading to the expected disposal, and the expected manner and timing of that disposal

- The gain, loss, or impairment recognized and, if not separately presented on the face of the Statement of Comprehensive Income, the caption in the Statement of Comprehensive Income that includes that gain or loss

- The segment in which the noncurrent asset or disposal group is presented (IFRS 8)

- In the period of the decision to **change the plan** to sell the noncurrent asset or disposal group, a description of the facts and circumstances leading to the decision and the effect of the decision on the results of operations for the period and any prior periods presented

18.6   FINANCIAL ANALYSIS AND INTERPRETATION

18.6.1 The requirements related to discontinued operations assist the analyst in distinguishing between ongoing or sustainable operations and future profitability, based on operations that management plans to continue.

18.6.2 IFRS requires that gains or losses on the disposal of depreciable assets be disclosed in the Statement of Comprehensive Income. If, however, the operations of a business are sold, abandoned, spun off, or otherwise disposed of, then this IFRS requires that the results of continuing operations be reported separately from discontinued operations to facilitate analysis of core business areas.

18.6.3 To facilitate analysis of profitability, any gain or loss from disposal of an entire business or segment should also be reported with the related results of discontinued operations as a separate item on the Statement of Comprehensive Income below income from continuing operations.

EXAMPLE: DISCONTINUED OPERATIONS

EXAMPLE 18.1

Outback Inc. specializes in camping and outdoor products and operates in three divisions: food, clothes, and equipment. Because of the high cost of local labor, the food division has incurred significant operating losses. Management has decided to close down the division and draws up a plan of discontinuance.

On May 1, 20X2, the board of directors approved and immediately announced the formal plan. The following data were obtained from the accounting records for the current and prior year ending June 30:

	20X2 ($'000)			20X1 ($'000)		
	Food	Clothes	Equip.	Food	Clothes	Equip.
Revenue	470	1,600	1,540	500	1,270	1,230
Cost of sales	350	500	510	400	400	500
Distribution costs	40	195	178	20	185	130
Administrative expenses	70	325	297	50	310	200
Other operating expenses	30	130	119	20	125	80
Taxation expenses or (benefit)	(6)	137	124	3	80	90

The following additional costs, which are directly related to the decision to discontinue, are not included in the table above.

Incurred between May 1, 20X2, and June 30, 20X2:

- Severance pay provision $85,000 (not tax deductible)

Budgeted for the year ending June 30, 20X3:

- Other direct costs $73,000
- Severance pay $12,000
- Bad debts $4,000

A proper evaluation of the recoverability of the assets in the food division, in terms of IAS 36, led to the recognition of an impairment loss of $19,000, which is included in the other operating expenses above and are fully tax deductible.

Apart from other information required to be disclosed elsewhere in the financial statements, the Statement of Comprehensive Income for the year ending June 30, 20X2, could be presented as follows:

Outback Inc. Statement of Comprehensive Income for the Year Ended June 30, 20X2	20X2 $'000	20X1 $'000
Continuing Operations (Clothes and Equipment)		
Revenue	3,140	2,500
Cost of sales	(1,010)	(900)
Gross profit	2,130	1,600
Distribution costs	(373)	(315)
Administrative expenses	(622)	(510)
Other operating expenses	(249)	(205)
Profit before Tax	886	570
Income tax expense	(261)	(170)
Net Profit for the Period	625	400
Discontinued Operation (Food)	(99)	7
Total Entity Net Profit for the Period	526	407
Detail in the Notes to the Financial Statement		
Discontinued Operations		
Revenue	470	500
Cost of sales	(350)	(400)
Gross profit	120	100
Distribution costs	(40)	(20)
Administrative expenses	(70)	(50)
Other operating expenses (30–19)	(11)	(20)
Impairment loss	(19)	–
Severance pay	(85)	–
(Loss) or Profit before Tax	(105)	10
Income tax benefit or (expense)	6	(3)
Net (Loss) or Profit for the Period	(99)	7

Chapter Nineteen

Exploration for and Evaluation of Mineral Resources (IFRS 6)

19.1 OBJECTIVE

IFRS 6 is guidance for entities that recognize assets used in the exploration for and evaluation of mineral resources. The key issues are the initial recognition criteria and measurement basis for these assets, measurement subsequent to recognition, and the tests for impairment of such assets in accordance with IAS 36.

19.2 SCOPE OF THE STANDARD

An entity should apply this IFRS to exploration and evaluation expenditures that it incurs.

IFRS 6 is specifically concerned with the initial recognition criteria for exploration and evaluation expenditure, the measurement basis thereafter (cost or revaluation model), and testing for any subsequent impairment of asset value. This standard does not address other aspects of accounting by entities engaged in the exploration for and evaluation of mineral resources.

An entity that has exploration and evaluation assets can test such assets for impairment on the basis of a cash-generating unit for exploration and evaluation assets, rather than on the basis of the cash-generating unit that might otherwise be required by IAS 36.

Entities with exploration and evaluation assets should disclose information about those assets, the level at which such assets are assessed for impairment, and any impairment losses recognized.

19.3 KEY CONCEPTS

19.3.1 A **cash-generating unit** is the smallest identifiable group of assets that generates cash inflows from continuing use that are largely independent of the cash inflows from other assets or groups of assets.

19.3.2 A cash-generating unit for exploration and evaluation assets should be no larger than a **business segment**. An entity should perform impairment tests of those assets under the accounting policies applied in its most recent annual financial statements.

19.3.3 **Exploration and evaluation assets** are expenditures for exploration and evaluation of mineral resources that are recognized as assets.

19.3.4 **Exploration and evaluation expenditures** are expenditures incurred by an entity in connection with the exploration for and evaluation of mineral resources.

19.3.5 Exploration for and evaluation of mineral resources is the search for mineral resources as well as the determination of the technical feasibility and commercial viability of extracting the mineral resource before the decision is made to develop the mineral resource.

19.4   ACCOUNTING TREATMENT

Initial Measurement

19.4.1 Exploration and evaluation assets should be measured at cost.

19.4.2 Expenditures related to the following activities are **potentially includable** in the initial measurement of exploration and evaluation assets:

- Acquisition of exploration rights
- Topographical, geological, geochemical, and geophysical studies
- Exploratory drilling
- Trenching
- Sampling
- Evaluating the technical feasibility and commercial viability of extracting mineral resources

19.4.3 Expenditures not to be included in the initial measurement of exploration and evaluation assets are

- the development of a mineral resource once technical feasibility and commercial viability of extracting a mineral resource have been established, and
- administration and other general overhead costs.

19.4.4 Any obligations for removal and restoration that are incurred during a particular period as a consequence of having undertaken the exploration for and evaluation of mineral resources is recognized in terms of IAS 20.

Subsequent Measurement

19.4.5 After recognition, an entity should apply either the **cost model** or the **revaluation model** to its exploration and evaluation assets. (IAS 16 and IAS 38 contain the key concepts that relate to cost, fair value, carrying value, and the impairment of assets.)

19.4.6 An entity that has recognized exploration and evaluation assets should assess those assets for **impairment** annually and should recognize any resulting impairment loss in accordance with IAS 36 (conditional exemption available at first application). Impairment might be indicated by the following:

- The period for which the entity has the right to explore in the specific area has expired during the period or will expire in the near future, and is not expected to be renewed.
- Further exploration for and evaluation of mineral resources in the specific area are neither budgeted nor planned in the near future.

- Significant changes have occurred with an adverse effect on the main assumptions, including prices and foreign exchange rates, underlying approved budgets, or plans for further exploration for and evaluation of mineral resources in the specific area.

- The decision not to develop the mineral resource in the specific area has been made.

- The entity plans to dispose of the asset at an unfavorable price.

- The entity does not expect the recognized exploration and evaluation assets to be reasonably recoverable from a successful development of the specific area or by the sale of the assets.

19.5   PRESENTATION AND DISCLOSURE

19.5.1 An entity should disclose information that identifies and explains the amounts recognized in its financial statements that arise from the exploration for and evaluation of mineral resources.

19.5.2 An entity should also disclose

- its **accounting policies** for exploration and evaluation **expenditures**;

- its **accounting policies** for the **recognition** of exploration and evaluation **assets**;

- the **amounts** of assets; liabilities; income; expense; and, if it presents its cash flow statement using the direct method, cash flows arising from the exploration for and evaluation of mineral resources; and

- the level at which the entity assesses exploration and evaluation assets for **impairment**.

19.6   FINANCIAL ANALYSIS AND INTERPRETATION

19.6.1 The **allocation over time of the original cost** of acquiring and developing natural resources is called **depletion**. It is similar to depreciation.

19.6.2 **Depletion** is the means of expensing the costs incurred in acquiring and developing natural resources. When depletion is accounted for using the units-of-production method, the formula appears as follows:

$$\text{Depletion Rate} = \frac{\text{Capitalized Cost of the Natural Resource Asset}}{\text{Estimated Number of Extractable Units}}$$

19.6.3 If, for example, a company buys oil and mineral rights for $5 million on a property that is believed to contain 2 million barrels of extractable oil, every barrel of oil extracted from the property is recorded as $2.50 of depletion expense on the Statement of Comprehensive Income, until the $5 million is written off. From the above formula, the depletion rate is

$$\text{Depletion Rate} = \frac{\$5,000,000}{2,000,000 \text{ bbls.}} = \$2.50/\text{bbl.}$$

19.6.4 Companies in some accounting jurisdictions might choose to capitalize only those costs that are associated with a successful discovery of a natural resource. Costs associated with unsuccessful efforts (that is, when the natural resources sought are not found) are expensed against income. This could be in line with paragraph 19.4.2 above, with the exception that an impairment test should determine which costs are not recoverable through depletion (depreciation). This is the more conservative method of accounting for acquisition and development costs, because it usually results in higher expenses and lower profits.

19.6.5 A company might buy, for example, oil and mineral rights on two properties for $6 million and $4 million, respectively. Ultimately, the company finds no oil on the first property and finds that the second property contains an estimated 2 million barrels of oil. Under the successful-efforts method, the accounting is as follows:

- At the time property rights are purchased:

	Dr	Cr
Oil and Mineral Rights (Statement of Financial Position Asset)	10,000,000	
Cash		10,000,000

- At the time when the first property is found to contain no oil, its cost is written off and the loss is taken immediately:

	Dr	Cr
Loss on Oil and Mineral Rights (Statement of Comprehensive Income)	6,000,000	
Oil and Mineral Rights (Statement of Financial Position)		6,000,000

19.6.6 Suppose, during the next year, 300,000 barrels of oil are extracted from the second property. This process is repeated every year until the Statement of Financial Position natural resource asset, Oil and Mineral Rights, is written down to zero:

	Dr*	Cr
Depletion Expense (Statement of Comprehensive Income)	600,000	
Oil and Mineral Rights (Statement of Financial Position)		600,000

$$\text{*Depletion Expense} = \left(\frac{\$4,000,000}{2,000,000 \text{ bbls}} \right) (300,000 \text{ bbls}) = \$600,000$$

19.6.7 For the following reasons, larger firms are more likely to expense as many costs as possible:

- Larger firms tend to hold reported earnings down, thereby making the firm less vulnerable to taxes and to political charges of earning windfall profits.

- The earnings volatility associated with this method is less harmful to large firms that engage in many more activities than just exploration.

- The negative impact on earnings is not severe for integrated oil companies that make substantial profits from marketing and refining activities, rather than just exploration activities.

EXAMPLE 19.1

Rybak Petroleum purchases an oil well for $100 million. It estimates that the well contains 250 million barrels of oil. The oil well has no salvage value. If the company extracts and sells 10,000 barrels of oil during the first year, how much depletion expense should be recorded?

a. $4,000

b. $10,000

c. $25,000

d. $250,000

EXPLANATION

Choice a. is correct. Depletion expense is

$$\text{Depletion rate} = \frac{\text{Current period production}}{\text{Total barrels of production}}$$

$$= \frac{10,000}{250,000,000}$$

$$= 0.00004$$

$$\text{Depletion expense} = \text{Purchase price} \times \text{Depletion rate}$$

$$= 100,000,000 \times 0.00004$$

$$= \underline{\$4,000}$$

Choice b. is incorrect. The choice incorrectly uses the depletion rate multiplied by the total barrels of oil in the well rather than the depletion rate multiplied by the purchase price.

Choice c. is incorrect. The choice incorrectly divides current production of 10,000 barrels by the purchase price, then multiplies this incorrect depletion rate by the total number of barrels of oil in the well.

Choice d. is incorrect. The choice incorrectly assumes a 0.001 depletion rate multiplied by the total number of barrels of oil in the well.

EXAMPLE 19.2

SunClair Exploration Inc. has just purchased new offshore oil drilling equipment for $35 million. The company's engineers estimate that the new equipment will produce 400 million barrels of oil over its estimated 15-year life, and have an estimated parts salvage value of $500,000. Assuming that the oil drilling equipment produced 22 million barrels of oil during its first year of production, what amount will the company record as depreciation expense for this equipment in the initial year using the units-of-production method of depreciation?

a. $2,300,000

b. $1,897,500

c. $1,925,000

d. $2,333,333

EXPLANATION

Choice b. is correct. Depreciation expense using units-of-production method is

$$\text{Depreciation rate per unit} = \frac{(\text{Original cost} - \text{Salvage value})}{\text{Est. production over useful life}}$$

$$= \frac{(\$35,000,000 - \$500,000)}{400,000,000 \text{ barrels}}$$

$$= 0.0863$$

$$\text{Depreciation expense} = \text{Depreciation rate} \times \text{Units produced}$$

$$= 0.0863 \times 22,000,000$$

$$= \underline{\$1,897,500}$$

Choice a. is incorrect. Units produced were multiplied by a useful life of 15 years, and the resulting number was then incorrectly used as the denominator of the depreciation rate calculation, rather than using the estimated 400 million–barrel estimated production over the useful life.

Choice c. is incorrect. This choice fails to subtract salvage value from original cost in the depreciation rate per unit calculation.

Choice d. is incorrect. This choice fails to subtract salvage value from the original cost in the depreciation rate per unit calculation, and incorrectly multiplies units produced by a useful life of 15 years as the denominator of the depreciation rate calculation.

Chapter Twenty

Provisions, Contingent Liabilities, and Contingent Assets (IAS 37)

Note: IAS 37 is currently under review, and an exposure draft of proposed amendments was issued in June 2005. The exposure draft emphasized that an asset or liability cannot be contingent. The definition for an asset or liability is either met, or not. Uncertainty is reflected in measurement, not in determining whether the asset or liability exists.

20.1 OBJECTIVE

Provisions and contingent liabilities have an increased level of inherent uncertainty. The prime objective of IAS 37 is to ensure that provisions are recognized only when established criteria of reliability of the obligation are met. In contrast, contingent liabilities and assets should not be recognized but should be disclosed so that such information is available in the financial statements.

20.2 SCOPE OF THE STANDARD

IAS 37 prescribes the appropriate accounting treatment as well as the disclosure requirements for all provisions, contingent liabilities, and contingent assets to enable users to understand their nature, timing, and amount.

The standard sets out the conditions that must be fulfilled for a provision to be recognized.

It guides the preparers of financial statements to decide when, with respect to a specific obligation, they should

- provide for it (recognize it),
- only disclose information, or
- disclose nothing.

IAS 37 is applicable to all entities when accounting for provisions and contingent liabilities or assets, except those resulting from

- financial instruments carried at fair value,
- executory contracts (for example, contracts under which both parties have partially performed their obligations to an equal extent),
- insurance contracts with policyholders, and
- events or transactions covered by another IAS (for example, income taxes and lease obligations).

20.3   KEY CONCEPTS

20.3.1 A **provision** is a liability of **uncertain timing** or **amount**. Provisions can be distinguished from other liabilities such as trade payables and accruals because there is uncertainty about the timing or amount of the future expenditure required in settlement.

20.3.2 A **liability** is defined in the framework as a **present obligation** of the entity arising from past events, the settlement of which is expected to result in an outflow from the entity of resources embodying economic benefits.

20.3.3 A **contingent liability** is either

- a **possible obligation**, because it has yet to be confirmed whether the entity has a present obligation that could lead to an outflow of resources embodying economic benefits; or

- a **present obligation** that does not meet the recognition criteria, either because an outflow of resources embodying economic benefits probably will not be required to settle the obligation, or because a sufficiently reliable estimate of the amount of the obligation cannot be made.

20.3.4 Contingent liabilities are not recognized because

- their existence will be confirmed by uncontrollable and uncertain future events (that is, not liabilities), or

- they do not meet the recognition criteria.

20.3.5 A **contingent asset** is a possible asset that arises from past events and whose existence will be confirmed only by uncertain future events not wholly within the control of the entity (for example, the entity is pursuing an insurance claim whose outcome is uncertain).

20.4   ACCOUNTING TREATMENT

Provisions

20.4.1 A provision should be **recognized** only when

- an entity has a present obligation (legal or constructive) as a result of a past event (obligating event),

- it is probable that an outflow of resources embodying economic benefits will be required to settle the obligation, and

- a reliable estimate can be made of the amount of the obligation.

20.4.2 A past event is deemed to give rise to a present obligation if it is more likely than not that a present obligation exists at Statement of Financial Position date.

20.4.3 A **legal** obligation normally arises from a contract or legislation. A **constructive** obligation arises only when **both** of the following conditions are present:

- The entity has indicated to other parties, by an established pattern of past practice, published policies, or a sufficiently specific current statement, that it will accept certain responsibilities.

- As a result, the entity has created a valid expectation on the part of those other parties that it will discharge those responsibilities.

20.4.4 The **amount recognized** as a provision should be the best estimate of the expenditure required to settle the present obligation at the Statement of Financial Position date.

20.4.5 Some or all of the expenditure required to settle a provision might be expected to be reimbursed by another party (for example, through insurance claims, indemnity clauses, or suppliers' warranties). These reimbursement are treated as follows:

- Recognize a **reimbursement** when it is virtually certain that reimbursement will be received if the entity settles the obligation. The amount recognized for the reimbursement should not exceed the amount of the provision.
- Treat the reimbursement as a separate asset.
- The expense relating to a provision can be presented net of the amount recognized for a reimbursement in the Statement of Comprehensive Income.

20.4.6 **Provisions** should be reviewed at each Statement of Financial Position date and adjusted to reflect the current best estimate.

20.4.7 A **provision** should be used only for expenditures for which the provision was originally recognized.

20.4.8 **Recognition and measurement** principles for (a) future operating losses, (b) onerous contracts, and (c) restructurings should be applied as follows:

a. Provisions should not be recognized for **future operating losses.** An expectation of future operating losses is an indication that certain assets of the operation could be impaired. IAS 36, Impairment of Assets, would then be applicable.

b. The present obligation under an **onerous contract** should be recognized and measured as a provision. An onerous contract is one in which the unavoidable costs of meeting the contract obligations exceed the economic benefits expected to be received under it.

c. A **restructuring** is a program planned and controlled by management that materially changes either the scope of business or the manner in which that business is conducted. A provision for restructuring costs is recognized when the normal recognition criteria for provisions are met. A constructive obligation to restructure arises only when an entity

- has a detailed formal plan for the restructuring, *and*
- has raised a valid expectation in those affected that it will carry out the restructuring by starting to implement that plan or announcing its main features to those affected by it.

    Where a restructuring involves the sale of an operation, no obligation arises for the sale until the entity is committed by a binding sale agreement.

Contingent Liabilities

20.4.9 An entity should *not* recognize a contingent liability. An entity should disclose a contingent liability unless the possibility of an outflow of resources embodying economic benefits is remote.

20.4.10 Contingent liabilities are assessed continually to determine whether an outflow of resources embodying economic benefits has become probable. When such an outflow becomes probable for an item previously dealt with as a contingent liability, a provision is recognized.

Contingent Assets

20.4.11 An entity should *not* recognize a contingent asset.

20.4.12 A contingent asset should be disclosed where an inflow of economic benefits is probable. When the realization of income is virtually certain, then the related asset is not a contingent asset and its recognition is appropriate under the framework.

20.5   PRESENTATION AND DISCLOSURE

20.5.1 Provisions: Disclose the following for *each* class separately:

- A detailed itemized reconciliation of the carrying amount at the beginning and end of the accounting period (comparatives are not required)
- A brief description of the nature of the obligation and the expected timing of any resulting outflows of economic benefits
- An indication of the uncertainties about the amount or timing of those outflows
- The amount of any expected reimbursement, stating the amount of any asset that has been recognized for that expected reimbursement

20.5.2 Contingent liabilities: Disclose the following for *each* class separately:

- Brief description of the nature of the liability
- Estimate of the financial effect
- Indication of uncertainties relating to the amount or timing of any outflow of economic benefits
- The possibility of any reimbursement

20.5.3 Contingent assets: Disclose the following for *each* class separately:

- Brief description of the nature of the asset
- Estimate of the financial effect

20.5.4 Exceptions allowed are as follows:

- If any information required for contingent liabilities or assets is not disclosed because it is not practical to do so, it should be so stated.
- In extremely rare cases, disclosure of some or all of the information required can be expected to seriously prejudice the position of the entity in a dispute with other parties regarding the provision, contingent liability, or contingent asset. In such cases, the information need not be disclosed; however, the general nature of the dispute should be disclosed, along with an explanation of why the information has not been disclosed.

20.5.5 Figure 20.1 summarizes the main requirements of IAS 37.

Figure 20.1—Decision Tree

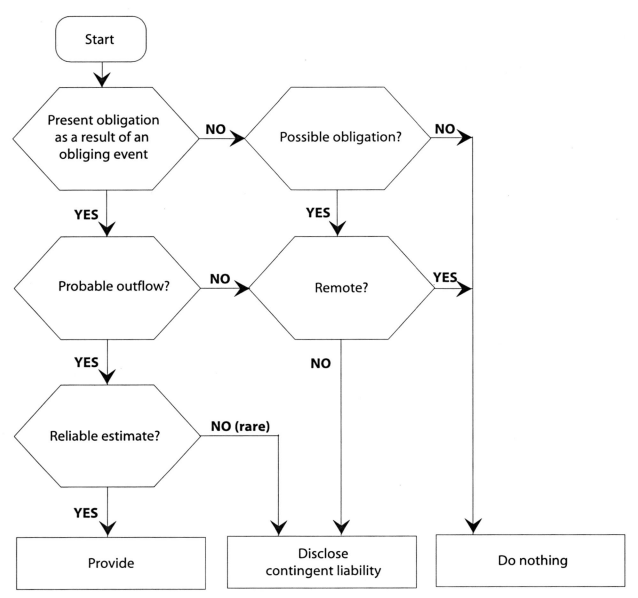

Source: IASCF, 2008, p. 1849.

EXAMPLE: PROVISIONS, CONTINGENT LIABILITIES, AND CONTINGENT ASSETS

EXAMPLE 20.1

The following scenarios relate to provisions and contingencies:

A. The Mighty Mouse Trap Company has just started to export mouse traps to the United States. The advertising slogan for the mouse traps is, "A girl's best friend." The Californian Liberation Movement is claiming $800,000 from the company because the advertising slogan allegedly compromises the dignity of women. The company's legal representatives believe that the success of the claim will depend on the judge who presides over the case. They estimate, however, that there is a 70 percent probability that the claim will be thrown out and a 30 percent probability that it will succeed.

B. Boss Ltd. specializes in the design and manufacture of an exclusive sports car. During the current financial year, 90 sports cars have been completed and sold. During the testing of the sports car, a serious defect was found in its steering mechanism.

All 90 clients were informed by letter of the defect and were told to bring their cars back to have the defect repaired at no charge. All the clients have indicated that this is the only remedy that they require. The estimated cost of the recall is $900,000.

The manufacturer of the steering mechanism, a listed company with sufficient funds, has accepted responsibility for the defect and has undertaken to reimburse Boss Ltd. for all costs that it might incur in this regard.

EXPLANATION

The matters above will be treated as follows for accounting purposes:

A. **Present obligation as a result of a past event:** The available evidence provided by the experts indicates that it is more likely that no present obligation exists at Statement of Financial Position date; there is a 70 percent probability that the claim will be thrown out. No obligating event has taken place.

Conclusion: No provision is recognized. The matter is disclosed as a contingent liability unless the 30 percent probability is regarded as being remote.

B. **Present obligation as a result of a past event:** The constructive obligation derives from the sale of defective cars.

Conclusion: The outflow of economic benefits is beyond any reasonable doubt. A provision is therefore recognized. However, as it is virtually certain that all of the expenditures will be reimbursed by the supplier of the steering mechanism, a separate asset is recognized in the Statement of Financial Position. In the Statement of Comprehensive Income, the expense relating to the provision can be shown net of the amount recognized for the reimbursement.

Chapter Twenty One

The Effects of Changes in Foreign Exchange Rates (IAS 21)

21.1 OBJECTIVE

Investments or balances in a foreign currency, or ownership in a foreign operation, expose an entity to foreign exchange gains or losses. IAS 21 considers the accounting treatment for foreign currency transactions and foreign operations. The principal aspects addressed are

- **exchange rate differences** and their effect on transactions in the financial statements, and
- **translation** of the financial statements of foreign operations (where the presentation currency differs from the functional currency).

21.2 SCOPE OF THE STANDARD

This standard prescribes the accounting treatment in relation to

- definition and distinction between **functional** and other currencies that give rise to exchange differences on transactions,
- definition and distinction between **presentation** and **functional currency** of a foreign operation that result in exchange differences on translation, and
- monetary and nonmonetary gains and losses.

IAS 21 does not apply to derivative transactions and balances that fall within the scope of IAS 39.

However, the standard does apply to the measurement of amounts relating to foreign currency assets, liabilities, and derivatives in the **functional currency,** and to the translation of foreign currency assets, liabilities, income and expenses into the **presentation currency**.

21.3 KEY CONCEPTS

21.3.1 **Foreign currency transactions** are transactions denominated in a currency other than the functional currency, including

- buying or selling goods or services,
- borrowing or lending funds,
- concluding unperformed foreign exchange contracts,
- acquiring or selling assets, and
- incurring or settling liabilities.

21.3.2 The **functional currency** is used to measure items in financial statements. It need not be the **local** currency of an entity. It is the currency of the primary economic environment in which the entity operates, for example,

- currency that mainly influences sales prices;
- currency of the country whose competitive forces and regulations determine the sales prices of goods and services; or
- currency that influences labor, material, and other costs.

21.3.3 The **presentation currency** of an entity is used to present the financial statements. It might be any currency, although many jurisdictions require the use of the **local** currency.

- The **functional currency of the parent** (or major) entity will usually determine the presentation currency.
- If the presentation currency is different from the functional currency, **translation** of financial statements from the functional currency to the presentation currency will be required.

21.3.4 The **functional currency of a foreign operation** is the **same** as the reporting entity's functional currency when

- foreign operations are an extension of the reporting entity,
- foreign operation's transactions with the reporting entity are high,
- cash flows of the foreign operation directly affect cash flows of the reporting entity,
- foreign operation's cash flows are available for remittance to the reporting entity, and
- foreign operation's cash flows are insufficient to service existing and normal debt obligations.

The **functional currency of a foreign operation** is **different** from the reporting entity's functional currency when the foreign operation's

- activities are carried out with a significant degree of autonomy,
- transactions with the reporting entity are low,
- cash flows do not directly affect cash flows of the reporting entity,
- cash flows are not readily available for remittance to the reporting entity, and
- cash flows are sufficient to service existing and normal debt obligations.

21.3.5 A **foreign operation** is a subsidiary, associate, joint venture, or branch of the reporting entity, the activities of which are based or conducted in a country other than the country of the reporting entity. (The foreign operation's functional currency will be determined by the degree of autonomy that it enjoys.)

21.3.6 **Exchange differences** arise on translation of financial statements measured using a functional currency that is different from the presentation currency.

21.3.7 Assets and liabilities are classified as follows to determine the rates at which items are **measured subsequent** to the initial transaction date:

- **Monetary items** are units of currency held and assets and liabilities to be received or paid in a fixed or determinable number of units of currency. The essential feature of a monetary item is a right to receive (or an obligation to deliver) a fixed or determinable number of units of currency. Monetary items include cash, receivables, loans, payables, long-term debt, provisions, employee benefit liabilities, and deferred tax assets and liabilities.

■ **Nonmonetary items** include equity securities; inventories; prepaid expenses; property, plant, equipment, and related accounts; goodwill; and intangible assets.

21.4 ACCOUNTING TREATMENT

Functional Currency Transactions

Recognition and Initial Measurement

21.4.1 For purposes of **recognition,** determine for **each entity** whether it is

■ a stand-alone entity,

■ an entity with foreign operations (parent), or

■ a foreign operation (subsidiary, branch).

21.4.2 On **initial recognition,** a foreign currency transaction should be reported in the functional currency by applying to the foreign currency amount the **spot exchange rate** between the functional currency and the foreign currency. Use the spot exchange rate on the transaction date.

Subsequent Measurement

21.4.3 At each Statement of Financial Position date, **subsequent measurement** takes place as follows:

■ **Monetary items** that remain unsettled are translated using the **closing rate** (the spot exchange rate on the date of the Statement of Financial Position).

■ **Nonmonetary items** are carried using the following measurements:

■ **Historical costs** are reported using the exchange rate at the **date of the transaction.** Approximate or average rates may be more appropriate for inventories or cost of sales, which affect the Statement of Comprehensive Income.

■ **Fair values** are reported using the exchange rate at the **date when the fair value** was determined.

21.4.5 Resulting **exchange differences** are included in profit or loss, regardless of whether they arise on the

■ **settlement** of monetary items, or

■ **translation** of monetary items at rates different from those at which they were translated on initial recognition.

21.4.6 The following exchange differences are **included in equity until disposal** of the related asset or liability, when they are transferred to profit or loss:

■ **Marked-to-market** gains or losses on available-for-sale financial assets. However, translation gains and losses on the principal portion of the asset are included in profit or loss.

■ **Nomonetary-item gains and losses** (for example, revaluation of property and plant).

- **Intragroup monetary items** that form part of an entity's net investment in a foreign entity.

- A **foreign liability** that is accounted for as a **hedge** of an entity's net investment in a foreign entity (IAS 39 criteria).

Presentation Currency: Translation from Functional Currency

21.4.7 The results and financial position of an entity whose functional currency is not the presentation currency should be translated into the presentation currency as follows:

- For **assets and liabilities,** use the **closing rate** at the Statement of Financial Position date.

- For **income and expenses,** use **spot rates** at the dates of transactions. Approximate or **average rates** can be used for practical reasons.

- **Goodwill and fair value adjustments** arising on the acquisition of a foreign operation should be treated as assets and liabilities of the foreign operation and are expressed in the functional currency of the foreign operation. Translation of goodwill and fair value adjustments is therefore at the **closing rate.**

21.4.8 All resulting **exchange differences** are included in a separate component of **equity** until disposal of the foreign operation, when they are included in profit or loss.

21.4.9 When the functional currency of a foreign operation is the currency of a **hyperinflationary** economy,

- the financial statements are restated for price changes in accordance with IAS 29, and

- the restated amounts for both the Statement of Financial Position and the Statement of Comprehensive Income are translated into the presentation currency using **closing rates.**

21.5   PRESENTATION AND DISCLOSURE

21.5.1 An entity should make the following disclosures:

- In its **Statement of Comprehensive Income**—the amount of exchange differences recognized in profit or loss **except** for those arising on financial instruments measured at fair value through profit or loss in accordance with IAS 39

- In its **Statement of Financial Position**—net exchange differences classified in a separate component of equity, and a reconciliation of the amount of such exchange differences at the beginning and end of the period

21.5.2 **The difference between the presentation and functional currency** should be stated, together with disclosure of the functional currency and the reason for using a different presentation currency.

21.5.3 Any **change** in the functional currency of an entity, and the reason for the change, should be disclosed.

21.5.4 When an entity **presents its financial statements in a currency that is different from its functional currency,** the entity should describe the financial statements as complying with

IFRS only if the statements comply with all the requirements of each applicable standard and interpretation.

21.6 FINANCIAL ANALYSIS AND INTERPRETATION

21.6.1 By placing the gain or loss from individual currency transactions on the Statement of Comprehensive Income, the accounting for foreign operations reports the volatility resulting from changes in exchange rates in profit or loss and, hence, earnings per share, which clearly reflects the underlying reality. The nature of this gain or loss must be understood by noting the root cause of its existence.

21.6.2 When entities hold foreign-currency-denominated monetary assets such as cash, they incur a gain when the value of that currency rises relative to the functional currency, and they incur a loss when the value of that currency falls.

When entities hold foreign-currency-denominated liabilities, they incur a loss when the value of the foreign currency rises and a gain when it falls.

21.6.3 Because entities typically hold both monetary assets and monetary liabilities that are denominated in foreign currencies, whether a rise (or fall) in the value of the foreign currency will result in a gain or loss depends on whether the net monetary position in these currencies is positive (that is, if assets exceed liabilities) or negative (that is, if liabilities exceed assets). In general, the gain or loss from currency translation is the product of the average net monetary position of an entity and the change in the exchange rate between the local and functional currencies. This requires an analysis of the changes in a company's net monetary position. Note that the reported net income from the foreign operations of an entity consists of three parts:

1. **Operational effects,** which is the net income that the entity would have reported in the reporting currency if exchange rates had not changed from their weighted average levels of the previous years.

2. **Flow effects** that have an impact on the amount of revenues and expenses that are reported on the Statement of Comprehensive Income, but which were received or incurred in foreign currencies. These can be calculated as a residual.

3. **Holding gain (loss) effects** that have an impact on the values of assets and liabilities reported on the Statement of Financial Position, but which are actually held or owed in foreign currencies.

21.6.4 The impact of the translation from functional currency to presentation currency falls on the equity portion of the Statement of Financial Position, and not on the Statement of Comprehensive Income. This means that presentation-currency-denominated net income and earnings-per-share figures will not be as volatile as when the individual transactions are translated (for instance, at spot or closing rates, with exchange differences flowing through the Statement of Comprehensive Income). However, the net worth (or equity) shown on the Statement of Financial Position becomes more volatile, because the translation adjustment is put on the Statement of Financial Position.

21.6.5 The analyst will find it easier to forecast earnings if there is no need to forecast any gain or loss from the foreign currency translation component to net income. As was previously discussed, the nature of the gain or loss from foreign currency translation can be understood by noting the root cause of its existence. When financial statements are translated, the net asset or liability position is critical (as compared with the net monetary position for individual transactions). If an entity has a net asset position in a foreign operation, it incurs a gain when the foreign currency rises and a loss when the currency falls. When the net position is a liability, it incurs a gain when the foreign currency falls and a loss when the currency appreciates.

EXAMPLE: THE EFFECTS OF CHANGES IN FOREIGN EXCHANGE RATES

EXAMPLE 21.1

Bark Inc. (whose functional currency is the U.S. dollar) purchased manufacturing equipment from the United Kingdom. The transaction was financed by a loan from a commercial bank in England.

Equipment costing £400,000 was purchased on January 2, 20X7, and the amount was paid over by the bank to the supplier on that same day. The loan must be repaid on December 31, 20X8, and interest is payable at 10 percent biannually in arrears. The Statement of Financial Position date is December 31.

The following exchange rates apply:

	£1 = $
January 2, 20X7	1.67
June 30, 20X7	1.71
December 31, 20X7	1.75
June 30, 20X8	1.73
December 31, 20X8	1.70

EXPLANATION

The **interest payments** would be recorded at the spot rates applicable on the dates of payment in the following manner:

	$
June 30, 20X7 (£20,000 × 1.71)	34,200
December 31, 20X7 (£20,000 × 1.75)	35,000
Total interest for 20X7	69,200
June 30, 20X8 (£20,000 × 1.73)	34,600
December 31, 20X8 (£20,000 × 1.70)	34,000
Total interest for 20X8	68,600

The **loan** is initially recorded on January 2, 20X7, and restated at the spot rate on December 31, 20X7, as well as December 31, 20X8, after which it is repaid at the spot rate. The movements in the balance of the loan are reflected as follows:

	$
Recorded at January 2, 20X7 (£400,000 × 1.67)	668,000
Foreign currency loss on restatement of loan	32,000
Restated at December 31, 20X7 (£400,000 × 1.75)	700,000
Foreign currency profit on restatement of loan	(20,000)
Restated and paid at December 31, 20X8 (£400,000 × 1.70)	680,000

The loan will be stated at an amount of $700,000 in the **Statement of Financial Position** on December 31, 20X7.

The manufacturing equipment remains at its historical spot rate of $668,000.

The following amounts will be recognized in the **Statement of Comprehensive Income**:

	20X8 $	20X7 $
Interest	68,600	69,200
Foreign currency loss (profit)	(20,000)	32,000

Part IV

Statement of Comprehensive Income

Income Statement

Chapter Twenty Two

Revenue (IAS 18)

22.1 OBJECTIVE

Revenue is defined as the inflow of economic benefits that derive from activities in the ordinary course of business. Key issues in IAS 18 are the definition of revenue, criteria for revenue recognition, and the distinction between revenue and other income (for example, gains on disposal of noncurrent assets or on translating foreign balances).

22.2 SCOPE OF THE STANDARD

This standard describes the accounting treatment of revenue. The following aspects are addressed:

- Revenue is distinguished from other income. (Income includes both revenue and gains.)
- Recognition criteria for revenue are identified.
- Practical guidance is provided on
    - moment of recognition,
    - amount to be recognized, and
    - disclosure requirements.

This standard deals with the accounting treatment of revenue that arises from

- sale of goods,
- rendering of services,
- use by others of entity assets yielding interest (see also IAS 39),
- royalties, and
- dividends (see also IAS 39).

Revenue excludes

- amounts collected on behalf of third parties, for example, a value-added tax;
- lease income (IAS 17);
- equity method investments (IAS 28);
- insurance contracts (IFRS 4);
- changes in fair value of financial assets and liabilities (IAS 39); and
- initial recognition and changes in fair value on biological assets (IAS 41).

22.3 KEY CONCEPTS

22.3.1 **Revenue** is defined as the gross inflow of economic benefits

- during the period,
- arising in the ordinary course of activities, and
- resulting in increases in equity, other than contributions by equity participants.

22.3.2 **Fair value** is the amount for which an asset could be exchanged, or a liability settled, between knowledgeable, willing parties in an arm's-length transaction.

22.3.3 **Effective yield** on an asset is the rate of interest required to discount the stream of future cash receipts expected over the life of the asset to equate to the initial carrying amount of the asset.

22.4 ACCOUNTING TREATMENT

Recognition

22.4.1 Revenue **cannot be recognized** when the expenses cannot be **measured reliably.** Consideration already received for the sale is **deferred** as a liability until revenue recognition can take place.

22.4.2 When goods or services are exchanged for that of a **similar nature** and value, no revenue recognition occurs. (Commercial substance of the transaction should govern.)

22.4.3 Revenue recognition from the **sale of goods** takes place when

- significant risks and rewards of ownership of the goods are transferred to the buyer,
- the entity retains neither continuing managerial involvement of ownership nor effective control over the goods sold,
- the amount of revenue can be measured reliably,
- it is probable that the economic benefits of the transaction will flow to the entity, and
- the costs of the transaction can be measured reliably.

22.4.4 Revenue recognition of **services** takes place as follows (similar to IAS 11—construction contracts):

- When the outcome of the transaction can be estimated reliably, costs and revenues are recognized according to the stage of completion at the Statement of Financial Position date.
- When the outcome of the transaction cannot be estimated reliably, recoverable contract costs will determine the extent of revenue recognition

22.4.5 Other revenues are recognized as follows:

- **Royalties** are recognized on an accrual basis (substance of the relevant agreements).
- **Dividends** are recognized when the right to receive payment is established (which is normally the dividend declaration date and not the "last day to register" for the dividend).

- **Repurchase agreements** arise when an entity sells goods and immediately concludes an agreement to repurchase them at a later date; the substantive effect of the transaction is negated, and the two transactions are dealt with as one.

- **Sales plus service** refers to when the selling price of a product includes an amount for subsequent servicing, and the service revenue portion is deferred over the period that the service is performed.

Initial Measurement

22.4.6 Revenue should be **measured** at the **fair value** of the consideration **received:**

- **Trade (cash) discounts** and **volume rebates** are deducted to determine fair value. However, payment discounts are nondeductible.

- When the inflow of cash is deferred (for example, the provision of interest-free credit), it effectively constitutes a financing transaction. The imputed rate of interest should be determined and the present value of the inflows calculated. The difference between the fair value and nominal amount of the consideration is separately recognized and disclosed as interest.

- When goods or services are rendered in exchange for dissimilar goods or services, revenue is measured at the fair value of the goods or services received.

22.4.7 **Interest income** should be recognized on a time-proportion basis that

- takes into account the effective yield on the asset (the effective interest rate method; see IAS 39); and

- includes amortization of any discount, premium, transaction costs, or other differences between initial carrying amount and amount at maturity.

Subsequent Measurement and Special Circumstances

22.4.8 **Financial service fees** are recognized as follows:

- Financial service fees that are an integral part of the effective yield on a financial instrument (such as an equity investment) carried at fair value are recognized immediately as revenue.

- Financial service fees that are an integral part of the effective yield on a financial instrument carried at amortized cost (for example, a loan) are recognized as revenue over the life of the asset as part of the application of the effective interest rate method.

- Origination fees on creation or acquisition of financial instruments carried at amortized cost, such as a loan, are deferred and recognized as adjustments to the effective interest rate.

- Most commitment fees to originate loans are deferred and recognized as adjustments to the effective interest rate or recognized as revenue on earlier expiration of the commitment.

Derecognition

22.4.9 **Uncertainty** about the collectability of an amount already included in revenue is treated as an expense rather than as an adjustment to revenue.

22.4.10 To determine the amount of an **impairment loss,** use the rate of interest that is used to discount cash flows.

22.5 PRESENTATION AND DISCLOSURE

22.5.1 Disclose the following **accounting policies**:

- Revenue measurement bases used
- Revenue recognition methods used
- Stage of completion method for services

22.5.2 The Statement of Comprehensive Income and notes should include

- amounts of significant revenue categories, including
  - sale of goods
  - rendering of services
  - interest
  - royalties
  - dividends
- amount of revenue recognized from the exchange of goods or services;
- accounting policies adopted for the recognition of revenue; and
- the methods adopted to determine the stage of completion of transactions involving the rendering of services.

22.6 FINANCIAL ANALYSIS AND INTERPRETATION

22.6.1 Accounting income is generated when revenues and their associated expenses are recognized on a Statement of Comprehensive Income. The recognition and matching principles determine when this occurs. IAS 18 sets out the criteria that must be met before revenue is earned (and hence recognized) in IFRS financial statements.

22.6.2 When a company intentionally distorts its financial results, financial condition, or both, it is engaging in financial manipulation. Generally, companies engage in such activities to hide operational problems. When they are caught, the company faces outcomes such as investors losing faith in management and a subsequent fall in the company's stock price. The two basic strategies underlying all accounting manipulation are

- to inflate current-period earnings through overstating revenues and gains or understating expenses, and
- to reduce current-period earnings by understating revenues or overstating expenses. A company is likely to engage in this strategy to shift earnings to a later period when they might be needed.

22.6.3 Financial manipulation tricks involving revenue can generally be grouped under four headings:

1. **Recording questionable revenue, or recording revenue prematurely:**
   - Recording revenue for services that have yet to be performed
   - Recording revenue prior to shipment or before the customer acquires control of the products
   - Recording revenue for items for which the customer is not required to pay

- Recording revenue for contrived sales to affiliated parties
- Engaging in quid pro quo transactions with customers

2. **Recording fictitious revenue:**
    - Recording revenue for sales that lack economic substance
    - Recording revenue that is, in substance, a loan
    - Recording investment income as revenue
    - Recording supplier rebates that are tied to future required purchases as revenue
    - Reporting revenue that was improperly withheld prior to a merger

3. **Recording one-time gains to boost income:**
    - Deliberately undervaluing assets, resulting in the recording of a gain on sale
    - Recording investment gains as revenue
    - Recording investment income or gains as a reduction in expenses
    - Reclassifying Statement of Financial Position accounts to create income

4. **Shifting revenues to future periods:**
    - Creating reserves that are reversed (reported as income) in later periods
    - Withholding revenues before an acquisition and then releasing these revenues in later periods

22.6.4 Not all manipulations are equal in their relative scale of importance to investors. For instance, inflation of revenues is more serious than manipulations that affect expenses. Companies recognize that revenue growth and the consistency of this growth are important to many investors in assessing that company's prospects. Therefore, identifying inflated revenues is of critical importance. The distortions that are used range from the relatively benign to the very serious.

22.6.5 The early warning signs that will help identify problem companies are

- few or no independent members on the board of directors,
- an incompetent external auditor or lack of auditor independence,
- highly competitive pressures on management, and
- management that is known or suspected to be of questionable character.

22.6.6 In addition, it is wise to watch companies with fast growth or companies that are financially weak. All fast-growth companies will eventually see their growth slow, and managers might be tempted to use accounting trickery to create the illusion of continuing rapid growth. Similarly, weak companies might use accounting manipulations to make investors believe that the companies' problems are less severe than they really are.

22.6.7 It is also wise to watch companies that are not publicly traded or that have recently made an initial public offering (IPO). Companies that are not publicly traded might not use outside auditors, which allows them more leeway to engage in questionable practices through the use of less-than-objective auditors or advisors.

EXAMPLE 22.1

Sykes and Anson, a high-tech company, is having a very poor year as a result of weak demand in the technology markets. The entity's controller, has determined that much of the inventory on hand is worth far less than the value recorded on the entity's books. He decides to write off this excess amount, which totals $10 million. Furthermore, he is worried that the inventory will fall in value next year and decides to take a further write-down of $5 million. Both of these write-offs occur in the current year.

Which of the following statements is true?

a. The company has engaged in a technique known as recording "sham" revenue.

b. The company has overstated its income in the current period.

c. The company has engaged in a technique that shifts future expenses into the current period.

d. The company should be applauded for being so conservative in its accounting for inventories.

EXPLANATION

Choice c. is correct. The company has overstated the amount of the current charge by $5 million. This expected decline in value should not be charged off until it occurs. It is conceivable that the market for Sykes and Anson's products will rebound and that the write-off was not needed. Effectively, the company has brought forward a potential future expense to the current period. The $10 million write-off is, however, appropriate.

Choice a. is incorrect. The facts do not support any issue concerning sham revenues.

Choice b. is incorrect. The company's income is understated, not overstated, in the current period, as a result of the excess $5 million write-off.

Choice d. is incorrect. Whereas conservative accounting is desirable, the entity has gone too far and is reporting results that are incorrect.

EXAMPLE 22.2

The information below comes from the 20X0 financial statements of Bear Corp. and Bull Co., both of which are based in Europe.

	Bear Corp.	Bull Co.
Acquisition accounting	The excess of acquisition cost over net fair value of assets acquired is charged to goodwill and written off over 10 years.	The excess of acquisition cost over net fair value of assets acquired is recorded as goodwill and written off over 20 years.
Soft costs	In anticipation or hope of future revenues, the company incorrectly defers certain costs incurred and matches them against future expected revenues.	The company expenses all costs incurred unless paid in advance and directly associated with future revenues.

Which company has a higher quality of earnings, as a result of its accounting for its soft costs?

a. Bull Co.

b. Bear Corp.

c. They are equally conservative.

d. Cannot be determined.

EXPLANATION

Choice a. is correct. Bull Co. is more conservative with soft cost reporting because it expenses all soft costs unless they are directly tied to future revenue.

Choice b. is incorrect. Bear Corp. is less conservative than Bull Co. with soft cost reporting because it defers costs in anticipation of matching them with future revenues.

Choice c. is incorrect. Bull Co.'s method of expensing all soft costs unless directly tied to future revenue is clearly more conservative.

Choice d. is incorrect.

Comment: Neither company is complying with IFRS with respect to goodwill. Goodwill should be tested for impairment on an annual basis.

EXAMPLE 22.3

A generous benefactor donates raw materials to an entity for use in its production process. The materials had cost the benefactor $20,000 and had a market value of $30,000 at the time of donation. The materials are still on hand at the Statement of Financial Position date. No entry has been made in the books of the entity. Should the entity recognize the donation as revenue in its books?

EXPLANATION

The proper accounting treatment of the above matter is as follows:

■ The accounting standard that deals with inventories, IAS 2, provides no guidance on the treatment of inventory acquired by donation. However, donations received meet the definition of revenue in IAS 18 (that is, the gross inflow of economic benefits during the period arising in the course of ordinary activities when those inflows result in increases in equity, other than increases relating to contributions from equity participants). It could be argued that receiving a donation is not part of the ordinary course of activities. In that case, the donation would be regarded as a capital gain. For purposes of this case study, the donation is regarded as revenue.

■ The donation should be recorded as revenue measured at the fair value ($30,000) of the raw materials received (because that is the economic benefit).

■ The raw materials received clearly meet the framework's definition of an asset, because the raw materials (resource) are now owned (controlled) by the corporation as a result of the donation (past event) from which a profit can be made in the future (future economic benefits). The recognition criteria of the framework, namely those of measurability and probability, are also satisfied.

■ Because the raw materials donated relate to trading items, they should be disclosed as inventory, with the fair value of $30,000 at the acquisition date being treated as the cost thereof.

Chapter Twenty Three

Construction Contracts (IAS 11)

23.1 OBJECTIVE

IAS 11 covers construction contracts for which the dates of contracting and of completion typically fall in different accounting periods. The standard applies to contracts for

- rendering services, and
- constructing or restoring assets and restoring the environment.

This standard deals with the appropriate criteria for recognition of construction contract revenue and costs, with a focus on the allocation of contract revenue and costs to the accounting periods in which construction work is performed.

23.2 SCOPE OF THE STANDARD

This standard applies to accounting for construction contracts in the financial statements of contractors. Two types of contracts are distinguished:

- **Fixed-price contracts**—usually a fixed contract price subject to cost escalation clauses
- **Cost-plus contracts**—the contract costs plus a percentage of such costs or a fixed fee

23.3 KEY CONCEPTS

23.3.1 A **construction contract** is a contract negotiated specifically for the construction of an asset or a combination of assets that are closely interrelated or interdependent in terms of their design, technology, and function, or in terms of their ultimate purpose or use. Construction contracts include those for the construction or restoration of assets and the restoration of the environment.

23.3.2 A **fixed-price contract** is a construction contract in which the contractor agrees to a fixed contract price, or a fixed rate per unit of output, which in some cases is subject to cost-escalation clauses.

23.3.3 A **cost-plus contract** is a construction contract in which the contractor is reimbursed for allowable or otherwise defined costs, plus a percentage of these costs or a fixed fee.

23.4 ACCOUNTING TREATMENT

Recognition and Initial Measurement

23.4.1 Contract revenue is measured at the fair value of the consideration received or receivable. The measurement of contract revenue is affected by a variety of uncertainties that depend on the outcome of future events. The estimates often need to be revised as events occur and uncertainties are resolved. Therefore, the amount of contract revenue may increase or decrease from one period to the next.

23.4.2 Contract revenues comprise

- the initial agreed contract amount; and
- variations, claims, and incentive payments to the extent that they will probably be realized and are capable of being reliably measured.

23.4.3 Contract costs comprise

- direct contract costs (for example, materials),
- general contract costs (for example, insurance), and
- costs specifically chargeable to the customer in terms of the contract (for example, administrative costs).

Subsequent Measurement

23.4.4 When the outcome of a construction contract can be reliably estimated, the excess of revenue over costs (profit) should be recognized based on the stage of completion (**percentage-of-completion method**).

23.4.5 The stage of completion is determined by reference to

- portion of costs incurred in relation to estimated total costs,
- surveys of work performed, and
- physical stage of completion.

23.4.6 When the outcome of a contract cannot be reliably estimated, revenue should be recognized to the extent that recovery of contract costs is probable.

23.4.7 Any expected excess of *total* contract costs over *total* contract revenue (loss) is recognized as an expense immediately.

23.4.8 The principles of IAS 11 are normally applied separately to each contract negotiated specifically for the construction of

- an asset (for example, a bridge); or
- a combination of assets that are closely interrelated or interdependent in terms of their design, technology, function, or use (for example, specialized production plants).

A group of contracts should be treated as a *single* construction contract if it was negotiated as a single package.

23.4.9 The following contracts should be treated as *separate* construction contracts:

- A contract for a number of assets if separate proposals have been submitted for each asset
- An additional asset constructed at the option of the customer that was not part of the original contract

23.5 PRESENTATION AND DISCLOSURE

23.5.1 Statement of Financial Position and notes include

- amount of advances received,
- amount of retention monies,
- contracts in progress being costs-to-date-plus-profits or costs-to-date-less-losses,
- gross amount due from customers (assets),
- gross amount due to customers (liabilities), and
- contingent assets and contingent liabilities (for example, claims).

23.5.2 The Statement of Comprehensive Income includes

- amount of contract revenue recognized.

23.5.3 Accounting policies include

- methods used for revenue recognition, and
- methods used for stage of completion.

23.6 FINANCIAL ANALYSIS AND INTERPRETATION

23.6.1 The use of the **percentage-of-completion method** requires that the total cost and total profit of a project be estimated at each Statement of Financial Position date. A pro rata proportion of the total estimated profit is then recognized in each accounting period during the performance of the contract. The pro rata proportion is based on the stage of completion at the end of the period and reflects the work performed during the period from an engineering perspective. (Production is the critical event that gives rise to income.)

23.6.2 At each Statement of Financial Position date, the percentage-of-completion method is applied to up-to-date estimates of revenue and costs so that any adjustment are reflected in the current period and future periods. Amounts recognized in prior periods are not adjusted.

23.6.3 Table 23.1 summarizes how the choice of accounting method affects the Statement of Financial Position, Statement of Comprehensive Income, statement of cash flows, and the key financial ratios when accounting for long-term projects. The effects are given for the early years of the project's life.

Table 23.1 Impact of Percentage-of-Completion Method on Financial Statements

Item or Ratio	Percentage-of-Completion Method (as opposed to a situation where the outcome of a contract cannot be reliably estimated)
Statement of Financial Position	Billings recorded but not received in cash are recorded as accounts receivable.
	Cumulative project expenses plus cumulative reported income less cumulative billings is recorded as a current asset if positive or a current liability if negative.
	Upon project completion, work-in-progress and advanced billings net to zero. Uncollected billings are accounts receivable.
Income Statement	Project costs are recorded as incurred.
	Revenues are recognized in proportion to the costs incurred during the period relative to the estimated total project cost.
	Reported earnings represent estimates of future operating cash flows.
	Estimated losses are recorded in their entirety as soon as a loss is estimated.
Statement of Cash Flows	Cash received from customers is reported as an operating cash inflow when received.
	Cash expended is recorded as an operating cash outflow when paid.
	Size of cash flow is the **same** because accounting choices have no effect on pretax cash flows.
Size of Current Assets	**Higher** if the cumulative work-in-progress (cumulative project costs and cumulative project income) exceeds cumulative billings.
	Same if cumulative billings equal or exceed work-in-progress.
Size of Current Liabilities	**Lower** as only receipts in excess of revenues are deferred as liabilities.
Net Worth	**Higher** because earnings are reported before the project is complete.
Profit Margin	**Higher** because earnings are reported during the project's life.
Asset Turnover	**Higher** because sales are reported during the project's life.
Debt or Equity	**Lower** because liabilities are lower and net worth is higher.
Return on Equity	**Higher** because earnings are higher percentage-wise than the higher equity.
Cash Flow	**Same** because accounting choices have no effect on cash flow.

EXAMPLE 23.1

A company undertakes a four-year project at a contracted price of $100 million that will be billed in four equal annual installments of $25 million over the project's life. The project is expected to cost $90 million, producing a $10 million profit. Over the life of the project, the billings, cash receipts, and cash outlays related to the project are as follows:

	Year 1 ($'000)	Year 2 ($'000)	Year 3 ($'000)	Year 4 ($'000)
Billings	25,000	25,000	25,000	25,000
Cash receipts	20,000	27,000	25,000	28,000
Cash outlays	18,000	36,000	27,000	9,000

Financial statements and schedules must be produced under the percentage-of-completion contract method, showing

    A. the cash flows from the project each year;

    B. the Statement of Comprehensive Income for the project each year;

    C. the Statement of Financial Position each year; and

    D. the profit margin, asset turnover, debt-to-equity, return on assets, return on equity, and the current ratio.

EXPLANATION

A. The cash flow is simply the difference between the cash received and paid every year as given in the problem:

	Year 1 ($'000)	Year 2 ($'000)	Year 3 ($'000)	Year 4 ($'000)
Cash receipts	20,000	27,000	25,000	28,000
Cash outlays	18,000	36,000	27,000	9,000
Cash flow	2,000	(9,000)	(2,000)	19,000
Cumulative cash flow (on Statement of Financial Position)	2,000	(7,000)	(9,000)	10,000

B. The revenues recorded on the Statement of Comprehensive Income each year are calculated as

$$\text{Revenues in a Year} = \frac{\text{Costs Incurred in Year}}{\text{Total Project Cost}} \times \text{Total Estimated Project Price}$$

Assuming the cash paid each year is the cost incurred in the year, with a total project cost of $90 million and the estimated project profit of $10 million, the Statement of Comprehensive Income schedule is as follows:

	Year 1 ($'000)	Year 2 ($'000)	Year 3 ($'000)	Year 4 ($'000)
Revenues $= \left(\dfrac{\text{Year's Expense}}{\$90,000,000} \times \$100,000,000 \right)$	20,000	40,000	30,000	10,000
Expense (cash paid)	18,000	36,000	27,000	9,000
Income	2,000	4,000	3,000	1,000
Cumulative income (retained earnings)	2,000	6,000	9,000	10,000

C. In constructing the Statement of Financial Position, the following is required:

- The difference between cumulative billings (to customers) and cumulative cash receipts (from customers) is recorded on the Statement of Financial Position as Accounts Receivable.
- The sum of the cumulative expenses and the cumulative reported income is a Work-in Progress current asset.
- Cumulative billings (to customers) are an Advanced Billings current liability.
- The *net* difference between the Work-in-Progress current assets and the Advanced Billings current liabilities is recorded on the Statement of Financial Position as a net current asset if it is positive or as a net current liability if it is negative.

A schedule of these items is as follows:

	Year 1 ($'000)	Year 2 ($'000)	Year 3 ($'000)	Year 4 ($'000)
Cumulative billings	25,000	50,000	75,000	100,000
Cumulative cash receipts	20,000	47,000	72,000	100,000
Accounts receivable (on Statement of Financial Position)	5,000	3,000	3,000	0
Cumulative expenses	18,000	54,000	81,000	90,000
Cumulative income	2,000	6,000	9,000	10,000
Work-in-progress	20,000	60,000	90,000	100,000
Less Cumulative billings	25,000	50,000	75,000	100,000
Net asset (liability) on Statement of Financial Position	(5,000)	10,000	15,000	0

The Statement of Financial Position's cash equals the cumulative cash based on the previous cash flow schedule.

Cumulative income is reported as retained earnings on the Statement of Financial Position.

The Statement of Financial Position is

	Year 1 ($'000)	Year 2 ($'000)	Year 3 ($'000)	Year 4 ($'000)
Cash (cumulative cash from the cash flow schedule)	2,000	(7,000)	(9,000)	10,000
Accounts receivable	5,000	3,000	3,000	0
Net asset (0 in last year)	–	10,000	15,000	0
Total assets	7,000	6,000	9,000	10,000
Net liability (0 in last year)	5,000	–	–	0
Retained earnings (cumulative income from Statement of Comprehensive Income)	2,000	6,000	9,000	10,000
Total liabilities and capital	7,000	6,000	9,000	10,000

D. The following illustrates the profit margin, asset turnover, debt-to-equity, return on assets, return on equity, and the current ratio:

Key Financial Ratios	Year 1	Year 2	Year 3	Year 4
Profit margin	10.0%	10.0%	10.0%	10.0%
Asset turnover	5.7x	6.2x	4.0x	1.1x
Debt-to-equity	2.5x	0.0x	0.0x	0.0x
Return on assets	57.1%	61.5%	40.0%	10.5%
Return on equity	200.0%	100.0%	40.0%	10.5%
Current ratio	1.4x	–	–	–

EXAMPLE 23.2

When comparing the use of the percentage-of-completion method with the completed-contract method during a long-term project's life, the percentage-of-completion method will result in which of the following:

    a. Earlier recognition of cash flows

    b. A higher return on assets

    c. A lower debt-to-equity ratio

    d. A higher asset turnover

EXPLANATION

    a. No. The choice of accounting method has no effect on cash flow.

    b. Yes. Because the periodic earnings will be higher under the percentage-of-completion method, the return on assets ratio will be higher.

    c. Yes. Because the percentage-of-completion method reports lower liabilities and higher net worth, the debt-to-equity ratio will be lower.

    d. Yes. The asset turnover ratio is higher under the percentage-of-completion method because sales are reported during the life of the project.

EXAMPLE 23.3

Omega Inc. started a four-year contract to build a dam. Activities commenced on February 1, 20X3. The total contract price amounted to $12 million, and it was estimated that the work would be completed at a total cost of $9.5 million. In the construction agreement the customer agreed to accept increases in wage tariffs additional to the contract price.

The following information refers to contract activities for the financial year ending December 31, 20X3:

1. Costs for the year:

	$'000
Material	1,400
Labor	800
Operating overhead	150
Subcontractors	180

2. Current estimate of total contract costs indicates the following:

   - Materials will be $180,000 higher than expected.
   - Total labor costs will be $300,000 higher than expected. Of this amount, only $240,000 will be the result of increased wage tariffs. The remainder will be caused by inefficiencies.
   - A savings of $30,000 is expected on operating overhead.

3. During the current financial year the customer requested a variation to the original contract, and it was agreed that the contract price would be increased by $900,000. The total estimated cost of this extra work is $750,000.

4. By the end of 20X3, certificates issued by quantity surveyors indicated a 25 percent stage of completion.

Determine the profit to date, based on

   - Option 1—contract costs in proportion to estimated contract costs
   - Option 2—percentage of the work certified

EXPLANATION

Contract profit recognized for the year ending December 31, 20X3, is as follows:

	Option 1 $'000	Option 2 $'000
Contract revenue (Calculation d)	3,107	3,285
Contract costs to date (Calculation a)	(2,530)	(2,530)
	577	755

Calculations	$'000	$'000
a. Contract costs to date		
Materials	1,400	
Labor	800	
Operating overhead	150	
Subcontractors	180	
	2,530	
b. Contract costs (revised estimated total costs)		
Original estimate	9,500	
Materials	180	
Labor	300	
Operating overhead	(30)	
Variation	750	
	10,700	
c. Contract revenue (revised estimate)		
Original amount	12,000	
Labor (wage increases added to contract price)	240	
Variation	900	
	13,140	
d. Stage of completion	Option 1	Option 2
Based on contract costs **in proportion to** estimated total contract costs:		
2,530 ÷ 10,700 × 13,140 (rounded off)	3,107	
Based on work certified: 25% × 3,140		3,285

Chapter Twenty Four

Employee Benefits (IAS 19)

24.1 OBJECTIVE

The fundamental issue addressed by IAS 19 is that entities should identify and recognize all the benefits that they are obliged to pay to employees, regardless of form or timing of the benefit.

24.2 SCOPE OF THE STANDARD

This standard prescribes the accounting recognition and measurement principles for all employee benefits, including those provided under both formal arrangements and informal practices.

The standard identifies five types of employee benefits:

1. Short-term employee benefits (for example, bonuses, wages, and social security)

2. Postemployment benefits (for example, pensions and other retirement benefits)

3. Long-term employee benefits (for example, long-service leave and, if not due within 12 months, profit sharing, bonuses, and deferred compensation)

4. Termination benefits

5. Equity compensation benefits (for example, employee share options per IFRS 2)

24.3 KEY CONCEPTS

24.3.1 **Employee benefits** are all forms of consideration given by an entity in exchange for service rendered by employees.

24.3.2 **Postemployment benefits** are employee benefits (other than termination benefits and equity compensation benefits) that are payable after the completion of employment.

24.3.3 **Equity compensation plans** are formal or informal arrangements under which an entity provides equity compensation benefits for one or more employees.

24.3.4 **Vested employee benefits** are employee benefits that are not conditional on future employment.

24.3.5 **Return on plan assets** comprises interest, dividends, and other revenue derived from the plan assets, together with realized and unrealized gains or losses on the plan assets, less any costs of administering the plan and less any tax payable by the plan itself.

24.3.6 **Actuarial gains and losses** comprise the effects of differences between the previous actuarial assumptions and what has actually occurred, as well as the effects of changes in actuarial assumptions.

24.3.7 In a **defined contribution plan,** the entity's legal or constructive obligation is limited to the amount it agrees to contribute to the fund. The actuarial risk (that the fund is insufficient to meet expected benefits) and the investment risk fall on the employee.

24.3.8 In a **defined benefit plan,** the entity's obligation is to provide the agreed benefits to current and former employees. Actuarial risk (that benefits will cost more than expected) and investment risk fall on the entity.

24.3.9 **Employee benefits** can be provided in terms of both the following:

- **Legal obligations,** which arise from the operation of law (for example, agreements and plans between the entity and employees or their representatives)
- **Constructive obligations,** which arise from informal practices that result in an obligation whereby the entity has no realistic alternative but to pay employee benefits (for example, the entity has a history of increasing benefits for former employees to keep pace with inflation even if there is no legal obligation to do so)

24.4   ACCOUNTING TREATMENT

Recognition

24.4.1 **Short-term employment benefits.** These should be recognized as an expense when the employee has rendered services in exchange for the benefits, *or* when the entity has a legal or constructive obligation to make such payments as a result of past events, for example, profit-sharing plans.

24.4.2 **Postemployment benefits.** An entity recognizes contributions to a **defined contribution plan** as an expense when an employee has rendered services in exchange for those contributions. When the contributions do not fall due within 12 months after the accounting period that services were rendered, they should be discounted.

24.4.3 **Equity compensation benefits.** Recognition and measurement requirements are specified in IFRS 2.

24.4.4 **Long-term benefits.** Virtually the same rules apply as for defined benefit retirement plans. However, a more simplified method of accounting is required for actuarial gains and losses as well as past-service costs, which are recognized immediately.

24.4.5 **Termination benefits.** When the event that results in an obligation is termination rather than employee service, an entity should recognize the benefits due only when it is demonstrably committed through a detailed formal plan to either

- terminate the employment of an employee or group of employees before the normal retirement date, or
- provide termination benefits to encourage voluntary redundancy.

Termination benefits falling due more than 12 months after the Statement of Financial Position date should be discounted.

Initial and Subsequent Measurement of Defined Benefit Plans

24.4.6 With regard to defined benefit plans, the following rules apply:

- An entity determines the present value of defined benefit **obligations** and the fair value of any **plan assets** with sufficient regularity.

- An entity should use the **projected unit credit method** to measure the present value of its defined benefit obligations and related current- and past-service costs. This method sees each period of service as giving rise to an additional unit of benefit entitlement and measures each unit separately to build up the final obligation.

- Unbiased and mutually compatible actuarial assumptions about demographic variables (for example, employee turnover and mortality) and financial variables (for example, future increases in salaries and certain changes in benefits) should be used.

- The difference between the fair value of any plan assets and the carrying amount of the defined benefit obligation is recognized as a liability or an asset.

- When it is virtually certain that another party will reimburse some or all of the expenditure required to settle a defined benefit obligation, an entity should recognize its right to reimbursement as a separate asset.

- Offsetting assets and liabilities of different plans is not allowed.

- The net total of current-service cost, interest cost, expected return on plan assets, any reimbursement rights, actuarial gains and losses, past-service cost, and the effect of any plan curtailments or settlements should be recognized as expense or income.

- Recognize past-service cost on a straight-line basis over the average period until the amended benefits become vested.

- Recognize gains or losses on the curtailment or settlement of a defined benefit plan when the curtailment or settlement occurs.

- Recognize a specified portion of the net cumulative actuarial gains and losses that exceed the *greater* of

  - 10 percent of the present value of the defined benefit obligation (before deducting plan assets), and

  - 10 percent of the fair value of any plan assets.

The minimum portion to be recognized for each defined benefit plan is the excess that falls outside the 10 percent "corridor" at the previous reporting date, divided by the expected average remaining working lives of the employees participating in that plan. Earlier recognition of these gains and losses is permitted.

24.5 PRESENTATION AND DISCLOSURE

24.5.1 The Statement of Financial Position and notes should include the following:

- Details about the recognized defined benefit assets and liabilities
- Reconciliation of the movements of the aforementioned

- Amounts included in the fair value of plan assets with respect to
  - the entity's own financial instruments, or
  - property occupied or assets used by the entity
- The actual return on plan assets
- Liability raised for equity compensation plans
- Financial instruments issued to and held by equity compensation plans as well as the fair values thereof
- Share options held by and exercised under equity compensation plans

24.5.2 The Statement of Comprehensive Income and notes should include the following:

- Expense recognized for defined contribution plans
- Expense recognized for defined benefit plans and the line items in which they are included
- Expense recognized for equity compensation plans

24.5.3 The following accounting policies should be disclosed:

- Methods applied for the recognition of the various types of employee benefits
- Description of postemployment benefit plans
- Description of equity compensation plans
- Actuarial valuation methods used
- Principal actuarial assumptions

24.6   FINANCIAL ANALYSIS AND INTERPRETATION

24.6.1 The complexity of the accounting standards applicable to pensions and other retirement benefits contributes to the wide range of differences among the companies offering these plans. As a result of this complexity and the fundamental differences in the two types of plans described below, analysts have a difficult time discerning the underlying economic substance of a firm's reported pension and other retirement benefits.

- **Defined contribution plans** require the employer to contribute a specific amount to a pension plan each year. The employee's retirement income is largely determined by the performance of the portfolio in which the contributions were invested.

- **Defined benefit plans** require the employer to pay specified pension benefits to retired employees. The investment risk is borne by the employer.

24.6.2 For **defined contribution plans,** the employer's annual pension expense is the amount that the company plan must contribute to the plan each year according to the contribution formula. Pension expense and cash outflow are the same, and there are no assets or liabilities recorded by the employer. A defined contribution pension plan obliges the employer only to make annual contributions to the pension plan based on a prescribed formula. When the contributions are made, the company has no further obligation that year.

24.6.3 For **defined benefit plans,** the annual pension expense and employer's liability are determined by calculating the present value of future benefits to be paid to retirees. Forecasting future benefits involves actuarial studies and assumptions about future events, including life expectancies of plan participants, labor turnover rates, future wage levels, discount rates, rates of return on plan assets, and so forth. Benefits promised to participants are defined by a specific formula that reflects these estimated future events. The estimated benefits are allocated to the years of service worked by employees to develop the annual pension expense. Companies with defined benefit pension plans accrue obligations to pay benefits, according to the benefit formula, as the employee performs work. However, these obligations are not discharged until after the employee retires.

24.6.4 Because pension **benefit formulas** relate the future benefits to the aggregate work performed by employees for the company until their retirement, there are several alternative ways of determining the size of the future obligations and their current values:

- **Actuarial estimates and defined benefit formulas.** Firms use actuaries to perform complex calculations to estimate the size of future obligations and their present value. Included in the computations are projections of employee salary growth, mortality, employee turnover, and retirement dates. These estimates are combined with the plan's benefit formula to generate a forecast of benefits to be paid in the future. This future benefit stream is discounted to present value, which is the employer's pension obligation each year.

- **Measures of the defined benefit pension obligation** are

  - accumulated benefit obligation (ABO)—the present value of pension benefits earned based on current salaries;

  - projected benefit obligation (PBO)—the present value of pension benefits earned, including projected salary increases; and

  - vested benefit obligation (VBO)—the portion of the benefit obligation that does not depend on future employee service (alternatively, the vested portion of the ABO).

24.6.5 With regard to **financial impact of assumptions,** for pay-related plans, PBO will be higher than ABO because of the inclusion of future salary increases. PBO and ABO will be the same for non-pay-related plans because salary increases have no effect on calculations. However, for non-pay-related plans, if there is enough evidence that past increases in benefits will be extended into the future, PBO will be higher than ABO after adjusting computations. For all defined benefit plans, calculations of PBO, ABO, and VBO must include automatic increases in benefits such as cost-of-living adjustments.

24.6.6 **Accounting** standards assume that pensions are forms of deferred compensation for work currently performed. Consequently, pension expenses are recognized on an accrual basis when earned by employees.

24.6.7 There are many **actuarial assumptions** that affect defined benefit pension obligations, the pension expense, and the funding requirements of the sponsoring firm:

- The discount rate
- The wage growth rate
- The expected return on plan assets
- The age distribution of the workforce
- The average service life of employees

24.6.8 In **analyzing the actuarial assumptions,** analysts need to determine whether the current assumptions are appropriate, particularly in comparison to the entity's competitors. In addition, if the assumptions have been changed, analysts need to determine the effect of a change in the following parameters on the financial statements:

- **Discount rate assumption.** If the discount rate is increased, the pension obligations will decrease, producing an actuarial gain for the year. If the discount rate is decreased, however, the pension obligation will increase, resulting in an actuarial loss for the year.

- **Wage growth rate assumption.** The wage growth rate assumption directly affects pension obligations and the service cost component of the reported pension expense. Therefore, a higher (lower) wage growth rate assumption will result in a higher (lower) pension obligation and a higher (lower) service cost component of the reported pension expense.

- **Expected rate of return on fund assets.** Because all funds should earn the same risk-adjusted return in the long run (if the market is efficient), deviations in this assumption from the norm that are unrelated to changes in a pension portfolio's asset mix might suggest that the pension expense is overstated or understated. In general, if the expected return on plan assets is too high, the pension expense is understated, boosting reported earnings; if the expected return on plan assets is too low, the pension expense is overstated, reducing reported earnings. Again, manipulating the expected return on plan assets will manipulate reported earnings and can be used to smooth earnings per share.

Table 24.1. Summary of Assumptions and Their Impact

	Higher (Lower) Discount Rate	Higher (Lower) Compensation Rate Increase	Higher (Lower) Expected Rate of Return on Plan Assets
PBO	Lower (Higher)	Higher (Lower)	No impact
ABO	Lower (Higher)	No impact	No impact
VBO	Lower (Higher)	No impact	No impact
Pension Expense	Lower (Higher)	Higher (Lower)	Lower (Higher)
Earnings	Higher (Lower)	Lower (Higher)	Higher (Lower)

EXAMPLE: EMPLOYEE BENEFITS

EXAMPLE 24.1

On December 31, 20X0, an entity's Statement of Financial Position includes a pension liability of $12 million. Management has decided to adopt IAS 19 as of January 1, 20X1, for the purpose of accounting for employee benefits. At that date, the present value of the obligation under IAS 19 is calculated at $146 million, and the fair value of plan assets is determined at $110 million. On January 1, 19X6, the entity had improved pension benefits. (Cost for nonvested benefits amounted to $16 million, and the average remaining period until vesting was eight years.)

EXPLANATION

The transitional liability is calculated as follows:

	$'000
Present value of the obligation	146,000
Fair value of plan assets	(110,000)
Past-service cost to be recognized in later periods (16 × 3/8)	(6,000)
Transitional liability	30,000
Liability already recognized	12,000
Increase in liability	18,000

The entity might (in terms of the transitional provisions of IAS 19) choose to either recognize the transitional liability of $18 million immediately or recognize it as an expense on a straight-line basis for up to five years. The choice is irrevocable. Subsequently, transitional arrangements are dealt with by IFRS 1.

EXAMPLE 24.2

Smith is analyzing three companies in the utilities industry: Northern Lights, Southeast Power, and Power Grid. After reviewing each company's pension footnotes, Smith made the following notes:

Assumption	Northern Lights		Southeast Power		Power Grid	
	20X0	20X1	20X0	20X1	20X0	20X1
Discount Rate	6.0%	5.5%	6.5%	6.5%	6.2%	6.0%
Assumed Rate of Compensation Growth	3.5%	3.5%	2.5%	3.0%	3.3%	3.0%
Expected Return on Assets	7.0%	7.0%	7.5%	7.2%	8.0%	8.5%

Issue 1: If Power Grid had left its expected rate of return on plan assets at 8 percent instead of raising it to 8.5 percent, what would the company have reported in 20X1?

    a. A lower accumulated benefit obligation (ABO)

    b. A higher projected benefit obligation (PBO)

    c. A lower funded status

    d. Higher pension expense

EXPLANATION

Choice d. is correct. The expected rate of return on plan assets is a direct (negative) component in the computation of pension expense. A lower rate would thus result in a higher pension expense. However, the ABO, PBO, and funded status are not affected by the expected return on plan assets.

Choice a. is incorrect. Only pension expense is affected by changes in the expected rate of return on plan assets. Therefore, there will not be a change in the ABO.

Choice b. is incorrect. Only pension expense is affected by changes in the expected rate of return on plan assets. Therefore, there will not be a change in the PBO.

Choice c. is incorrect. Only pension expense is affected by changes in the expected rate of return on plan assets. Therefore, there will not be a change in the funded status.

Issue 2: Based on the statistics and assumptions provided, which company has the most conservative pension accounting (that is, the one that will produce the highest PBO, ABO, and pension expense)?

  a. Northern Lights

  b. Southeast Power

  c. Power Grid

  d. Cannot be determined

EXPLANATION

Choice a. is correct. Northern Lights has the most conservative pension plan assumptions, including the lowest discount rate, highest compensation growth, and the lowest expected return on plan assets. These assumptions result in a higher ABO and PBO, as well as higher pension expense than either Southeast Power or Power Grid.

Choice b. is incorrect. All of Southeast Power's assumptions are more aggressive than the assumptions made by Northern Lights.

Choice c. is incorrect. All of Power Grid's assumptions are more aggressive than the assumptions made by Northern Lights.

Choice d. is incorrect. Enough information was provided in the table above to determine that the assumptions made by Northern Light are the most conservative, resulting in a higher ABO, PBO, and pension expense than either Southeast Power or Power Grid.

Issue 3: When Power Grid lowers its discount rate in 20X1 to 6 percent from 6.2 percent in 20X0, what will be the effects on the PBO and ABO?

	PBO	ABO
a.	Increase	Increase
b.	Decrease	Increase
c.	Decrease	Decrease
d.	Increase	Decrease

EXPLANATION

Choice a. is correct. The discount rate is used to calculate the present value of future benefits owed. Therefore, a decrease in the discount rate will increase both the PBO and the ABO.

Choice b. is incorrect. The PBO will not decrease when the discount rate decreases, because the discount rate is used to calculate the present value of future benefits.

Choice c. is incorrect. The discount rate is used to calculate the present value of future benefits. Therefore, a decrease in the discount rate will not decrease either the PBO or the ABO.

Choice d. is incorrect. The ABO will not decrease when the discount rate decreases, because the discount rate is used to calculate the present value of future benefits.

Chapter Twenty Five

Impairment of Assets (IAS 36)

25.1 OBJECTIVE

The objective of IAS 36 is to prescribe the procedures that an entity applies to ensure that its assets are carried at no more than the recoverable amount. The key concept is the identification and recognition of movements in asset value subsequent to initial recognition when such movements result in a reduction of asset value.

25.2 SCOPE OF THE STANDARD

IAS 36 prescribes

- the circumstances in which an entity should calculate the recoverable amount of its assets, including internal and external indicators or impairment;

- the measurement of recoverable amount for individual assets and cash-generating units; and

- the recognition and reversal of impairment losses.

This standard covers most noncurrent assets, with the exception of financial assets and noncurrent assets classified as held for sale.

25.3 KEY CONCEPTS

25.3.1 An **impairment loss** is the amount by which the carrying amount of an asset or a cash-generating unit exceeds its recoverable amount.

25.3.2 The **recoverable amount** of an asset or a cash-generating unit is the higher of its fair value less costs to sell and its value in use. **Value in use** is the present value of the future cash flows expected to be derived from an asset or a cash-generating unit. If either the net selling price or the value in use of an asset exceeds its carrying amount, the asset is not impaired.

25.3.3 **Fair value less costs to sell** is the amount obtainable from the sale of an asset or a cash-generating unit in an arm's-length transaction between knowledgeable, willing parties less the costs of disposal.

25.3.4 In determining the **value in use** of an asset, an entity should use cash flow projections and the pretax discount rate.

Cash flow projections (before income taxes and finance costs) for the asset or cash-generating unit in its current condition should be based on reasonable and supportable assumptions that

- reflect management's best estimate of the range of economic conditions that will exist over the remaining useful life of the asset,

- are based on the most recent financial budgets and forecasts approved by management for a maximum period of five years, and

- base any projections beyond the period covered by the most recent budget and forecasts on those budget and forecasts using a steady or declining growth rate unless an increasing rate can be justified.

- The **pretax discount rate** must reflect current market assessments of the time value of money and the risks specific to the asset or cash-generating unit. The discount rate should not reflect risks for which future cash flows have been adjusted.

25.4 ACCOUNTING TREATMENT

25.4.1 The **recoverable amount** of an asset should be estimated if, at the Statement of Financial Position date, there is an indication that the asset could be impaired. The recoverable amount of an asset should also be estimated annually for

- intangible assets with an indefinite useful life,

- intangible assets not yet ready for use, and

- goodwill.

25.4.2 The entity should consider, at a minimum, the following:

- **External sources of information,** for example, decline in an asset's market value, significant changes that have an adverse effect on the entity, increases in market interest rates, and so on

- **Internal sources of information,** for example, evidence of obsolescence or physical damage, significant changes in the extent to which or the manner in which the assets are used or are expected to be used, and evidence from internal reporting indicating an asset is performing worse than expected

25.4.3 An impairment loss should be recognized in the **profit or loss** unless the asset is carried at the revalued amount in accordance with IAS 16 or some other IFRS, in which case it should be dealt with as a revaluation decrease (see chapter 10). After recognition of the impairment loss, the depreciation charge for subsequent periods is based on the revised carrying amount.

25.4.4 An entity should reassess at each Statement of Financial Position date whether there is any indication that an impairment loss recognized in a prior period no longer exists or has decreased. If any such indication exists, the entity should estimate the recoverable amount of that asset. An impairment loss recognized in prior periods should be **reversed** if, and only if, there has been a change in the estimates used to determine recoverable amount since the last impairment loss was recognized. If that is the case, the carrying amount of the asset should be increased to its recoverable amount, but only to the extent that it does not increase the carrying amount of the asset above the carrying amount that would have been determined for the asset (net of amortization or depreciation) if no impairment loss had been recognized in prior years. For example, the previous impairment of a security held to maturity or available for sale, in terms of IAS 39, cannot be reversed to a higher value than what the amortized value would have been had the impairment not taken place.

25.4.5 For the purpose of **impairment testing,** goodwill should be allocated to each of the acquirer's cash-generating units or groups of cash-generating units that are expected to benefit from a combination, regardless of whether other assets or liabilities of the acquiree are allocated to that unit or those units. A cash-generating unit is the smallest identifiable group of assets that generates cash inflows from continuing use that are largely independent of the cash inflows from other assets or groups of assets.

25.4.6 A recoverable amount should be estimated for an individual asset. If it is not possible to do so, an entity should determine the recoverable amount for the **cash-generating unit** to which the asset belongs. The recoverable amount of a cash-generating unit is determined in the same way as that of an individual asset. The entity should identify all the corporate assets that relate to the cash-generating unit under review. When corporate assets cannot be allocated to cash-generating units on a reasonable and consistent basis, the entity should identify the group of units to which the corporate assets can be allocated on a reasonable and consistent basis and perform the impairment test for that group of units.

25.4.7 An impairment loss for a cash-generating unit should be allocated to reduce the carrying amount of the assets of the unit in the following order:

- Goodwill
- Other assets on a pro rata basis

The carrying amount of any asset should not be reduced below the highest of its fair value less costs to sell, its value in use, and zero.

25.4.8 A reversal of an impairment loss should be recognized in **profit or loss** unless the asset is carried at the revalued amount in accordance with IAS 16 or another IFRS when the reversal is treated as a revaluation increase in accordance with that standard.

25.4.9 An **impairment loss for goodwill** should not be reversed.

25.5   PRESENTATION AND DISCLOSURE

25.5.1 The following should be disclosed for *each* class of assets and for *each* reportable segment, based on the entity's primary format (where IAS 14, Segment Reporting, is applicable):

- Amount recognized in the Statement of Comprehensive Income for
  - impairment losses
  - reversals of impairment losses
- Amount recognized directly in equity for
  - impairment losses
  - reversals of impairment losses

25.5.2 If an impairment loss for an individual asset or a cash-generating unit is recognized or reversed and is **material** to the financial statements, the following should be disclosed:

- Events and circumstances that led to the loss being recognized or reversed

- Amount recognized or reversed
- Details about the nature of the asset or the cash-generating unit and the reportable segments involved
- Whether the recoverable amount is the net selling price or value in use
- The basis used to determine the net selling price *or* the discount rate used to determine value in use, and any previous value in use

25.6   FINANCIAL ANALYSIS AND INTERPRETATION

25.6.1 An **impaired asset** is an asset that is going to be retained by the entity and whose book value is not expected to be recovered from future operations. Lack of recoverability is indicated by such factors as

- a significant decrease in market value, physical change, or use of the asset;
- adverse changes in the legal or business climate;
- significant cost overruns; and
- current, historical, and probable future operating or cash flow losses from the asset.

25.6.2 Management makes the decisions about whether or not an asset's value is impaired by reference to internal and external sources of information, using cash flow projections based on reasonable and supportable assumptions and its own most recent budgets and forecasts. In IFRS financial statements, the need for a write-down, the size of the write-down, and the timing of the write-down are determined by objective and supportable evidence rather than at management's discretion. Impairment losses, therefore, cannot be used in IFRS financial statements to smooth or manipulate earnings in some other way. The discount rate used to determine the present value of future cash flows of the asset in its recoverability test must be determined objectively, based on market conditions.

25.6.3 From an external analyst's perspective, it is difficult to forecast impairment losses. However, the impairment losses themselves and the related disclosures provide the analyst with useful information about management's projections of future cash flows.

25.6.4 When impairment losses are recognized, the financial statements are affected in several ways:

- The carrying amount of the asset is reduced by the impairment loss. This reduces the carrying amount of the entity's total assets.
- The deferred tax liability is reduced and deferred tax income is recognized if the entity cannot take a tax deduction for the impairment loss until the asset is sold or fully used.
- Retained earnings and, hence, shareholders' equity is reduced by the difference between the impairment loss and any associated reduction in the deferred tax liability.
- Profit before tax is reduced by the amount of the impairment loss.
- Profit is reduced by the difference between the impairment loss and any associated reduction in deferred tax expense.

25.6.5 In addition, the impairment loss affects the following financial ratios and elements:

- **Asset turnover** ratios increase because of the lower asset base.

- The **debt-to-equity** ratios rise because of the lower equity base.
- **Profit margins** suffer a one-time reduction because of the recognition of the impairment loss.
- The **book value** (shareholders' equity) of the entity is reduced because of the reduction in equity.
- **Future depreciation charges** are reduced because the carrying amount of the asset is reduced.
- Lower future depreciation charges tend to cause the **future profitability** of the firm to increase (because the losses are taken in the current year).
- Higher future profitability and lower asset values tend to increase **future returns on assets.**
- Higher future profitability and lower equity values tend to increase **future returns on equity.**

25.6.6 Impairment losses do not directly affect cash flows because the cash outflows for the asset have already occurred; tax deductions, and hence tax payments, might not be affected. However, the impairment loss is an indicator that future operating cash flows could be lower than previously forecast.

EXAMPLE: IMPAIRMENT OF ASSETS

EXAMPLE 25.1

The following information relates to individual equipment items of an entity at a Statement of Financial Position date:

	Carrying amount $	Fair value less costs to sell $	Value in use $
Item #1	119,000	121,000	114,000
Item #2 (note 1)	237,000	207,000	205,000
Item #3 (note 1)	115,000	117,000	123,000
Item #4	83,000	75,000	79,000
Item #5 (note 2)	31,000	26,000	–

Notes

1. Items #2 and #3 are carried at revalued amounts, and the cumulative revaluation surpluses included in equity for the items are $12,000 and $6,000, respectively. Both items are manufacturing equipment.

2. Item #5 is a bus used for transporting employees in the mornings and evenings. It is not possible to determine the value in use of the bus separately because the bus does not generate cash inflows from continuing use that are independent of the cash flows from other assets.

EXPLANATION

The major issues related to the possible impairment of the above-mentioned items can be analyzed as follows:

Item #1

The recoverable amount is defined as the **higher** of an asset's net selling price and its value in use. No impairment loss is recognized because the recoverable amount of $121,000 is higher than the carrying amount of $119,000.

Item #2

Item #2 is impaired because its recoverable amount ($207,000) is lower than its carrying amount ($237,000), giving rise to an impairment loss of $30,000. According to IAS 36 (par. 60), the loss should be treated as a revaluation decrease. Therefore, $12,000 of the loss is debited to revaluation surplus in equity, and the balance of the loss ($18,000) is recognized in profit or loss.

Item #3

Item #3 is not impaired.

Item #4

Item #4 is impaired because its recoverable amount ($79,000) is lower than its carrying amount ($83,000), giving rise to an impairment loss of $4,000, which is recognized as an expense in profit or loss.

Item #5

The recoverable amount of the bus cannot be determined because the asset's value in use cannot be estimated to be close to its net selling price, and it does not generate cash inflows from continuing use that are largely independent of those from other assets. Therefore, management must determine the cash-generating unit to which the bus belongs and estimate the recoverable amount of this unit as a whole. If this unit consists of items #1 to #5, the carrying amount of the cash-generating unit (after recognizing the impairment losses on items #2 and #4) is $551,000. The fair value less costs to sell of the cash-generating unit is $546,000 (assuming that the assets could not be sold for more than the aggregate of their individual fair values). The value in use of the cash-generating unit is $521,000 (assuming, again, that the assets do not collectively produce cash flows that are higher than those used in the determination of their individual values in use). Therefore, the recoverable amount of the cash-generating unit is $546,000, giving rise to a further impairment loss of $5,000. The loss should be allocated on a pro rata basis to items #1, #3, and #5, provided that the carrying amount of each item is not reduced below the highest of its fair value less costs to sell and value in use. This means, in practice, that the whole of the loss is allocated to item #5, the bus.

Chapter Twenty Six

Borrowing Costs (IAS 23)

26.1   OBJECTIVE

The acquisition, construction, or production of some assets can take longer than one accounting period. If borrowing costs incurred during a period are directly attributable to specific assets, it might be legitimate to regard these costs as forming part of the costs of getting such assets ready for their intended use or sale. The major issue is the appropriate criteria that should be applied to capitalize these costs.

26.2   SCOPE OF THE STANDARD

IAS 23 is to be applied in accounting for all borrowing costs, which are defined as interest and other costs incurred by an entity in connection with borrowing funds.

IAS 23 prescribes that borrowing costs *attributable directly* to the acquisition, construction, or production of an asset be capitalized—provided they meet the criteria of resulting probable benefit and can be measured reliably.

Other borrowing costs are recognized as an expense in the period in which they are incurred.

26.3   KEY CONCEPTS

26.3.1 **Qualifying assets** are those assets that require a substantial time to bring them to their intended use or saleable condition, for example

- inventories requiring a substantial period to bring them to a saleable condition; and
- manufacturing plants, power generation facilities, and investment properties.

26.3.2 Arguments **in favor of capitalization** of borrowing costs include the following:

- Interest will be included in any contract, whether explicitly stated or not—no contractor will be willing to produce free of finance costs.
- Borrowing costs form part of acquisition costs.
- Costs included in assets are matched against revenue of future periods.
- Capitalization results in better comparability between assets purchased and constructed.

26.3.3 Arguments **against capitalization** of borrowing costs include the following:

- The attempt to link borrowing costs to a specific asset is arbitrary.
- Different financing methods can result in different amounts capitalized for the same asset.
- Expensing borrowing costs causes better comparable results.

26.4 ACCOUNTING TREATMENT

Recognition and Initial Measurement

26.4.1 Borrowing costs directly attributable to the acquisition, construction, or production of a qualifying asset must be **capitalized** when

- it is **probable** that they will result in future economic benefits to the entity, and
- the costs can be **measured reliably** (see effective interest rate method per IAS 39).

26.4.2 When the **carrying value** of an asset, inclusive of capitalized interest, exceeds the net realizable value, the asset should be written down to the latter value.

26.4.3 Capitalization **commences** when

- expenditures on a qualifying asset are being incurred,
- borrowing costs are being incurred, and
- activities necessary to prepare the asset for its intended sale or use are in progress.

Measurement

26.4.4 The **amount to be capitalized** is the borrowing costs that could have been **avoided** if the expenditure on the qualifying asset had not been made:

- If funds are **specifically borrowed** to obtain a particular asset, the amount of borrowing costs qualifying for capitalization is the actual costs incurred during the period, less income earned on temporary investment of those borrowings.
- If funds are **borrowed generally** and used to obtain an asset, the amount of borrowing costs to be capitalized should be determined by applying the weighted average of the borrowing costs to the expenditure on that asset. The amount capitalized during a period should not exceed the amount of borrowing costs incurred during that period.

26.4.5 Capitalization should **not cease**

- when all of the components required before any part of the asset (for example, a plant) can be sold or used are not yet completed,
- for brief interruptions in activities,
- during periods when substantial technical and administrative work is being carried out, or
- for delays that are inherent in the asset acquisition process (for example, wines that need long periods of maturity).

Derecognition

26.4.6 Capitalization should **cease** when

- the asset is materially ready for its intended use or sale,
- active development is suspended for extended periods, or
- construction is completed in part and the completed part can be used independently (for example, a business center).

26.5 PRESENTATION AND DISCLOSURE

The following should be disclosed:

- Accounting policy adopted for borrowing costs
- Capitalization rate used to calculate capitalized borrowing costs
- Total borrowing costs incurred, with a distinction between
    - the amount recognized as an expense, and
    - the amount capitalized.

26.6 FINANCIAL ANALYSIS AND INTERPRETATION

26.6.1 **Capitalized interest** becomes a part of the historical cost of the asset. Included in capitalized interest are explicit interest costs and interest related to a finance lease. This capitalized interest requirement does not apply to

- inventories routinely produced or purchased for sale or use,
- assets that are not being made ready for use, or
- assets that could be used immediately, whether or not they are actually being used.

26.6.2 The amount of interest cost to be capitalized is that portion of interest expense incurred during the asset's construction period that theoretically could have been avoided if the asset had been acquired ready to use. This includes any interest on borrowings that are made specifically to finance the construction of the asset, and any interest on the general debt of the company, up to the amount invested in the project. The capitalized interest cost cannot exceed the total interest expense that the entity incurred during the period.

26.6.3 Before the asset is operational, the interest portion should be included and recorded on the Statement of Financial Position as an **asset in course of construction.** That capitalized interest will subsequently be expensed over the life of the asset by means of depreciation of the asset.

26.6.4 The capitalization of interest expense that is incurred during the construction of an asset reduces interest expense during the period in which the interest was paid. As a result, capitalized interest causes accounting profit to be greater than cash flow.

26.6.5 For analytical purposes, especially when comparing two companies that do not have similar borrowing patterns, analysts often remove the capitalized interest expense from the asset portion of the Statement of Financial Position and treat that capitalized interest as an interest expense. If this adjustment is not made, analysts reason that important ratios—such as the interest coverage ratio—will be higher than those of comparable companies. However, IFRS no longer provides a choice of expensing interest and now requires capitalization of interest on qualifying assets. The financial statements of companies that have not capitalized such interest should therefore be adjusted.

EXAMPLE 26.1

Morskoy Inc. is constructing a warehouse that will take about 18 months to complete. It began construction on January 1, 20X2. The following payments were made during 20X2:

	$'000
January 31	200
March 31	450
June 30	100
October 31	200
November 30	250

The first payment on January 31 was funded from the entity's pool of debt. However, the entity succeeded in raising a medium-term loan for an amount of $800,000 on March 31, 20X2, with simple interest of 9 percent per annum, calculated and payable monthly in arrears. These funds were specifically used for this construction. Excess funds were temporarily invested at 6 percent per annum monthly in arrears and payable in cash. The pool of debt was again used for a $200,000 payment on November 30, which could not be funded from the medium-term loan.

The construction project was temporarily halted for three weeks in May, when substantial technical and administrative work was carried out.

Morskoy adopted the accounting policy of capitalizing borrowing costs.

The following amounts of debt were outstanding at the Statement of Financial Position date, December 31, 20X2:

	$'000
Medium-term loan (see description above)	800
Bank overdraft	1,200
(The weighted average amount outstanding during the year was $750,000, and total interest charged by the bank amounted to $33,800 for the year.)	
A 10%, 7-year note dated October 1, 19x7, with simple interest payable annually at December 31	9,000

EXPLANATION

The amount to be capitalized to the cost price of the warehouse in 20X2 can be calculated as follows:

	$
Specific loan	
$800,000 × 9 percent × 9/12	54,000
Interest earned on unused portion of loan available during the year:	
April 1 to June 30 [(800,000 − 450,000) × 3/12 × 6%]	(5,250)
July 1 to October 31 [(800,000 − 550,000) × 4/12 × 6%]	(5,000)
November 1 to November 30 [(800,000 − 750,000) × 1/12 × 6%]	(250)
	43,500
General pool of funds	
Capitalization rate is 9.58 percent (Calculation a)	
Paid on January 31 (200,000 × 11/12 × 9.58%)	17,563
Paid on November 30 (200,000 × 1/12 × 9.58%)	1,597
	19,160
Total Amount to Be Capitalized	62,660

Note: Although the activities had been interrupted by technical and administrative work during May 20X2, capitalization is not suspended for this period according to IAS 23.

Calculation a	$
Capitalization rate for pool of debt	
Total interest paid on these borrowings	
Bank overdraft	33,800
7-year note (9,000,000 × 10%)	900,000
	933,800
Weighted average total borrowings	
Bank overdraft	750,000
7-year note	9,000,000
	9,750,000

Capitalization rate = 933,800 ÷ 9,750,000
= 9.58% (rounded)

EXAMPLE 26.2

A company has a building under construction that is being financed with $8 million of debt, $6 million of which is a construction loan directly on the building. The rest is financed out of the general debt of the company. The company will use the building when it is completed. The debt structure of the firm is as follows:

	$'000
Construction loan @ 11%	6,000
Long-term debentures @ 9%	9,000
Long-term subordinated debentures @ 10%	3,000

The debentures and subordinated debentures were issued at the same time.

Issue 1: What is the interest payable during the year?

    a. $660,000

    b. $1,800,000

    c. $1,770,000

    d. $1,140,000

EXPLANATION

Choice c. is correct $(0.11 (\$6,000,000) + 0.09 (\$9,000,000) + 0.10 (\$3,000,000) = \$1,770,000)$.

Issue 2: The capitalized interest cost to be recorded as an asset on the Statement of Financial Position, according to IAS 23, is

    a. $660,000

    b. $850,000

    c. $845,000

    d. $1,770,000

EXPLANATION

Choice c. is correct.

The effective interest rate on the construction loan is 11 percent.

The effective average interest rate on the company's other debt is

$$\frac{9,000,000}{12,000,000} \times 9\% + \frac{3,000,000}{12,000,000} \times 10\% = 9.25\%$$

These two rates are used to calculate the capitalized interest:

$$\begin{aligned} \text{Capitalized Interest} &= \$6,000,000 (0.11) + 2,000,000 (0.0925) \\ &= \$660,000 + 185,000 = \$845,000 \end{aligned}$$

Issue 3: What amount of interest expense should be reported on the Statement of Comprehensive Income?

   a. $920,000

   b. $1,140,000

   c. $925,000

   d. $1,770,000

EXPLANATION

Choice c. is correct ($1,770,000 − 845,000 = $925,000).

Chapter Twenty Seven

Accounting for Government Grants and Disclosure of Government Assistance (IAS 20)

27.1 OBJECTIVE

IAS 20 deals with the accounting of grants and assistance from the government:

- **Government grants** are transfers of resources from the government to an enterprise in return for past or future compliance with conditions relating to the operating activities.

- **Government assistance** is action by government to provide a specific economic benefit for an entity (or entities). It excludes benefits provided indirectly through action affecting general trading conditions (for example, provision of infrastructure).

The key issue is whether the entity will continue to comply with the grant/assistance conditions and hence be allowed to recognize the grant as income.

27.2 SCOPE OF THE STANDARD

This standard addresses the following aspects of accounting for government grants and other forms of government assistance:

- Definition of government grants (assets and income grants) and government assistance
- The recognition criteria for grants
- Disclosure of the extent of the benefit (benefits) recognized or received and other forms of government assistance in each accounting period

IAS 41 (see chapter 12) deals with government grants related to biological assets.

27.3 KEY CONCEPTS

27.3.1 The term **government** refers to government, government agencies, and similar bodies, whether local, national, or international.

27.3.2 **Government grants** are assistance by government in the form of transfers of resources. The following distinction is made between the two types of government grants:

- **Grants related to assets:** Grants whereby an enterprise qualifying for them should purchase, construct, or otherwise acquire long-term assets
- **Grants related to income:** Government grants other than those related to assets

27.3.3 Government assistance includes

- free technical and marketing advice,
- provision of guarantees,
- government procurement policy that is responsible for a portion of the enterprise's sales, and
- loans at nil or low interest rates. (The benefit is not quantified by the imputation of interest.)

27.4 ACCOUNTING TREATMENT

Recognition

27.4.1 Government grants should be recognized as income on a systematic basis over the periods necessary to **match** them with related costs that they should compensate. Examples include the following:

- Grants related to depreciable assets are recognized as income over the periods and in the proportions to which depreciation is charged by reducing costs or deferring income.
- A grant of land can be conditional upon the erection of a building on the site. Income is normally then recognized over the life of the building.

27.4.2 A government grant as compensation for expenses or losses already incurred or immediate financial support with no future related costs is recognized as income of the period in which it becomes receivable.

27.4.3 Government grants, including nonmonetary grants at fair value, should be **recognized** only when there is reasonable assurance that

- the enterprise will comply with the conditions attached to them, and
- the grants will be received.

A grant received in cash or as a reduction of a liability to government is accounted for similarly.

Initial Measurement

27.4.4 Nonmonetary grants (for example, land or other resources) is assessed and recorded at fair value. Alternatively, the grant and asset (assets) are recorded at a nominal amount.

27.4.5 A **forgivable loan** (where the lender undertakes to waive repayment of loans under prescribed conditions) is treated as a grant when there is reasonable assurance that the terms for forgiveness of the loan will be met. This conflicts with IAS 39, but it is not currently addressed in IFRS.

Subsequent Measurement

27.4.6 A repayment of a government grant is accounted for as a revision of an accounting estimate (refer to IAS 8) as follows:

- Repayment related to income is first applied against an unamortized deferred grant credit.
- Repayment in excess of a deferred grant credit is recognized as an expense.
- Repayment related to an asset is recorded by increasing the carrying amount of the asset or reducing a deferred income balance. (Cumulative additional depreciation that would have been recognized to date is recognized immediately.)

27.5 PRESENTATION AND DISCLOSURE

27.5.1 Presentation

- **Asset-related grants.** Present in the **Statement of Financial Position** by either
    - setting up the grant as deferred income, or
    - deducting it from the carrying amount of the asset.
- **Income-related grants.** Present in the **Statement of Comprehensive Income** as either
    - separate credit line item, or
    - deduction from the related expense.

27.5.2 Disclosure

- Describe the **accounting policies** related to method of presentation and method of recognition.
- Include the following in the **Statement of Comprehensive Income and notes:**
    - Government grants: describe the nature, extent, and amount
    - Government assistance: describe the nature, extent, and duration
    - Unfulfilled conditions
    - Contingencies attached to assistance

EXAMPLE: ACCOUNTING FOR GOVERNMENT GRANTS AND DISCLOSURE OF GOVERNMENT ASSISTANCE

EXAMPLE 27.1

Jobworld Inc. obtained a grant of $10 million from a government agency for an investment project to construct a manufacturing plant costing at least $88 million. The principal term is that the grant payments relate to the level of capital expenditure. The secondary intention of the grant is to safeguard 500 jobs. The grant will have to be repaid pro rata if there is an underspending on capital. Twenty percent of the grant will have to be repaid if the jobs are not safeguarded until 18 months after the date of the last asset purchase.

The plant was completed on January 1, 20X4, at a total cost of $90 million. The plant has an expected useful life of 20 years and is depreciated on a straight-line basis with no residual value.

EXPLANATION

The grant should be recognized as income on a systematic basis over the periods that will match it with the related costs it is intended to compensate. Difficulties can arise where the terms of the grant do not specify precisely the expenditure to which it is intended to contribute. Grants might be intended to cover costs consisting of both capital and revenue expenditure. This would require a detailed analysis of the terms of the grant.

The employment condition should be seen as an additional condition to prevent replacement of labor by capital, rather than as the reason for the grant. This grant should therefore be regarded as an **asset-related grant.** IAS 20 allows two acceptable methods of presentation of such grants. The application of each method is demonstrated for the first three years of operation:

1. Setting grant up as deferred income

The plant would be reflected as follows in the Statement of Financial Positions at December 31 of the years indicated:

	20X6 $'000	20X5 $'000	20X4 $'000
Plant	90,000	90,000	90,000
Historical cost	(13,500)	(9,000)	(4,500)
Accumulated depreciation	76,500	81,000	85,500
Carrying value	**10,000**	**10,000**	**10,000**
Deferred income	500	1,000	1,500

The following amounts would be recognized in the Statement of Comprehensive Income of the respective years:

	20X6 $'000	20X5 $'000	20X4 $'000
Depreciation (expense) (90,000,000 ÷ 20)	4,500	4,500	4,500
Government grant (income) (10,000,000 ÷ 20)	(500)	(500)	(500)

The above amounts are treated as separate Statement of Comprehensive Income items and should not be offset under this method of presentation.

2. Deducting grant in arriving at carrying amount of asset

The adjusted historical cost of the plant would be $80 million, which is the total cost of $90 million less the $10 million grant.

The plant would be reflected as follows in the respective Statement of Financial Positions:

	20X6 $'000	20X5 $'000	20X4 $'000
Plant			
Historical cost	80,000	80,000	80,000
Accumulated depreciation	(12,000)	(8,000)	(4,000)
	68,000	72,000	76,000

The Statement of Comprehensive Income would reflect an annual depreciation charge of $4 million ($80,000,000 ÷ 20). This charge agrees with the net result of the annual amounts recognized in the Statement of Comprehensive Income under the first alternative.

Chapter Twenty Eight

Share-Based Payment (IFRS 2)

28.1 OBJECTIVE

Share-based payments occur when an entity uses a transfer of shares instead of satisfying an obligation using conventional cash. IFRS 2 covers situations where the entity makes any share-based payment transaction, including transactions with employees or other parties, to be settled in cash, equity, or the entity's equity instruments. The main issues relate to if and when the share-based payment should be recognized and when these transactions should be reflected as expenses in the Statement of Comprehensive Income.

28.2 SCOPE OF THE STANDARD

This IFRS should be applied for all share-based payment transactions. IFRS 2 covers more than just employee share options, because it also deals with the issuance of shares (and rights to shares) in return for services and goods. The standard specifically covers

- the criteria for defining a share-based payment; and

- the distinction and accounting for the various types of share-based payments, namely equity settled, cash settled, and transactions in which the entity receives or acquires goods or services and where there is an option to settle via equity instruments.

An entity should reflect in its profit and loss and financial position statements the effects of share-based payment transactions, including expenses associated with transactions in which employees receive share options.

28.3 KEY CONCEPTS

28.3.1 A **share-based payment transaction** is a transaction in which the entity receives goods or services as consideration for equity instruments of the entity (including shares or share options), or acquires goods or services by incurring liabilities to the supplier of those goods or services for amounts that are based on the price of the entity's shares or other equity instruments of the entity. Share-based payment transactions include transactions where the terms of the arrangement provide either the entity or the supplier of those goods or services with a choice of whether the entity settles the transaction in cash (or other assets) or through the issuance of equity instruments.

28.3.2 In an **equity-settled share-based payment transaction,** the entity receives goods or services (including shares or share options) as consideration for the entity's equity instruments. An **equity instrument** is a contract that evidences a residual interest in the assets of an entity after deducting all of its liabilities. An equity instrument granted is the right to an equity instrument of the entity conferred by the entity on another party, under a share-based payment arrangement.

28.3.3 In a **cash-settled share-based payment transaction**, the entity acquires goods or services by incurring a liability to transfer cash or other assets to the supplier of those goods or services for amounts that are based on the price or value of the entity's shares or other equity instruments.

28.3.4 The **grant date** is the date at which the entity and another party (including an employee) agree to a share-based payment arrangement. At grant date, the entity confers on the counterparty the right to cash, other assets, or the entity's equity instruments, provided that the specified vesting conditions are met.

28.3.5 **Employees and others providing similar services** are individuals who render personal or similar services to the entity.

28.3.6 Under a share-based payment arrangement, a counterparty's right to receive the entity's cash, other assets, or equity instruments **vests** upon satisfaction of any specified vesting conditions. Vesting conditions include service conditions. The **vesting period** is the period during which all the specified vesting conditions of a share-based payment arrangement should be satisfied.

28.3.7 **Fair value** is the amount for which an asset could be exchanged, a liability settled, or an equity instrument granted between knowledgeable, willing parties in an arm's-length transaction.

28.3.8 **Intrinsic value** is the difference between the fair value of the shares to which the counterparty has the right to subscribe or which it has the right to receive, and the price the counterparty is required to pay for those shares.

28.3.9 **Market condition** is a condition that is related to the market price of the entity's equity instruments.

28.3.10 A **share option** is a contract that gives the holder the right but not the obligation to subscribe to the entity's shares at a fixed or determinable price for a specified period of time.

28.4   ACCOUNTING TREATMENT

28.4.1 Share-based payments could be

- cash settled, that is, by a cash payment based on the value of equity instruments;
- equity settled, that is, by the issue of equity instruments; or
- cash or equity settled (by choice of the entity or supplier).

28.4.2 An entity should recognize **the goods or services received or acquired** in a share-based payment transaction when it obtains the goods or as the services are received.

28.4.3 Share-based payment transactions should be measured at

- the fair value of the goods or services received in the case of all third party, nonemployee transactions, unless it is not possible to measure the fair value of those goods or services reliably; or
- the fair value of the equity instruments in all other cases, including all employee transactions.

Equity-Settled Share-Based Payment Transactions

28.4.4 The fair value of the equity instruments issued or to be issued should be measured

- at grant date for transactions with employees and others providing similar services; and
- at the date on which the entity receives the goods or the counterparty renders the services in all other cases.

28.4.5 The fair value of the equity instruments issued or to be issued should be based on market prices, taking into account market vesting conditions (for example, market prices or reference to an index) but not other vesting conditions (for example, service periods). Listed shares should be measured at market price. Options should be measured

- on the basis of the market price of any equivalent traded options,
- using an option pricing model in the absence of such market prices, or
- at intrinsic value when the options cannot be measured reliably on the basis of market prices or on the basis of an option pricing model.

28.4.6 In the rare cases where the entity is required to measure the equity instruments at their **intrinsic value,** it remeasures the instruments at each reporting date until final settlement and recognizes any **change in intrinsic value in profit or loss.**

28.4.7 The entity should recognize an asset (for example, inventory) or an expense (for example, services received or employee benefits) and a corresponding increase in equity if the goods or services were received in an **equity-settled** share-based payment transaction. Therefore, an entity recognizes an asset or expense and a corresponding increase in equity

- on grant date if there are no vesting conditions or if the goods or services have already been received,
- as the services are rendered if nonemployee services are rendered over a period, or
- over the vesting period for employee and other share-based payment transactions where there is a vesting period.

28.4.8 If the equity instruments granted do not **vest** until the counterparty completes a specified period of service, the amount recognized should be adjusted over any vesting period for changes in the estimate of the number of securities that will be issued, but not for changes in the fair value of those securities. Therefore, on the vesting date, the amount recognized is the exact number of securities that can be issued as of that date, measured at the fair value of those securities at grant date.

28.4.9 If the entity **cancels or settles a grant** of equity instruments during the vesting period (other than a grant canceled by forfeiture when the vesting conditions are not satisfied), the following accounting requirements apply:

- The entity accounts for the cancellation or settlement as an acceleration of vesting by recognizing immediately the amount that otherwise would have been recognized over the remainder of the vesting period.
- The entity recognizes in equity any payment made to the employee on the cancellation or settlement to the extent that the payment does not exceed the fair value at the repurchase date of the equity instruments granted.

- The entity recognizes as an expense the excess of any payment made to the employee on the cancellation or settlement over the fair value at the repurchase date of the equity instruments granted.

- The entity accounts for new equity instruments granted to the employee as replacements for the cancelled equity instruments as a modification of the original grant. The difference between the fair value of the replacement equity instruments and the net fair value of the cancelled equity instruments at the date the replacement equity instruments are granted is recognized as an expense.

Cash-Settled Share-Based Payment Transaction

28.4.10 The entity should recognize an asset (for example, inventory) or an expense (for example, services received or employee benefits) and a liability if the goods or services were received in a **cash-settled** share-based payment transaction.

28.4.11 Until the liability is settled, the entity should remeasure the fair value of the liability at each reporting date and at the date of settlement, with any changes in fair value recognized in profit or loss for the period.

Share-Based Payment Transactions with Cash Alternatives

28.4.12 For **share-based payment transactions** in which the terms of the arrangement provide either the entity or the counterparty with the choice of whether the entity settles the transaction in cash (or other assets) or by issuing equity instruments, the entity should account for that transaction, or the components of that transaction, as a cash-settled share-based payment transaction if, and to the extent that, the entity has incurred a liability to settle in cash or other assets. If no such liability has been incurred, the entity should account for the transaction as an equity-settled share-based payment transaction.

28.5   PRESENTATION AND DISCLOSURE

28.5.1 An entity should disclose information that enables users of the financial statements to understand the **effect of share-based payment transactions on the entity's profit or loss** for the period and on its financial position.

28.5.2 An entity should disclose information that enables users of the financial statements to understand **the nature and extent** of share-based payment arrangements that existed during the period.

28.5.3 An entity should provide **a description** of

- each type of share-based payment arrangement that existed at any time during the period; and

- the general terms and conditions of each arrangement, such as vesting requirements, the maximum term of options granted, and the method of settlement (for example, whether in cash or equity).

28.5.4 An entity should provide the **number and weighted average exercise prices** of share options for each of the following groups of options:

- Outstanding at the beginning of the period
- Granted during the period
- Forfeited during the period
- Exercised during the period
- Expired during the period
- Outstanding at the end of the period
- Exercisable at the end of the period

28.5.5 For **share options granted** during the period, the weighted average fair value of those options at the measurement date and information on how that fair value was measured should be disclosed, including

- the option pricing model used and the inputs to that model, including
    - the weighted average share price,
    - exercise price,
    - expected volatility,
    - option life,
    - expected dividends,
    - the risk-free interest rate, and
    - any other inputs to the model, including the method used and the assumptions made to incorporate the effects of expected early exercise;
- how expected volatility was determined, including an explanation of the extent to which expected volatility was based on historical volatility; and
- whether and how any other features of the option grant were incorporated into the measurement of fair value, such as a market condition.

28.5.6 An entity should disclose information that enables users of the financial statements to understand how the **fair value of the goods or services received** or the fair value of the equity instruments granted during the period was determined.

28.5.7 For share **options exercised** during the period, an entity should disclose the weighted average share price at the date of exercise.

28.5.8 For share **options outstanding** at the end of the period, an entity should disclose the range of exercise prices and weighted average remaining contractual life.

28.6 FINANCIAL ANALYSIS AND INTERPRETATION

28.6.1 Share-based earnings complicate the analysis of various operating areas, in particular operating cash flow.

28.6.2 When an employee exercises such share options, the cash payment by the employees are typically classified as operating cash flows. This effect could be large and may not necessarily be sustainable, especially if the options were to become out-of-the-money and their exercise therefore no longer attractive.

28.6.3 The variables used to measure the fair value of an equity instrument issued under IFRS 2 have a significant impact on that valuation, and the determination of these variables requires significant professional judgment. A minor change in a variable, such as volatility or expected life of an instrument, could have a quantitatively material impact on the fair value of the instruments granted. In the end, the selection of variables must be based on entity-specific information.

28.6.4 One of the most difficult issues in applying IFRS 2 will be determining the fair value of share-based payments, which requires numerous estimates and the application of careful judgment. Measurement difficulties may arise because the final value of the share-based payment transaction is determined when the transaction is settled at some point in the future but must be estimated at the date of grant.

28.6.5 The determination of the model an entity uses is an accounting policy choice and should be applied consistently to similar share-based payment transactions. Improvements to a model would be considered a change in estimate, and IAS 8 should be applied when an entity changes models (for example, from Black-Scholes to a binomial model).

28.6.6 The major strength of the Black-Scholes model is that it is a generally accepted method for valuing share options. It has gained wide acceptance from both regulators and users. Nearly all companies with share option plans use the Black-Scholes model to compute the fair value of their share options today. The consistent use of this model also enhances the comparability between entities.

28.6.7 Another strength of Black-Scholes is that the formula required to calculate the fair value is relatively straightforward and can be easily included in spreadsheets.

28.6.8 The binomial model is described as an "open form solution," as it can incorporate different values for variables (such as volatility) over the term of the option. The model can also be adjusted to take account of market conditions and other factors.

28.6.9 Many factors should be considered when estimating expected volatility. For example, the estimation of volatility might first focus on implied volatilities for the terms that were available in the market and compare the implied volatility to the long-term average historical volatility for reasonableness. In addition to implied and historical volatility, IFRS 2 suggests the following factors be considered in estimating expected volatility:

- The length of time an entity's shares have been publicly traded

- Appropriate and regular intervals for price observations

- Other factors indicating that expected future volatility might differ from past volatility (for example, extraordinary volatility in historical share prices)

28.6.10 Typically, the shares underlying traded options are acquired from existing shareholders and therefore have no dilutive effect. Capital structure effects of nontraded options, such as dilution, can be significant and are generally anticipated by the market at the date of grant. Nevertheless, except in the most unusual cases, dilutive considerations should have no impact on the individual employee's decision. The market's anticipation will depend on, among other matters, whether the process of share returns is the same or is altered by the dilution and the cash infusion. In many situations the number of employee share options issued relative to the number of shares outstanding is not significant, and the effect of dilution on share price can therefore be ignored.

IFRS 2 suggests that the issuer consider whether the possible dilutive effect of the future exercise of options granted has an effect on the fair value of those options at grant date by an adjustment to option pricing models.

EXAMPLE: DISCLOSURE OF SHARE-BASED PAYMENT

EXAMPLE 28.1

Summary of Significant Accounting Policies

Share-based payments

On January 1, 20X5, the Group applied the requirements of IFRS 2 share-based payments. In accordance with the transition provisions, IFRS 2 was applied to all grants after November 7, 20X2, that were unvested as of January 1, 20X5.

The Group issues equity-settled and cash-settled share-based payments to certain employees. Equity-settled share-based payments are measured at fair value at the date of grant. The fair value determined at the grant date of the equity-settled share-based payments is expensed on a straight-line basis over the vesting period, based on the Group's estimate of shares that will eventually vest. A liability equal to the portion of the goods or services received is recognized at the current fair value determined at each Statement of Financial Position date for cash-settled share-based payments.

Fair value is measured by use of the Black-Scholes pricing model. The expected life used in the model has been adjusted, based on management's best estimate, for the effects of nontransferability, exercise restrictions, and behavioral considerations.

The Group also provides employees the ability to purchase the Group's ordinary shares at 85 percent of the current market value. The Group records an expense based on its best estimate of the 15 percent discount related to shares expected to vest on a straight-line basis over the vesting period.

Note XX: Share-based payments.

Equity-settled share option plan

The Group plan provides for a grant price equal to the average quoted market price of the Group shares on the date of grant. The vesting period is generally 3 to 4 years. If the options remain unexercised after 10 years from the date of grant, the options expire. Furthermore, options are forfeited if the employee leaves the Group before the options vest.

	20X4		20X5	
	Options	Weighted average exercise price in €	Options	Weighted average exercise price in €
Outstanding at the beginning of the period	42,125	64.26	44,440	65.75
Granted during the period	11,135	68.34	12,120	69.68
Forfeited during the period	(2,000)	65.67	(1,000)	66.53
Exercised during the period	(5,575)	45.32	(8,300)	53.69
Expired during the period	(1,245)	82.93	(750)	82.93
Outstanding at the end of the period	44,440	65.75	46,510	66.33
Exercisable at the end of the period	23,575	46.47	24,650	52.98

Source: Deloitte Touche Tohmatsu, IFRS 2: Share-based payments, pp. 61–63

The weighted average share price at the date of exercise for share options exercised during the period was €53.69. The options outstanding at December 31, 20X5, had a weighted average exercise price of €66.33, and a weighted average remaining contractual life of 8.64 years. The inputs into the Black-Scholes model were as follows:

	20X4	20X5
Weighted average share price	68.34	69.68
Weighted average exercise price	68.34	69.68
Expected volatility	40%	35%
Expected life	3–8 years	4–9 years
Risk-free rate	3%	3%
Expected dividends	none	none

Expected volatility was determined by calculating the historical volatility of the Group's share price over the previous nine years. The expected life used in the model was adjusted, based on management's best estimate, for the effects of nontransferability, exercise restrictions, and behavioral considerations.

During 20X5, the Group repriced certain of its outstanding options. The strike price was reduced from €82.93 to the then-current market price of €69.22. The incremental fair value of €125,000 will be expensed over the remaining vesting period (two years). The Group used the inputs noted above to measure the fair value of the old and new shares.

The Group recognized total expenses of €775,000 and €750,000 related to equity-settled share-based payment transactions in 20X4 and 20X5, respectively.

Cash-settled share-based payments

The Group issues to certain employees share appreciation rights (SARs) that require the Group to pay the intrinsic value of the SAR to the employee at the date of exercise. The Group has recorded liabilities of €1,325,000 and €1,435,000 in 20X4 and 20X5, respectively. Fair value of the SARs is determined using the Black-Scholes model using the assumptions noted in the above table. The Group recorded total expenses of €325,000 and €110,000 in 20X4 and 20X5, respectively. The total intrinsic value at 20X4 and 20X5 was €1,150,000 and €1,275,000, respectively.

Other share-based payment plans

The employee share purchase plans are open to almost all employees and provide for a purchase price equal to the daily average market price on the date of grant, less 15 percent. The shares can be purchased during a two-week period each year. The shares so purchased are generally placed in the employee share savings plan for a five-year period. Pursuant to these plans, the Group issued 2,123,073 ordinary shares in 20X5 at a weighted average share prices of €64.35.

Chapter Twenty Nine

Events After the Balance Sheet Date (IAS 10)

29.1 OBJECTIVE

Certain balance sheet (Statement of Financial Position) events occur subsequent to the balance sheet date but before the date that the financial statements are approved for issue. These events might indicate the need for adjustments to the amounts recognized in the financial statements or require disclosure. IAS 10 addresses the effect of such events on the information that is provided in the financial statements.

29.2 SCOPE OF THE STANDARD

IAS 10 should be applied in the accounting and disclosure of all post–balance sheet (Statement of Financial Position) events, both favorable and unfavorable, that occur before the date on which the financial statements are authorized for issue. This standard prescribes the appropriate accounting treatment for such events and whether adjustments or simple disclosure is required.

This standard also requires that an entity not prepare its financial statements on a going-concern basis if events after the balance sheet date indicate that the going-concern assumption is not appropriate.

29.3 KEY CONCEPTS

29.3.1 Events after the balance sheet date are those events that

- provide evidence of conditions that existed at the balance sheet date, and
- are indicative of conditions that arose after the balance sheet date.

29.3.2 Two types of events can be distinguished:

- Conditions existing at the balance sheet (Statement of Financial Position) date: **adjusting events** providing additional evidence of conditions existing at the Statement of Financial Position date (the origin of the event is in the current reporting period)
- **Nonadjusting events,** indicative of conditions arising after the Statement of Financial Position date

29.4 ACCOUNTING TREATMENT

29.4.1 Amounts recognized in the financial statements of an entity are **adjusted** for events occurring after the Statement of Financial Position date that provide additional information about conditions existing at the Statement of Financial Position date, and therefore allow these amounts to be estimated more accurately. For example, adjustments could be required for a loss recognized on a trade debtor that is confirmed by the bankruptcy of a customer after the Statement of Financial Position date.

29.4.2 If events occur after the Statement of Financial Position date that do not affect the condition of assets and liabilities at the Statement of Financial Position date, **no adjustment** is required. However, disclosure should be made of such events if they are of such importance that nondisclosure would affect decisions made by users of the financial statements. For example, it should be disclosed if an earthquake destroys a major portion of the manufacturing plant of the entity after the Statement of Financial Position date or an event were to alter the current or noncurrent classification of an asset at the Statement of Financial Position date, per IAS 1.

29.4.3 Dividends stated should be in respect of the period covered by the financial statements; those that are proposed or declared after the Statement of Financial Position date but before approval of the financial statements should not be recognized as a liability at the Statement of Financial Position date.

29.4.4 An entity should not prepare financial statements on a going-concern basis if management determines after the Statement of Financial Position date that it intends to either liquidate the entity or cease trading (or that it has no realistic alternative but to do so). For example, if a fire destroys a major part of the business after the year-end, going-concern considerations would override all considerations (even if an event technically did not require disclosure) and the financial statements would be adjusted.

29.4.5 The process of **authorization** for issue of financial statements will depend on the form of the entity and its management structure. The date of authorization for issue would normally be the date on which the financial statements are authorized for release outside the entity.

29.5 PRESENTATION AND DISCLOSURE

29.5.1 Disclosure requirements related to the **date of authorization for issue** are as follows:

- Date when financial statements were authorized for issue
- Name of the person who gave the authorization
- Name of the party (if any) with the power to amend the financial statements after issuance

29.5.2 For **nonadjusting events** that would affect the ability of users to make proper evaluations and decisions, the following should be disclosed:

- Nature of the event
- Estimate of the financial effect
- A statement if such an estimate cannot be made

29.5.3 Disclosures that relate to conditions that existed at the Statement of Financial Position date should be updated in light of any new information about those conditions that is received after the Statement of Financial Position date.

EXAMPLE 29.1

A corporation with a Statement of Financial Position date of December 31 has a foreign long-term liability that is not covered by a foreign exchange contract. The foreign currency amount was converted at the closing rate on December 31, 20X4, and is shown in the accounting records at the local currency (LC) 2.0 million.

The local currency dropped significantly against the U.S. dollar on February 27, 20X5, resulting in a loss of LC4.0 million. On this date, management decided to hedge further exposure by taking out a foreign currency forward-exchange contract, which limited the eventual liability to LC6.0 million. If this situation were to apply at the Statement of Financial Position date, it would result in the corporation's liabilities exceeding the fair value of its assets.

EXPLANATION

The situation above falls within the definition of **post–balance sheet events** and specifically those events that refer to conditions arising *after* the Statement of Financial Position date.

The loss of LC4.0 million that arose in 20X5 must be recognized in the 20X5 Statement of Comprehensive Income. No provision with respect to the loss can be made in the financial statements for the year ending December 31, 20X4.

However, consideration should be given to whether it would be appropriate to apply the **going-concern** concept in the preparation of the financial statements. The date and frequency of repayment of the liability will have to be considered.

The following information should be **disclosed in a note** to the financial statements for the year ending December 31, 20X4:

- The nature of the events
- An estimate of the financial effect, in this case, a loss of LC4.0 million

Part V

Disclosure

Chapter Thirty

Related-Party Disclosures (IAS 24)

30.1 OBJECTIVE

A related-party relationship between entities or individuals is one where the arrangement is not of the normal independent business type. A related-party relationship can have an effect on the financial position and operating results of the reporting entity. The objective of this IAS is to define related-party relationships and transactions and to enhance their disclosure.

30.2 SCOPE OF THE STANDARD

An entity's financial statements should contain the disclosures necessary to draw attention to the possibility that the financial position and profit or loss could have been affected by the existence of related parties and by transactions and outstanding balances with them.

This IAS should be applied when identifying related-party relationships and related-party transactions, such as outstanding balances or the circumstances under which these aspects should be reported.

30.3 KEY CONCEPTS

30.3.1 **Parties are considered to be related** if one party has the ability to control, jointly control, or exercise significant influence over the other party.

30.3.2 A **related-party transaction** is a transfer of resources, services, or obligations between related parties, regardless of whether a price is charged.

30.3.3 Related-party relationships include

- entities that directly control, are controlled by, or are under common control with the reporting entity (for example, a group of companies),
- associates,
- individuals, including close family members, who either directly or indirectly own interest in the voting power in the reporting entity that gives them significant influence,
- key management personnel (including directors, officers, and close family members) responsible for planning, directing, and controlling the activities,
- entities in which a substantial interest in the voting power is held, either directly or indirectly, by individuals (key personnel and close family members), or entities over which these people can exercise significant influence,
- parties with joint control over the entity,

- joint ventures in which the entity is a venturer, and

- postemployment benefit plans for the benefit of employees of an entity, or of any entity that is a related party to that entity.

30.3.4 **Close members of the family** of an individual are family members who might be expected to influence, or be influenced by, that individual in their dealings with the entity. They may include

- the individual's domestic partner and children,

- children of the individual's domestic partner, and

- dependants of the individual or the individual's domestic partner.

30.3.5 **Compensation** includes all employee benefits (see also IAS 19 and IFRS 2) and all forms of such consideration paid, payable, or provided by the entity, or on behalf of the entity, in exchange for services rendered to the entity. It also includes such consideration paid on behalf of a parent of the entity in respect of the entity. Compensation includes

- short-term employee benefits and nonmonetary benefits for current employees,

- postemployment benefits,

- other long-term employee benefits,

- termination benefits, and

- share-based payment.

30.4 ACCOUNTING TREATMENT

30.4.1 A related-party transaction comprises a transfer of resources or obligations between related parties, regardless of whether a price is charged; this transfer of resources includes transactions concluded on an arm's length basis. The following are examples of these transactions:

- Purchase or sale of goods

- Purchase or sale of property or other assets

- Rendering or receipt of services

- Agency arrangements

- Lease agreements

- Transfer of research and development

- License agreements

- Finance, including loans and equity contributions

- Guarantees and collaterals

- Management contracts

30.4.2 Related-party relationships are normal features in commerce. Many entities carry on separate parts of their activities through subsidiaries, associates, joint ventures, and so on. These parties sometimes enter into transactions through atypical business terms and prices.

30.4.3 Related parties have a degree of flexibility in the price-setting process that is not present in transactions between nonrelated parties. For example, they can use a

- comparable uncontrolled price method,
- resale price method, or
- cost-plus method.

30.5 PRESENTATION AND DISCLOSURE

30.5.1 Relationships between parent and subsidiaries should be disclosed, irrespective of whether there have been transactions between the parties. The name of the parent and, if different, the name of the ultimate controlling party should be disclosed.

30.5.2 Compensation of key management personnel should be disclosed in total and for each of the following categories of compensation:

- Short-term employee benefits
- Postemployment benefits
- Other long-term benefits
- Termination benefits
- Equity compensation benefits

30.5.3 If **related-party transactions** occur, the following should be disclosed:

- Nature of related-party relationships
- Nature of the transactions
- Transactions and outstanding balances, including
  - amount of transactions and outstanding balances,
  - terms and conditions,
  - guarantees given or received, and
  - provisions for doubtful debts and bad and doubtful debt expense.

30.5.4 The matters in 30.5.3 should be separately disclosed for

- the parent,
- entities with joint control or significant influence over the entity,
- subsidiaries,
- associates,
- joint ventures in which the entity is a venturer,
- key management personnel of the entity or its parent, and
- other related parties.

30.6 FINANCIAL ANALYSIS AND INTERPRETATION

30.6.1 Transactions with related parties often raise questions of governance, especially when the impact is not clear from the amounts disclosed.

30.6.2 These types of transactions and the related approval processes can give rise to negative publicity. For example, amounts paid to management and directors have been the focus of significant attention in terms of governance processes in recent years.

30.6.3 For this reason, the disclosure of pricing policies and approval processes for related-party transactions should be taken into account when considering the impact of those transactions on the business.

30.6.4 The potential disempowerment of groups such as minority shareholders should be considered, particularly where payments are made to other group companies.

EXAMPLE: RELATED-PARTY DISCLOSURES

EXAMPLE 30.1

Habitat Inc. is a subsidiary in a group structure, as indicated by the following diagram.

Habitat Inc.

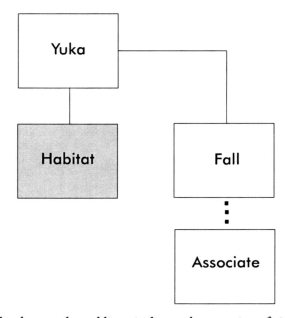

Solid lines indicate **control,** whereas dotted lines indicate the exercise of **significant influence.**

During the year, Habitat acquired plant and equipment from Associate at an amount of $23 million, on which Associate earned a profit of $4 million.

EXPLANATION

Habitat and Associate are deemed to be related parties in terms of IAS 24. The full details of the transaction should therefore be disclosed in the financial statement of **both** entities as required by IAS 24, namely

- nature of the related-party relationship,
- the nature of the transaction,
- amount involved, and
- any amount still due from Habitat to Associate.

Chapter Thirty One

Earnings per Share (IAS 33)

31.1 OBJECTIVE

Earning per share is a prime variable used for evaluating the performance of an entity. IAS 33 prescribes principles for the determination and presentation of earnings per share, focusing on the denominator (per share amount) of the calculation. The standard distinguishes between the notions of basic as well as diluted earnings per share.

31.2 SCOPE OF THE STANDARD

This standard applies to entities whose shares are **publicly traded** (or in the process of being issued in public securities markets) and other entities that choose to disclose earnings per share. It is applicable to consolidated information only if the parent prepares consolidated financial statements.

The standard requires and prescribes the form of calculation and disclosure of **basic** as well as **diluted** earnings per share.

31.3 KEY CONCEPTS

31.3.1 An **ordinary share** is an equity instrument that is subordinate to all other classes of equity instruments. An entity may issue more than one class of ordinary shares.

31.3.2 **Dilution** is a reduction in earnings per share or an increase in loss per share resulting from the assumption that convertible instruments are converted, that options or warrants are exercised, or that ordinary shares are issued upon the satisfaction of specified conditions.

31.3.3 A **potential ordinary share** is a financial instrument or other contract that can entitle its holder to ordinary shares (for example, debt or equity instruments that are convertible into ordinary shares, and share warrants and options that give the holder the right to purchase ordinary shares).

31.3.4 **Options, warrants, and their equivalents** are financial instruments that give the holder the right to purchase ordinary shares at a specified price.

31.3.5 **Put options** on ordinary shares are contracts that give the holder the right to sell ordinary shares at a specified price for a given period.

31.4 ACCOUNTING TREATMENT

31.4.1 Basic earnings per share are calculated by dividing the profit or loss for the period attributable to ordinary equity holders of the parent entity by the weighted average number of ordinary shares outstanding during the period.

31.4.2 Basic earnings are profit or loss attributable to ordinary equity holders and (if presented) profit or loss from continuing operations attributable to those equity holders.

Profit or loss is adjusted for the following amounts related to preference dividends:

- Differences arising on the settlement of the preference shares
- Other similar effects of preference shares classified as equity

Qualifying preference dividends are

- the amount declared for the period on noncumulative preference shares; and
- the full amount of **cumulative preference dividends** for the period, whether or not declared.

31.4.3 When calculating the weighted number of shares, the following aspects must be considered:

- The **weighted number of shares** are the average number of shares outstanding during the period (that is, the number of ordinary shares outstanding at the beginning of the period, adjusted by those bought back or issued during the period) multiplied by a time-weighting factor.
- Contingency **issuable shares** are included in the computation of basic earnings per share, but only from the date when all necessary conditions have been satisfied.
- The number of shares for **current** and all **previous periods** presented should be adjusted for changes in shares without a corresponding change in resources (for example, bonus issue and share split).
- The number of **ordinary shares** should be adjusted for all periods prior to a rights issue (which includes a bonus element), multiplied by the following factor:

$$\frac{\text{Fair value per share immediately prior to the exercise of rights}}{\text{Theoretical ex-rights fair value per share}}$$

31.4.4 Diluted earnings are the profit or loss attributable to ordinary equity holders of the parent entity and (if presented) profit or loss from continuing operations attributable to those equity holders, adjusted for the effects of all dilutive potential ordinary shares.

31.4.5 Diluted earnings consist of the basic earnings *adjusted for after-tax effects* of the following items associated with dilutive potential ordinary shares:

- Dividends or other items
- Interest for the period
- Other changes in income or expense that would result from a conversion of shares. (For example, the savings on interest related to these shares can lead to an increase in the expense relating to a nondiscretionary employee profit-sharing plan.)

31.4.6 The following adjustments are made to the **weighted number of shares:**

- The weighted average number of shares for basic earnings per share (EPS), **plus** those to be issued on conversion of all dilutive potential ordinary shares. Potential ordinary shares are treated as dilutive when their conversion would decrease net profit per share from continuing ordinary operations.

- These shares are deemed to have been converted into ordinary shares at the beginning of the period or, if later, at the date the shares were issued.

- Options, warrants (and their equivalents), convertible instruments, contingently issuable shares, contracts that can be settled in ordinary shares or cash, purchased options, and written put options should be considered.

31.4.7 EPS amounts should be **restated** in the following circumstances:

- If the number of shares outstanding is affected as a result of a capitalization, bonus issue, share split, or a reverse share split, the calculation of basic EPS and diluted EPS should be adjusted retrospectively.

- If these changes occur after Statement of Financial Position date but before issue of financial statements, the per-share calculations are based on the new number of shares.

31.4.8 Basic EPS and diluted EPS for all periods presented are adjusted for the effect of

- prior period errors, or
- changes in accounting policies.

31.5 PRESENTATION AND DISCLOSURE

31.5.1 Basic EPS and diluted EPS are shown with equal prominence on the face of the Statement of Comprehensive Income for **each** class of ordinary shares with different rights for

- profit or loss from continuing operations attributable to ordinary equity holders of the parent entity,

- profit or loss attributable to ordinary equity holders of the parent entity, and

- any reported discontinued operation.

31.5.2 Basic and diluted **losses** per share are disclosed when they occur.

31.5.3 Amounts used as numerators for basic EPS and diluted EPS and a reconciliation of those amounts to the net profit or loss for the period must be disclosed.

31.5.4 If an EPS figure in addition to the one required by IAS 33 is disclosed,

- Basic and diluted amounts per share should be disclosed with equal prominence.

- That figure should be disclosed in notes, not on the face of the Statement of Comprehensive Income.

- The basis on which the numerator is determined should be indicated, including whether amounts are before or after tax.

- Reconciliation of the numerator and reported line item should be provided in the Statement of Comprehensive Income of the denominator.

- The same denominator should be used as for basic EPS or dilutive EPS (as appropriate).

31.5.5 The weighted average number of ordinary shares used as the denominator in calculating basic EPS and diluted EPS, and a reconciliation of these denominators to each other, must be disclosed.

31.6 FINANCIAL ANALYSIS AND INTERPRETATION

31.6.1 When discussing companies, investors and others commonly refer to **earnings per share.** If a company has a simple capital structure—one that contains no convertible bonds or preferred shares, no warrants or options, and no contingent shares—it will present only its **basic earnings per share.**

31.6.2 For complex capital structures, both basic earnings per share and **diluted earnings per share** are generally reported. A complex capital structure is one where the company does have one or more of the following types of securities: convertible bonds, preferred shares, warrants, options, and contingent shares.

EXAMPLE 31.1

The issued and fully paid share capital of Angli Inc., unchanged since the date of incorporation until the financial year ended March 31, 20X4, include the following:

- 1,200,000 ordinary shares with no par value
- 300,000 6% participating preference shares of $1 each

The corporation has been operating at a profit for a number of years. As a result of a very conservative dividend policy in previous years, there is a large accumulated profit balance on the Statement of Financial Position. On July 1, 20X4, the directors decided to issue to all ordinary shareholders two capitalization shares for every one previously held.

The following abstract was taken from the (noncompliant) consolidated Statement of Comprehensive Income for the year ending March 31, 20X5:

	20X5 $	20X4 $
Profit after Tax	400,000	290,000
Minority Interest (not IFRS compliant)	(30,000)	(20,000)
Net Profit from Ordinary Activities	370,000	270,000
Extraordinary Item (not IFRS compliant)	–	(10,000)
Profit for the Year	370,000	260,000

The following dividends have been paid or declared at the end of the reported periods:

	20X5 $	20X4 $
Ordinary	165,000	120,000
Preference	34,500	30,000

The participating preference shareholders are entitled to share profits in the same ratio in which they share dividends, after payment of the fixed preference dividend. The shareholders will share the same benefits if the company is liquidated.

EXPLANATION

The earnings per share (required by IAS 33) and the dividends per share (required by IAS 1) to be presented in the group financial statements for the year ending March 31, 20X5, are calculated as follows:

	20X5	20X4
EARNINGS PER SHARE		
Attributable earnings (Calculation b) divided by weighted number of shares (Calculation c)		
Ordinary Shares	320,000	220,000
	3,600,000	3,600,000
	= $0.089	= $0.061
Participating Preference Shares		
	50,000	40,000
	300,000	300,000
	= $0.167	= $0.133
	20X5	**20X4**
DIVIDENDS PER SHARE		
Dividends divided by actual number of shares in issue		
Ordinary Shares	165,000	120,000
(20X4 adjusted for the capitalization issue for the purposes of comparability)	3,600,000	3,600,000
	= $0.046	= $0.033
Preference Shares	34,500	30,000
	300,000	300,000
	= $0.115	= $0.10

CALCULATIONS

a. Percentage of profits attributable to classes of equity shares

	20X5 $	20X4 $
Total preference dividend	34,500	30,000
Fixed portion (6% x $300,000)	(18,000)	(18,000)
	16,500	12,000
Dividend paid to ordinary shareholders	165,000	120,000

Therefore, the participating preference shareholders share profits in the ratio 1:10 with the ordinary shareholders after payment of the fixed preference dividend out of profits.

b. Earnings per class of share

	20X5 $	20X4 $
Net profit for the period	370,000	260,000
Fixed preference dividend	(18,000)	(18,000)
	352,000	242,000
Attributable to ordinary shareholders: 10/11	320,000	220,000
Attributable to participating preference shareholders: 1/11	2,000	22,000
Fixed dividend	18,000	18,000
	50,000	40,000

c. Weighted number of ordinary shares in issue

	20X5 Shares	20X4 Shares
Balance, April 1, 20X3	1,200,000	1,200,000
Capitalization issue	2,400,000	2,400,000
	3,600,000	3,600,000

EXAMPLE 31.2

L. J. Pathmark reported net earnings of $250,000 for the year ending 20X1. The company had 125,000 shares of $1 par value common stock and 30,000 shares of $40 par value convertible preference shares outstanding during the year. The dividend rate on the preference shares was $2 per share. Each share of the convertible preference shares can be converted into two shares of L. J. Pathmark Class A common shares. During the year no convertible preference shares were converted.

What were L. J. Pathmark's basic earnings per share?

    a. $0.89 per share

    b. $1.52 per share

    c. $1.76 per share

    d. $2.00 per share

EXPLANATION

Choice b. is correct. The answer was derived from the following calculation:

$$\text{Basic earnings per share} = \frac{\left(\text{Net income} - \text{Preference dividends}\right)}{\left(\text{Weighted average common shares}\right)}$$

$$= \frac{\$250,000 - (\$2 \times 30,000 \text{ shares})}{125,000 \text{ shares}}$$

$$= \frac{\$190,000}{125,000}$$

$$= \$1.52 \text{ per share}$$

Choice a. is incorrect. This answer does not correctly apply the formula above.

Choice c. is incorrect. The preference dividends were improperly determined by using the shares (only), and not deriving a dollar dividend.

Choice d. is incorrect. When determining the basic EPS, preference dividends were not subtracted.

EXAMPLE 31.3

L. J. Pathmark reported net earnings of $250,000 for the year ending 20X1. The company had 125,000 shares of $1 par value common stock and 30,000 shares of $40 par value convertible preference shares outstanding during the year. The dividend rate on the preference shares was $2 per share. Each share of the convertible preference shares can be converted into two shares of L. J. Pathmark Class A common shares. During the year no convertible preference shares were converted.

What were L. J. Pathmark's diluted earnings per share?

    a. $0.70 per share.

    b. $1.35 per share.

    c. $1.68 per share.

    d. $2.00 per share.

EXPLANATION

Choice b. is correct. The answer was derived from the following calculation:

$$\text{Diluted earnings per share} = \frac{\left(\begin{array}{c}\text{Net income}\end{array} - \begin{array}{c}\text{Preference dividends}\end{array} + \begin{array}{c}\text{Dividends on converted securities}\end{array}\right)}{\begin{array}{c}\text{Shares outstanding}\end{array} + \begin{array}{c}\text{Additional shares if securities were converted}\end{array}}$$

$$= \frac{(\$250{,}000 - \$60{,}000 + \$60{,}000)}{125{,}000 + (30{,}000 \times 2)}$$

$$= \frac{\$250{,}000}{185{,}000}$$

$$= \$1.35 \text{ per share}$$

Choice a. is incorrect. Dividends on converted securities were incorrectly subtracted in the numerator.

Choice c. is incorrect. Preference dividends were ignored in the numerator of the calculation.

Choice d. is incorrect. This represents an incorrect application of both fully diluted and basic EPS, as net income is divided by shares outstanding.

Chapter Thirty Two

Financial Instruments: Presentation (IAS 32)

Note: IAS 32, IAS 39, and IFRS 7 were issued as separate standards but are applied in practice as a unit because they deal with the same accounting phenomenon.

32.1 OBJECTIVE

Users need information that will enhance their understanding of the significance of on–Statement of Financial Position and off-balance-sheet financial instruments regarding an entity's existing financial position, performance, and cash flows, as well as the amounts, timing, and certainty of future cash flows associated with those instruments.

IAS 32 prescribes requirements for the presentation of on-balance-sheet financial instruments.

32.2 SCOPE OF THE STANDARD

The standard deals with **all types of financial instruments**, both recognized and unrecognized, and should be applied to contracts to buy or sell a nonfinancial item that **can be settled** net

- in cash,
- by another financial instrument, or
- by exchanging financial instruments, as if the contracts were financial instruments.

Presentation issues addressed by IAS 32 relate to

- distinguishing liabilities from equity;
- classifying compound instruments;
- reporting interest, dividends, losses, and gains; and
- offsetting financial assets and liabilities.

IAS 32 applies to all risks arising from all financial instruments, except

- interests in subsidiaries, associates, and joint ventures (IAS 27, 28, and 31);
- employers' rights and obligations arising from employee benefit plans (IAS 19);
- financial instruments within the scope of IFRS 2;
- contracts for contingent consideration in a business combination (IFRS 3); and
- insurance contracts and financial instruments within the scope of IFRS 4 (except for derivatives that are embedded in insurance contracts if IAS 39 requires the entity to account for them separately).

32.3 KEY CONCEPTS

32.3.1 A **financial instrument** is any contract that gives rise to both a financial asset of one entity and a financial liability or equity instrument of another.

32.3.2 A **financial asset** is any asset that is

- cash (for example, cash deposited at a bank);
- a contractual right to receive cash or a financial asset (for example, the right of a debtor and derivative instrument);
- a contractual right to exchange financial instruments under potentially favorable conditions;
- a contract that will or may be settled in an entity's own equity instruments; or
- an equity instrument of another entity (for example, investment in shares).

Physical assets (for example, inventories and patents) are not financial assets because they do not give rise to a present contractual right to receive cash or other financial assets.

32.3.3 A **financial liability** is a contractual obligation to

- deliver any financial asset,
- exchange financial instruments under potentially unfavorable conditions, or
- be settled in the entity's own equity instruments.

Liabilities imposed by statutory requirements (for example, income taxes) are not financial liabilities because they are not contractual.

32.3.4 An **equity instrument** is any contract that evidences a residual interest in the assets of an entity after deducting all of its liabilities. An obligation to issue an equity instrument is not a financial liability because it results in an increase in equity and cannot result in a loss to the entity.

32.3.5 **Fair value** is the amount for which an asset could be exchanged, or a liability settled, between knowledgeable, willing parties in an arm's-length transaction.

32.4 PRESENTATION

32.4.1 The issuer of a financial instrument should classify the instrument, or its component parts, **on initial recognition** as a financial liability, a financial asset, or an equity instrument in accordance with the substance of the contractual arrangement and the definitions of a financial liability, a financial asset, and an equity instrument.

32.4.2 The issuer of a **compound financial instrument** that contains **both** a liability and equity element (for example, convertible bonds) should classify the instrument's component parts separately, for example: total amount – liability portion = equity portion. Once so classified, the classification is not changed, even if economic circumstances change. No gain or loss arises from recognizing and presenting the parts separately.

32.4.3 **Interest, dividends, losses, and gains** relating to a financial liability should be reported in the Statement of Comprehensive Income as expense or income. Distributions to holders of an equity instrument should be debited **directly** to equity. The classification of the financial instrument therefore determines its accounting treatment:

- Dividends on shares classified as liabilities would thus be classified as an expense in the same way that interest payments on a loan are classified as an expense. Furthermore, such dividends would have to be accrued over time.

- Gains and losses (premiums and discounts) on redemption or refinancing of instruments classified as liabilities are reported in the Statement of Comprehensive Income, whereas gains and losses on instruments classified as equity of the issuer are reported as movements in equity.

32.4.4 A financial asset and a financial liability should be **offset** only when

- a legal enforceable right to set off exists, and

- an intention exists to either settle on a net basis or to realize the asset and settle the related liability simultaneously.

32.5   DISCLOSURE

See chapter 33 (IFRS 7) for information about disclosure requirements.

Chapter Thirty Three

Financial Instruments: Disclosures (IFRS 7)

33.1 OBJECTIVE

Users of financial statements need information about an entity's exposure to risks and how those risks are managed. Such information can influence a user's assessment of the financial position and financial performance of an entity or of the amount, timing, and uncertainty of its future cash flows. Greater transparency regarding those risks allows users to make more informed judgments about risk and return.

IFRS 7 requires entities to provide disclosures in their financial statements that enable users to evaluate the **significance of financial instruments** for the entity's financial position and performance. Entities should describe the **nature and extent of risks** arising from financial instruments to which they are exposed during the period under review and at the reporting date, and how they manage those risks.

33.2 SCOPE OF THE STANDARD

IFRS 7 applies to all entities and for all risks arising from all financial instruments, whether recognized or unrecognized (for example, some loan commitments and other instruments falling outside the direct scope of IAS 39), except the following:

- Interests in subsidiaries, associates, and joint ventures (IAS 27, 28, and 31)
- Employers' rights and obligations arising from employee benefit plans (IAS 19)
- Contracts for contingent consideration in a business combination (IFRS 3)
- Insurance contracts as defined in IFRS 4 (except for derivatives that are embedded in insurance contracts if IAS 39 requires the entity to account for them separately)

IFRS 7 requires disclosure of the following:

- Significance of financial instruments, in each category of asset (assets held at fair value through profit and loss, assets available for sale, assets held to maturity, and loans and receivables) or liability (liabilities at fair value and liabilities shown at amortized cost) and by class of instrument
- Carrying values of financial assets and financial liabilities
- Nature and extent of the risk exposures arising from financial instruments used by the entity
- Qualitative and quantitative information about exposure to credit risk, liquidity risk, and market risk arising from financial instruments
- Management's objectives, policies, and processes for managing those risks

33.3   KEY CONCEPTS

33.3.1 Four classes of financial assets: Assets carried at fair value through profit and loss, held-to-maturity securities, available-for-sale securities, and loans and receivables.

33.3.2 Two classes of financial liabilities: Liabilities carried at fair value through profit and loss, and liabilities measured at amortized cost (see also chapter 17).

33.3.3 Classes of financial instruments: Financial instruments must be grouped into classes that

- are appropriate to the nature of the information disclosed, and
- take into account the characteristics of those financial instruments.

33.3.4 Reconciliations: Sufficient information must be provided to enable reconciliations with items presented in the Statement of Financial Position.

33.4   ACCOUNTING TREATMENT/DISCLOSURE OVERVIEW

33.4.1 Macro view of disclosure requirements (tables 33.1 and 33.2). IFRS 7 requires a determination of the significance of key disclosures, as well as the financial instruments affected, for the financial position and performance of an entity. In addition, the qualitative and quantitative nature and extent of risks arising from financial instruments must be disclosed.

Table 33.1 Disclosure Overview

Measurement	Instruments	Nature & Extent of Risks	Significance	Statement of Financial Position	Statement of Comprehensive Income	Hedging
Assets						
Fair value through profit and loss (P&L)	Trading securities			Carrying values	Net gains & losses	Description
	Designated fair value assets			Reclassification	Net gains & losses - separate disclosure of movements through equity - AFS assets	Gains & losses
	Derivatives	Qualitative & quantitative risk arising from assets & liabilities	Value of financial instruments must be stated on Statement of Financial Position	Derecognition	Total interest income & expense (using effective interest rate method)	Effectiveness
Fair value through equity	Available-for-sale securities	Credit risk - per class of asset	and	Collateral - for assets pledged		Ineffective portions transferred from equity - where applicable
Amortized securities	Held-to-maturity securities (HTM)	Liquidity risk - all financial liabilities	Related amounts on Statement of Comprehensive Income			
Amortized assets - other	Loans & receivables	Market risk by type - all assets & liabilities		Impairments - by class		
Liabilities						
Fair value through P&L	Trading securities			Embedded equity derivatives		
	Designated fair value assets					
	Derivatives			Defaults & breaches (loans payable)		
Amortized liabilities	Other liabilities					

Table 33.2 Information to Be Disclosed and Financial Instruments Affected

Information to Be Disclosed and Financial Instruments Affected
A. Determination of Significance (for example, evidenced by carrying value) for Financial Position and Performance
A1. Statement of Financial Position
A2. Statement of Comprehensive Income and Equity
A3. Other Disclosures—accounting policies, hedge accounting, and fair value
B. Nature and Extent of Risks Arising from Financial Instruments
B1. Qualitative disclosures (nature and how arising)—not necessarily by instrument
B2. Quantitative disclosures

33.4.2 Overview of Statement of Financial Position disclosure (see table 33.3). The carrying values of all financial assets and liabilities must be disclosed. The broad categories of Statement of Financial Position disclosures relate to credit risk and related collateral issues, recognition and reclassification issues, liabilities with embedded options, and loans payable but in default.

Table 33.3 Overview of Statement of Financial Position Disclosures

Information to Be Disclosed	Financial Instruments Affected
Carrying values	All financial assets and financial liabilities
Credit risk	Loans and receivables at fair value, liabilities at fair value
Reclassification	All financial assets
Derecognition—transfers of assets not qualifying	All financial assets
Collateral given or held	Financial assets pledged and pledged assets received
Allowance for credit losses—impairments in a separate account	Financial assets impaired—per class
Structured liabilities with equity components—using interdependent multiple embedded derivatives	Financial liabilities with multiple embedded derivatives
Loans payable—defaults and breaches	Loans payable—currently in default

33.4.3 Overview of Statement of Comprehensive Income disclosure (see table 33.4). Statement of Comprehensive Income disclosures focus on net gains and losses on financial assets and liabilities, with a split between the different classes of assets and liabilities—to enable the reader to distinguish between designated fair value financial instruments, amortized instruments, and traded fair value instruments.

Table 33.4 Overview of Statement of Comprehensive Income Disclosure

Information to Be Disclosed	Financial Instruments Affected
Net gains and losses	All financial instruments—except available-for-sale assets
Net gains and losses—amounts recognized and amounts removed from equity to be separated	Available-for-sale financial assets
Total interest income and total interest expense—using effective interest rate method	All financial assets *and* financial liabilities measured at amortized cost

33.4.4 Overview of other disclosure types. IFRS 7 also requires that the annual financial statements provide information regarding the accounting policies and measurement bases used when preparing those financial statements—in addition to detailed disclosure regarding hedge accounting for all hedge types—and fair value information for all classes of financial assets and financial liabilities.

33.4.5 Overview of disclosure of nature and extent of risks arising from financial instruments. Once the entity has complied with Statement of Financial Position and Statement of Comprehensive Income disclosures, the user needs qualitative and quantitative information regarding the different types of risks arising from all financial instruments, as well as specific quantitative information with regard to credit, liquidity, and market risks. Table 33.5 summarizes the required disclosures of risk.

Table 33.5 Nature and Extent of Risks Arising from Financial Instruments

Information to Be Disclosed	Financial Instruments Affected
Qualitative disclosures (nature and how arising)—not necessarily by instrument	Each type of risk arising from all financial assets *and* financial liabilities
Quantitative disclosures	Each type of risk arising from all financial assets *and* financial liabilities
Credit risk	Financial assets and financial liabilities—per class
Liquidity risk	All financial liabilities
Market risk	Each type of *market* risk arising from all financial assets and financial liabilities

33.5 DISCLOSURE—DETAILED/MICRO VIEW

33.5.1 Credit risk on the Statement of Financial Position. The credit risk related to loans and receivables as well as liabilities, both measured at fair value, must be disclosed.

For loans and receivables designated at fair value through profit and loss, disclose the following:

- Maximum exposure to credit risk
- Mitigation by using credit derivatives
- The change in fair value attributable to credit risk (not market risk events) as well as the methods used to achieve this specific credit risk disclosure
- The change in the fair value of credit derivatives for the current period and cumulatively since the loan was designated at fair value

For liabilities at fair value, disclose the following:

- The change in fair value attributable to credit risk (not market risk events) as well as the methods used to achieve this specific credit risk disclosure
- The difference between the current carrying amount and the required contractual payment when the liability matures

33.5.2 Reclassification of Statement of Financial Position items. Reclassification of Statement of Financial Position items must be disclosed for all financial assets when items are reclassified

- between cost, amortized cost, or fair value;
- out of fair value and the reason therefore; and
- into fair value and the reason therefore.

33.5.3 Derecognition of Statement of Financial Position items. All transfers of assets not qualifying for derecognition must be identified as follows:

- The nature of assets transferred that do not qualify for derecognition (for example, certain special-purpose vehicles for asset-backed securities)
- The nature of the risks/rewards still exposed
- The carrying amount of assets still recognized—disclose the original total and associated liabilities

33.5.4 Collateral related to items on the Statement of Financial Position. The following has to be disclosed:

- Collateral given or held for financial assets pledged and pledged assets received
- For financial assets pledged,
    - the carrying amount of assets pledged
    - the terms and conditions of assets pledged
- For financial assets received as a pledge and available to be sold,
    - the fair value of collateral held if available to be sold or repledged (even if the owner does not default)
    - the fair value of collateral sold or repledged (whether there is any obligation to return the collateral at the contract maturity)
    - terms and conditions for the use of collateral

33.5.5 Allowance for credit losses on the Statement of Financial Position. Reconciliation of changes during the current period should be provided for all impaired financial assets, by class of asset.

33.5.6 Embedded options in the Statement of Financial Position (structured liabilities with equity components using interdependent multiple embedded derivatives). Disclose the existence of features and interdependencies for all financial liabilities with multiple embedded derivatives.

33.5.7 Loans payable in default. For loans payable, where loans are in default or conditions have been breached, disclose the following:

- The carrying amount of such liabilities
- Details related to the principal, interest, sinking fund, or redemption terms
- Any remedy of default or renegotiation of loan terms that had taken place prior to the issue of the financial statements

33.5.8 Hedge accounting in the financial statements. The types of hedges and risks related to hedging activities must be disclosed as follows (table 33.6):

Table 33.6 Disclosure of Hedging Activities

Information to Be Disclosed	Financial Instruments Affected
Description of each type of hedge	All hedge types
Description of financial instruments designated as hedging instruments	Financial instruments used as hedging instruments
Fair value of financial instruments designated as hedging instruments	
Periods when cash flows will occur—when impact on profit and loss is expected	Cash flow hedges
Description of forecast transactions where hedge accounting was previously used—no longer expected to occur	
Amount recognized in equity during the period	
Amount removed from equity into profit and loss—per Statement of Comprehensive Income line item	
Amount removed from equity into initial cost/carrying amount of forecast hedged nonfinancial instrument	
Ineffectiveness recognized in profit and loss	
Gains or losses on hedging instrument	Fair value hedges
Gains or losses on hedged item attributable to the hedged risk	
Ineffectiveness recognized in profit and loss	Hedges of net investments in foreign operations

33.5.9 Fair value disclosure in the financial statements. For all classes of financial assets and financial liabilities, the following fair value financial information has to be disclosed:

- Information that is reconcilable with corresponding amounts in the Statement of Financial Position

- Methods and valuation techniques used

- Market price reference if used

- Valuation techniques using assumptions not supported by observable/quoted market prices as well as the change in fair value recognized in profit and loss, using this technique

- Effects of reasonable or possible alternatives for assumptions used in valuation techniques

- Carrying amounts and descriptions where fair value is not used, including the reasons why it is not used, the market for such instruments, and how disposals might occur

- Carrying amount and profit and loss on derecognition of instruments whose fair value could not be measured reliably

Fair value need not be disclosed where the carrying value is a reasonable approximation of fair value (for example, short-term trade receivables/payables, equities shown at cost per IAS 39, certain IFRS 4 discretionary participation contracts). However, sufficient information for users to make their own judgments should be disclosed.

33.5.10 Nature and extent of risks arising from financial instruments: qualitative disclosures.
Qualitative disclosures (the nature of risks and how they arose) do not necessarily have to be broken down by individual financial instruments. However, each type of risk arising from all financial assets and financial liabilities must be discussed, as follows:

- The exposure to risk and how risks arise
- The objectives, policies, and processes to manage risk, as well as any changes in risk management processes from the previous period
- The methods used to measure risk as well as any changes in risk measurement processes from the previous period

33.5.11 Quantitative disclosures. For each type of risk arising from all financial assets and financial liabilities, provide the following:

- Summary quantitative data as supplied internally to key management personnel
- Detail of all risk concentrations
- Further information if data provided are not representative of the risk during the period
- Credit, liquidity, and market risk information (specified below), where material

33.5.12 Credit risk: quantitative disclosures. The maximum exposure (ignoring collateral or netting outside IAS 32—credit enhancements) to credit risk must be provided for each class of financial asset and financial liability. In addition, the following information must be provided for each class of financial asset:

- A description of any collateral held
- Information regarding the credit quality of financial assets that are neither past due nor impaired
- The carrying value of assets renegotiated
- An age analysis of past due (but not impaired) items, including the fair value of any collateral held
- Analysis of impaired items, including any factors considered in determining the impairment as well as the fair value of collateral
- A discussion of the nature and carrying value of collateral acquired and recognized, including the policies for disposal or usage of collateral

33.5.13 Liquidity risk: quantitative disclosures. For all financial liabilities, the following must be provided:

- An analysis of remaining contractual maturities
- A description of the management of inherent liquidity risk

33.5.14 Market risk: quantitative disclosures. For each type of market risk arising from all financial assets and financial liabilities, the following must be disclosed:

- Sensitivity analysis, including the impact on income and equity. Value at risk (VAR) may be used, as long as objectives and key parameters are disclosed.
- Methods and assumptions used for sensitivity analysis, as well as changes from the previous period.
- Further information if data provided are not representative of risk during the period.

33.6.1 Historically, generally accepted accounting practices did not place heavy burdens of disclosure of financial risk management practices. This situation changed in the 1990s with the introduction of IAS 30 (subsequently scrapped with introduction of IFRS 7) and IAS 32 (disclosure requirements transferred to IFRS 7). IAS 30 and IAS 32, which are now largely superseded by IFRS 7, required many financial regulators to adopt a "full disclosure" approach. IAS 30 encouraged management to add comments on financial statements describing the way liquidity, solvency, and other risks associated with the operations of a bank were managed and controlled.

33.6.2 Users need information to assist them with their evaluation of an entity's financial position, financial performance, and risk management so that they are in a position to make economic decisions (based on their evaluation). Of key importance are a realistic valuation of assets, including sensitivities to future events and adverse developments, and the proper recognition of income and expenses. Equally important is the evaluation of the entire risk profile, including on- and off-balance-sheet items, capital adequacy, the capacity to withstand short-term problems, and the ability to generate additional capital.

33.6.3 Market participants also need information that enhances their understanding of the significance of on- and off-balance-sheet financial instruments to an entity's financial position, performance, and cash flows. This information is necessary to assess the amounts, timing, and certainty of future cash flows associated with such instruments. For several years, but especially in the wake of the East Asia financial crises of the late 1990s, there has been criticism regarding deficiencies in accounting practices that have resulted in the incomplete and inadequate presentation of risk-based financial information in annual financial reports. Market participants perceived the opacity of financial information as not only an official oversight, but also as the Achilles heel of effective corporate governance and market discipline.

33.6.4 Disclosure is an effective mechanism to expose financial risk management practices to market discipline. Disclosure should be sufficiently comprehensive to meet the needs of users within the constraints of what can reasonably be required. Improved transparency through better disclosure may reduce the chances of a systemic financial crisis or the effects of contagion because creditors and other market participants will be better able to distinguish between the financial circumstances that face different institutions or countries.

33.6.5 Lastly, disclosure requirements should be accompanied by active regulatory enforcement—and perhaps even fraud laws—to ensure that the information disclosed is complete, timely, and not deliberately misleading. Regulatory institutions should also have adequate enforcement capacities. IFRS 7 aims to rectify some of the remaining gaps in financial risk disclosure by adding the following requirements to the existing accounting standards:

- New disclosure requirements for loans and receivables designated as fair value through profit or loss

- Disclosure of the amount of change in a financial liability's fair value that is not attributable to changes in market conditions

- The method used to determine the effects of changes from a benchmark interest rate

- Where an impairment of a financial asset is recorded through an allowance account (for example, a provision for doubtful debts as opposed to a direct reduction to the carrying amount of the receivable), a reconciliation of changes in carrying amounts in that account during the period, for each class of financial asset

- The amount of ineffectiveness recognized in profit or loss on cash flow hedges and hedges of net investments
- Gains or losses in fair value hedges arising from remeasuring the hedging instrument and on the hedged item attributable to the hedged risk
- The net gain or loss on held-to-maturity investments, loans and receivables, and financial liabilities measured at amortized cost

33.6.6 Table 33.7 presents a summary of the information to be disclosed and the financial instruments affected by such disclosure.

Table 33.7 IFRS 7-Information to Be Disclosed and Financial Instruments Affected

A. Determination of Significance for Financial Position and Performance	
Statement of Financial Position	
Information to Be Disclosed	**Financial Instruments Affected**
Carrying Values	All financial assets and financial liabilities
Credit Risk	
Maximum exposure to credit risk	Loans and receivables designated at fair value
Mitigation by using credit derivatives	Loans and receivables designated at fair value
Fair value change of credit derivatives—current period and cumulatively since loan was designated	Derivatives
Change in fair value attributable to credit risk (not market risk events). Methods used to determine this specific credit risk disclosure.	Liabilities at fair value
Difference—carrying amount and required contractual payment at maturity	Liabilities at fair value
Reclassification	
Reclassification between cost, amortized cost and fair value	All financial assets
Reclassified out of fair value and the reason therefore	All financial assets
Reclassified into fair value and the reason therefore	All financial assets
Derecognition—Transfers of Assets Not Qualifying	
Nature of assets transferred that do not qualify for derecognition (certain special-purpose vehicles for asset-backed securities)	All financial assets
Nature—risks/rewards still exposed	All financial assets
Carrying amount of assets still recognized; disclose as original total and associated liabilities	All financial assets

Statement of Financial Position (continued)	
Information to Be Disclosed	**Financial Instruments Affected**
Collateral Given or Held	
Carrying amount of assets pledged	Financial assets pledged
Terms and conditions of assets pledged	Financial assets pledged
Fair value of collateral held if available to be sold or repledged (even if owner does not default)	Financial assets received as a pledge and available to be sold
Fair value of collateral sold or repledged—obligation to return. Terms and conditions for use of collateral.	Financial assets received as a pledge and available to be sold
Allowance for Credit Losses—Impairments in a Separate Account	
Reconciliation of changes during period	Financial assets impaired—per class
Structured Liabilities with Equity Components—Using Interdependent Multiple Embedded Derivatives	
Disclose existence of features and interdependencies	Financial liabilities with multiple embedded derivatives
Loans Payable—Defaults and Breaches	
Carrying amount	Loans payable in default
Details of principal, interest, sinking fund, or redemption terms	Loans payable in default
Any remedy of default renegotiation of loan terms prior to issue of financial statements	Loans payable in default

Statement of Comprehensive Income and Equity	
Information to Be Disclosed	**Financial Instruments Affected**
Net gains and losses	*Trading* financial assets *Designated* financial assets and liabilities held at fair value
Net gains and losses—amounts recognized and amounts removed from equity to be shown separately	Available-for-sale financial assets
Net gains and losses	All other financial assets not measured at fair value and financial liabilities measured at amortized cost (neither at fair value through profit and loss)
Total interest income and total interest expense—using effective interest rate method	Financial assets not measured at fair value and financial liabilities measured at amortized cost (neither at fair value through profit and loss)

Other Disclosures—Three Types

Information to Be Disclosed	Financial Instruments Affected
1. Accounting policies—measurement basis used in preparing financial statements	Annual financial statements
2. Hedge accounting (types of hedges and risks)	
Description of each type of hedge	All hedge types
Description of financial instruments designated as hedging instruments	Financial instruments used as hedging instruments
Fair value of financial instruments designated as hedging instruments	Financial instruments used as hedging instruments
Periods when cash flows will occur—when impact on profit and loss is expected	Cash flow hedges
Description of forecast transactions where hedge accounting previously used—no longer expected to occur	Cash flow hedges
Amount recognized in equity during the period	Cash flow hedges
Amount removed from equity into profit and loss—per Statement of Comprehensive Income line item	Cash flow hedges
Amount removed from equity into initial cost/carrying amount of forecast hedged nonfinancial instrument	Cash flow hedges
Ineffectiveness recognized in profit and loss	Cash flow hedges
Gains or losses on hedging instrument	Fair value hedges
Gains or losses on hedged item attributable to the hedged risk	Fair value hedges
Ineffectiveness recognized in profit and loss	Hedges of net investments in foreign operations
3. Fair value	
Disclosure reconcilable with corresponding amount in the Statement of Financial Position	All financial assets *and* financial liabilities—per class
Methods and valuation techniques used—market price reference if used	All financial assets *and* financial liabilities—per class
Valuation techniques using assumptions not supported by observable/quoted market prices—change in fair value recognized in profit and loss using this technique	All financial assets *and* financial liabilities—per class
Effects of reasonable/possible alternatives for assumptions used in valuation techniques	All financial assets *and* financial liabilities—per class
Carrying amounts and descriptions where fair value not used—include reasons why not used, the market for such instruments, and how disposals might occur	All financial assets *and* financial liabilities—per class
Carrying amount and profit and loss on derecognition of instruments whose fair value could not be measured reliably	Instruments whose fair value could not be measured reliably
Fair value need not be disclosed where carrying value is reasonable approximation of fair value—disclose sufficient information for users to make own judgments.	Instruments where fair value is a reasonable approximation of fair value, e.g., short-term trade receivables/payables, equities shown at cost per IAS 39, certain IFRS 4 discretionary participation contracts

B. Nature and Extent of Risks Arising from Financial Instruments

Information to Be Disclosed	Financial Instruments Affected
Qualitative Disclosures (Nature and How Arising)— Not Necessarily by Instrument	
Exposure to risk and how risks arise	Each type of risk arising from all financial assets *and* financial liabilities
Objectives, policies, processes to *manage* risk—changes from previous period	Each type of risk arising from all financial assets *and* financial liabilities
Methods used to *measure* risk—changes from previous period	Each type of risk arising from all financial assets *and* financial liabilities
Quantitative Disclosures	
Summary quantitative data as supplied internally to key management personnel	Each type of risk arising from all financial assets *and* financial liabilities
Risk concentrations	Each type of risk arising from all financial assets *and* financial liabilities
Further information if data provided are not representative of risk during period	Each type of risk arising from all financial assets *and* financial liabilities
Credit, liquidity, and market risk information as below, where material	Each type of risk arising from all financial assets *and* financial liabilities
Credit Risk	
Maximum exposure (ignoring collateral or netting outside IAS 32—credit enhancements)	All financial assets *and* financial liabilities—per class
Description of collateral held	All financial assets—per class
Information regarding credit quality of financial assets—not past due nor impaired	All financial assets—per class
Carrying value of assets renegotiated	All financial assets—per class
Age analysis of *past due* (but not impaired) items—fair value of collateral	All financial assets—per class
Analysis of impaired items—including factors considered in determining impairment—fair value of collateral	All financial assets—per class
Nature and carrying value of *collateral acquired* and recognized (or recognizable)—policies for disposal or usage	All financial assets—per class
Liquidity Risk	
Analysis of remaining contractual maturities	All financial liabilities
Description of management of inherent liquidity risk	All financial liabilities
Market Risk	
Sensitivity analysis, including the impact on income *and* equity (may use value-at-risk, disclose objectives and key parameters)	Each type of *market* risk arising from all financial assets and financial liabilities
Methods and assumptions used for sensitivity analysis—changes from previous period	Each type of *market* risk arising from all financial assets and financial liabilities
Further information if data provided are not representative of risk during period	Each type of *market* risk arising from all financial assets and financial liabilities

EXAMPLE: FINANCIAL INSTRUMENTS: DISCLOSURE AND PRESENTATION

The following extracts were adopted from a *World Bank Annual Report*.

EXAMPLE 33.1

Liquidity management

Liquid assets of the International Bank for Reconstruction and Development (IBRD) are held principally in obligations of governments and other official entities, time deposits, and other unconditional obligations of banks and financial institutions, currency and interest rate swaps, asset-backed securities, and futures and options contracts pertaining to such obligations.

Liquidity risk arises in the general funding of IBRD's activities and in the management of its financial positions. It includes the risk of being unable to fund its portfolio of assets at appropriate maturities and rates and the risk of being unable to liquidate a position in a timely manner at a reasonable price. The objective of liquidity management is to ensure the availability of sufficient cash flows to meet all of IBRD's financial commitments.

Under IBRD's liquidity management policy, aggregate liquid asset holdings should be kept at or above a specified prudential minimum. That minimum is equal to the highest consecutive six months of expected debt service obligations for the fiscal year, plus one-half of net approved loan disbursements as projected for the fiscal year. The fiscal 20X3 prudential minimum liquidity level has been set at $18 billion, unchanged from that set for fiscal 20X2. IBRD also holds liquid assets over the specified minimum to provide flexibility in timing its borrowing transactions and to meet working capital needs.

- Liquid assets may be held in three distinct subportfolios—stable, operational, and discretionary—each with different risk profiles and performance benchmarks.
- The stable portfolio is principally an investment portfolio holding the prudential minimum level of liquidity, which is set at the beginning of each fiscal year.
- The operational portfolio provides working capital for IBRD's day-to-day cash flow requirements.

Financial risk management

IBRD assumes various kinds of risk in the process of providing development banking services. Its activities can give rise to four major types of financial risk: credit risk, market risk (interest rate and exchange rate), liquidity risk, and operational risk. The major inherent risk to IBRD is country credit risk or loan portfolio risk.

Governance Structure

The risk management governance structure includes a Risk Management Secretariat supporting the Management Committee in its oversight function. The Risk Management Secretariat was established in fiscal 20X1 to support the Management Committee, particularly in the coordination of different aspects of risk management and in connection with risks that cut across functional areas.

For financial risk management, there is an Asset/Liability Management Committee chaired by the chief financial officer. The Asset/Liability Management Committee makes recommendations in the areas of financial policy, the adequacy and allocation of risk capital, and oversight of financial reporting. Two subcommittees that report to the Asset/Liability Management Committee are the Market Risk and Currency Management Subcommittee and the Credit Risk Subcommittee.

The **Market Risk and Currency Management** Subcommittee develops and monitors the policies under which market and commercial credit risks faced by IBRD are measured, reported, and managed. The subcommittee also monitors compliance with policies governing commercial credit exposure and currency management. Specific areas of activity include establishing guidelines for limiting Statement of Financial Position and market risks, the use of derivative instruments, setting investment guidelines, and monitoring matches between assets and their funding. The Credit Risk Subcommittee monitors the measurement and reporting of country credit risk and reviews the impact on the provision for losses on loans and guarantees of any changes in risk ratings of borrowing member countries or movements between the accrual and nonaccrual portfolios.

Country credit risk, the primary risk faced by IBRD, is identified, measured, and monitored by the Country Credit Risk Department, led by the chief credit officer. This unit is independent from IBRD's business units. In addition to continuously reviewing the creditworthiness of IBRD borrowers, this department is responsible for assessing loan portfolio risk, determining the adequacy of provisions for losses on loans and guarantees, and monitoring borrowers that are vulnerable to crises in the near term.

Market risks, liquidity risks, and counterparty credit risks in IBRD's financial operations are identified, measured, and monitored by the Corporate Finance Department, which is independent from IBRD's business units. The Corporate Finance Department works with IBRD's financial managers, who are responsible for the day-to-day management of these risks, to establish and document processes that facilitate, control, and monitor risk. These processes are built on a foundation of initial identification and measurement of risks by each of the business units.

The processes and procedures by which IBRD manages its risk profile continually evolve as its activities change in response to market, credit, product, and other developments. The executive directors, particularly the Audit Committee members, periodically review trends in IBRD's risk profiles and performance, as well as any significant developments in risk management policies and controls.

Market Risk

IBRD faces risks that result from market movements, primarily interest and exchange rates. In comparison to country credit risk, IBRD's exposure to market risks is small. IBRD has an integrated asset/liability management framework to flexibly assess and hedge market risks associated with the characteristics of the products in IBRD's portfolios.

The objective of asset/liability management for IBRD is to ensure adequate funding for each product at the most attractive available cost, and to manage the currency composition, maturity profile and interest rate sensitivity characteristics of the portfolio of liabilities supporting each lending product in accordance with the particular requirements for that product and within prescribed risk parameters. The current-value information is used in the asset/liability management process.

Use of Derivatives

As part of its asset/liability management process, IBRD employs derivatives to manage and align the characteristics of its assets and liabilities. IBRD uses derivative instruments to adjust the interest rate repricing characteristics of specific Statement of Financial Position assets and liabilities, or groups of assets and liabilities with similar repricing characteristics, and to modify the currency composition of net assets and liabilities. Table 33.8 details the current-value information of each loan product, the liquid asset portfolio, and the debt allocated to fund these assets.

Table 33.8 Financial Instrument Portfolios

In millions of U.S. dollars

	At June 30, 20X2			At June 30, 20X1		
	Carrying Value	Contractual Yield	Current Value Mark	Carrying Value	Contractual Yield	Current Value Mark
Loans[a]	$116,240	4.09%	$6,353	$121,589	5.06%	$4,865
Variable-Rate Multicurrency Pool Loans	22,728	4.62	2,447	28,076	5.03	1,766
Single-Currency Pool Loans	20,490	6.95	1,682	25,585	8.12	1,987
Variable-Spread Loans	36,424	1.62	44	33,031	2.44	54
Fixed-Rate Single-Currency Loans	15,315	6.45	1,756	15,873	6.59	969
Special Structural and Sector Adjustment Loans	8,454	3.33	8	11,505	4.22	15
Fixed-Spread Loans	12,414	3.18	401	7,017	4.00	57
Other Fixed-Rate Loans	415	7.92	15	502	7.86	17
	At June 30, 20X2			At June 30, 20X1		
	Carrying Value	Contractual Yield	Current Value Mark	Carrying Value	Contractual Yield	Current Value Mark
Liquid Asset Portfolio[e,f]	**$26,423**	**1.35%**		**$24,886**	**2.11%**	
Borrowings (including swaps)[e]	**$107,845**	**2.75%**	**$4,946**	**$114,261**	**3.61%**	**$3,499**
Variable-Rate Multicurrency Pools	13,615	3.96	2,624	17,875	4.09	1,780
Single-Currency Pools	12,857	5.68	1,046	16,996	7.03	1,260
Variable-Spread	25,151	1.05	(186)	22,106	1.96	(229)
Fixed-Rate Single Currency	12,400	6.13	1,451	13,727	5.83	774
Special Structural and Sector Adjustment	8,012	1.04	(22)	11,916	1.79	(74)
Fixed-Spread	7,146	2.61	133	5,055	3.13	(85)
Other Debt	28,664	1.42	(100)	26,586	2.27	73

a. Contractual yield is presented before the application of interest waivers.
b. Excludes fixed-rate single-currency pool loans, which have been classified in other fixed-rate loans.
c. Includes fixed-rate single-currency loans for which the rate had not yet been fixed at fiscal year-end.
d. Includes loans with nonstandard terms.
e. Carrying amounts and contractual yields are on a basis that includes accrued interest and any unamortized amounts, but does not include the effects of applying FAS 133.
f. The liquid asset portfolio is carried and reported at market value and excludes investment assets associated with certain other postemployment benefits.
g. Includes amounts not yet allocated at June 30, 20X2, and June 30, 20X1.

Interest Rate Risk

There are two main sources of potential interest rate risk to IBRD. The first is the interest rate sensitivity associated with the net spread between the rate IBRD earns on its assets and the cost of borrowings, which fund those assets. The second is the interest rate sensitivity of the income earned from funding a portion of IBRD assets with equity. In general, lower nominal interest rates result in lower lending rates, which, in turn, reduce the nominal earnings on IBRD's equity. In addition, as the loan portfolio shifts from pool loans to LIBOR-based loans, the sensitivity of IBRD's income to changes in market interest rates will increase.

Exchange Rate Risk

To minimize exchange rate risk in a multicurrency environment, IBRD matches its borrowing obligations in any one currency (after swap activities) with assets in the same currency. In addition, IBRD's policy is to minimize the exchange rate sensitivity of its equity-to-loans ratio. It carries out this policy by undertaking currency conversions periodically to align the currency composition of its equity to that of its outstanding loans. This policy is designed to minimize the impact of market rate fluctuations on the equity-to-loans ratio, thereby preserving IBRD's ability to better absorb potential losses from arrears, regardless of the market environment.

Operational Risk

Operational risk is the potential for loss resulting from inadequate or failed internal processes or systems, human factors, or external events. Operational risk includes business disruption and system failure; transaction processing failures; and failures in execution of legal, fiduciary, and agency responsibilities. IBRD, like all financial institutions, is exposed to many types of operational risks. IBRD attempts to mitigate operational risk by maintaining a system of internal controls that is designed to keep that risk at appropriate levels in view of the financial strength of IBRD and the characteristics of the activities and markets in which IBRD operates.

Fair Value of Financial Instruments

Under the current-value basis of reporting, IBRD carries all of its financial assets and liabilities at estimated values. Under the reported basis, IBRD carries its investments and derivatives, as defined by FAS 133, on a fair value basis. These derivatives include certain features in debt instruments that, for accounting purposes, are separately valued and accounted for as either assets or liabilities. When possible, fair value is determined by quoted market prices. If quoted market prices are not available, then fair value is based on discounted cash flow models using market estimates of cash flows and discount rates.

All the financial models used for input to IBRD's financial statements are subject to both internal and external verification and review by qualified personnel. These models use market-sourced inputs, such as interest rate yield curves, exchange rates, and option volatilities. Selection of these inputs may involve some judgment. Imprecision in estimating these factors, and changes in assumptions, can affect net income and IBRD's financial position as reported in the Statement of Financial Position.

Table 33.9 Investments and Borrowings
In millions of U.S. dollars

	20X2	20X1
INVESTMENTS – TRADING PORTFOLIO		
Options and futures		
■ Long position	$9,590	$6,300
■ Short position	222	976
■ Credit exposure due to potential nonperformance by counterparties	*	1
Currency swaps		
■ Credit exposure due to potential nonperformance by counterparties	92	51
Interest rate swaps		
■ Notional principal	4,575	10,705
■ Credit exposure due to potential nonperformance by counterparties	50	8
BORROWING PORTFOLIO		
Currency swaps		
■ Credit exposure due to potential nonperformance by counterparties	6,949	2,092
Interest rate swaps		
■ Notional principal	82,112	82,533
■ Credit exposure due to potential nonperformance by counterparties	5,079	3,084

Chapter Thirty Four

Operating Segments (IFRS 8)

34.1 OBJECTIVE

IFRS 8 establishes principles for reporting information by business segments, that is, information about the different business activities of an entity and the different economic environments in which it operates. This helps users make more informed judgments by more completely describing the entity's past performance and risks and returns.

IFRS 8 requires identification of operating segments on the basis of internal reports that top management uses when determining the allocation of resources to a segment and assessing its performance.

34.2 SCOPE OF THE STANDARD

This standard applies to all individual entities (or consolidated financial statements with a parent) whose equity or debt securities are traded in a public securities market or that are in the process of issuing such instruments. Other entities that voluntarily choose disclosure under this standard should comply fully with the requirements of IFRS 8.

A parent entity is required to present segment information only on the basis of its consolidated financial statements. If a subsidiary's own securities are publicly traded, it will present segment information in its own separate financial report. (Financial statement disclosure of equity information for associated investments would mirror this requirement.)

34.3 KEY CONCEPTS

34.3.1 An **operating segment** is a component of an entity

- that engages in business activities from which it may earn revenues and incur expenses,
- whose operating results are regularly reviewed by the entity's chief operating decision maker for allocating resources to the segment and assessing its performance, and
- for which discrete financial information is available.

Business activities include revenues and expenses from transactions with other components of the same entity.

34.3.2 A reportable segment is an operating segment that meets any of the following quantitative thresholds:

- Its reported **revenue**—including both sales to external customers and intersegment sales or transfers—is 10 percent or more of the combined revenue (internal and external) of all operating segments.

- Its absolute reported **profit** is 10 percent or more of the combined reported profit of all operating segments that did not report a loss, or its absolute reported **loss** is 10 percent or more of the combined reported loss of all operating segments that reported a loss.

- Its **assets** are 10 percent or more of the combined assets of all operating segments.

34.4 ACCOUNTING TREATMENT

34.4.1 Segment information should conform to the accounting policies adopted for preparing and presenting the consolidated financial statements.

34.4.2 The amount of each segment item reported is the measure reported to the chief operating decision maker for the purposes of allocating resources to the segment and assessing its performance.

34.4.3 An entity must explain the measurements of segment profit or loss, segment assets, and segment liabilities for each reportable segment. At a minimum, an entity must disclose the nature of any differences between the following:

- Basis of accounting for any transactions between reportable segments

- Measurements of the reportable segments' profits or losses and the entity's profit or loss

- Measurements of the reportable segments' assets and the entity's assets

- Measurements of the reportable segments' liabilities and the entity's liabilities

- Accounting periods in the measurement methods used to determine reported segment profit or loss and the effect of those differences on the measure of segment profit or loss

- Allocations to reportable segments—for example, if the entity allocates depreciation expense to a segment without allocating the related depreciable assets to that segment

34.4.4 Operating segments often exhibit similar long-term financial performance if they have similar economic characteristics. For example, similar long-term average gross margins would be expected for two operating segments with similar economic characteristics. Two or more operating segments may be aggregated into a single operating segment for disclosure purposes if aggregation is consistent with the core principle of IFRS 8, the segments have similar economic characteristics, and the segments are similar in each of the following respects:

- Products and services

- Production processes

- The type or class of customer for their products and services

- The methods used to distribute their products or provide their services

- The nature of the regulatory environment (for example, banking, insurance, or public utilities)

34.4.5 Decide whether segments are reportable segments. If the total revenue from external customers for all *reportable* segments combined is less than 75 percent of the total entity revenue, additional reportable segments should be identified until the 75 percent level is reached.

34.4.6 Operating segments that do not meet any of the quantitative thresholds may be considered reportable, and separately disclosed, if management believes that information about the segment would be useful to users of the financial statements.

34.4.7 Small segments might be combined as one if they share a substantial number of factors that define a business or geographical segment, or they might be combined with a similar significant reportable segment. If they are not separately reported or combined, they are included as an unallocated reconciling item.

34.4.8 A segment that is not judged to be a reportable segment in the current period should nonetheless be reported if it is significant for decision-making purposes (for example, future market strategy).

34.5   PRESENTATION AND DISCLOSURE

34.5.1 An entity must disclose the factors used to identify its reportable segments, including

- the basis of organization (products and services, geographic areas, regulatory environments, or a combination thereof);
- whether operating segments have been aggregated; and
- types of products and services from which each reportable segment derives its revenues.

34.5.2 An entity must report

- a measure of profit or loss and total assets for each reportable segment, and
- a measure of liabilities for each reportable segment if such an amount is regularly provided to the chief operating decision maker.

34.5.3 An entity must also disclose the following about each reportable segment if the specified amounts are included in the measure of segment profit or loss reviewed by the chief operating decision maker, or are otherwise regularly provided to the chief operating decision maker:

- Revenues from external customers
- Revenues from transactions with other operating segments of the same entity
- Interest revenue
- Interest expense
- Depreciation and amortization
- Material items of income
- The entity's interest in the profit or loss of associates and joint ventures accounted for by the equity method
- Income tax expense
- Material noncash items other than depreciation and amortization

EXAMPLE 34.1

Hollier Inc. is a diversified entity that operates in nine operating segments organized around differences in products and geographical areas. The following financial information relates to the year ending June 30, 20X5.

	Total Sales	External Sales	Total Profit	Total Assets
Nature of Business				
Beer	2,249	809	631	4,977
Beverages	1,244	543	-131	3,475
Hotels	4,894	4,029	714	5,253
Retail	3,815	3,021	-401	1,072
Packaging	7,552	5,211	1,510	8,258
Totals	19,754	13,613	2,323	23,035
Geographical Areas				
Finland	7,111	6,841	1,536	9,231
France	1,371	1,000	-478	5,001
United Kingdom	3,451	2,164	494	3,667
Australia	7,821	3,608	771	5,136
Totals	19,754	13,613	2,323	23,035

EXPLANATION

The **first** step in identifying the reportable segments of the entity is to identify those which represent at least 10 percent of any of the entity's sales, profit, or assets.

	Exceeds 10 % of			Qualify
	Total Sales = $ 1975	Total Profit / Absolute Loss = $ 232	Total Assets = $ 2303	
Nature of Business				
Beer	Yes	Yes	Yes	Yes
Beverages	No	No	Yes	Yes
Hotels	Yes	Yes	Yes	Yes
Retail	Yes	No	No	Yes
Packaging	Yes	Yes	Yes	Yes
Geographical Areas				
Finland	Yes	Yes	Yes	Yes
France	No	No	Yes	Yes
United Kingdom	Yes	Yes	Yes	Yes
Australia	Yes	Yes	Yes	Yes

The **second** step would be to check if total external revenue attributable to reportable segments constitutes at least 75 percent of the total consolidated or entity revenue of $13,613,000.

As all operating segments qualify as reportable segments, the external revenue requirement of 75 percent is met.

If that had not been the case, IFRS 8 would have required that additional operating segments be identified as reportable even if they do not meet the 10 percent thresholds in step one.

Chapter Thirty Five

Interim Financial Reporting (IAS 34)

35.1 OBJECTIVE

Interim financial information enhances the accuracy of forecasting earnings and share prices. IAS 34 is concerned with the following for interim financial reports:

- Minimum content
- Principles for recognition and measurement

35.2 SCOPE OF THE STANDARD

This standard applies to all entities that publish interim financial reports covering a period shorter than a full financial year (for example, a half year or a quarter). This standard applies whether such reporting is **required** by law or regulations or if the entity **voluntarily** publishes such reports.

IAS 34 defines and prescribes the minimum content of an interim financial report, including disclosures, and identifies the accounting recognition and measurement principles that should be applied in an interim financial report.

35.3 KEY CONCEPTS

35.3.1 An **interim financial report** is a financial report that contains either a complete or condensed set of financial statements for a period shorter than an entity's full financial year.

35.3.2 A **condensed Statement of Financial Position** (balance sheet) is produced at the end of an interim period with comparative balances provided for the end of the prior full financial year.

35.3.3 A **condensed Statement of Comprehensive Income** (income statement) is produced for the current interim period and cumulative for the current financial year to date, with comparatives for the comparable interim periods of the prior financial year. An entity that publishes interim financial reports quarterly would, for example, prepare four Statements of Comprehensive Income in its third quarter: one for the nine months cumulatively since the beginning of the year, one for the third quarter only, and comparative Statements of Comprehensive Income for the exact comparable periods of the prior financial year.

35.3.4 A **condensed cash flow statement** is a cumulative statement for the current financial year to date, and a comparative statement for the comparable interim period of the prior financial year.

35.3.5 **Condensed changes in equity statements** are cumulative for the current financial year to date and comparative for the comparable interim period of the prior financial year.

35.4   ACCOUNTING TREATMENT

35.4.1 An interim financial report includes the following:

- Condensed Statement of Financial Position (balance sheet)
- Condensed Statement of Comprehensive Income (income statement)
- Condensed cash flow statement
- Condensed changes in equity
- Selected explanatory notes

35.4.2 Following are the required **form and content** of an interim financial report:

- It must include at a minimum
    - each of the headings and subtotals that were included in the most recent annual financial statements, and
    - selected explanatory notes required by IAS 34.
- Basic and diluted earnings per share must be presented on the face of the Statement of Comprehensive Income.
- A parent should prepare the report on a consolidated basis.

35.4.3 An entity should apply the same **accounting policies** in its interim financial statements as in its latest annual financial statements, except for accounting policy changes made subsequent to the last annual financial statements.

35.4.4 The frequency of interim reporting (for example, semiannually or quarterly) does not affect the **measurement** of an entity's annual results. Measurements for interim reporting purposes are therefore made on a year-to-date basis, the so-called **discrete method.**

35.4.5 **Revenues** received seasonally, cyclically, or occasionally should not be recognized or deferred as of an interim date if recognition or deferral would not be appropriate at the end of the entity's financial year. For example, an entity that earns all its revenue in the first half of a year does not defer any of that revenue until the second half of the year.

35.4.6 **Costs** incurred unevenly during the financial year should not be recognized or deferred as of the interim date if recognition or deferral would not be appropriate at the end of the financial year. To illustrate, the cost of a planned major periodic maintenance that is expected to occur late in the year is not anticipated for interim reporting purposes unless the entity has a legal or constructive obligation. Similarly, development costs incurred are not deferred in an earlier period in the hope that they will meet the asset recognition criteria in a later period.

35.4.7 Measurements in both annual and interim financial reports are often based on reasonable estimates, but the preparation of interim financial reports generally will require a greater **use of estimation methods** than annual financial reports. For example, full stock-taking and valuation procedures cannot be realistically carried out for inventories at interim dates.

35.4.8 A change in accounting policy should be reflected by **restating** the financial statements of prior interim periods of the current financial year **and** the comparable interim periods of prior years in terms of IAS 8 (if practicable).

35.5 PRESENTATION AND DISCLOSURE

35.5.1 Selected **explanatory notes** in interim financial reports are intended to provide an update since the last annual financial statements. The following should be included at a minimum:

- A statement that accounting policies have been applied consistently or a description of any changes made since the last annual financial statements

- Explanatory comments about seasonality or cyclicality of operations

- Nature and amount of items affecting assets, liabilities, equity, net income, or cash flows that are unusual because of their nature, size, or incidence

- Changes in estimates of amounts reported in prior interim periods of the current year or amounts reported in prior years

- Changes in outstanding debt or equity, including uncorrected defaults or breaches of a debt covenant

- Dividends paid

- Revenue and results of business segments or geographical segments, whichever is the primary format of segment reporting

- Events occurring after the Statement of Financial Position date

- Purchases or disposals of subsidiaries and long-term investments, restructurings, and discontinued operations

- Changes in contingent liabilities or assets

- The fact that the interim financial report complies with IAS 34

35.5.2 If an estimate of an amount reported in an interim period is changed significantly during the **final interim period** of the financial year but a separate financial report is not published for that final interim period, the nature and amount should be disclosed in a note to the annual financial statements.

35.6 FINANCIAL ANALYSIS AND INTERPRETATION

35.6.1 Because the tax expense in interim financial statements should be based on the expected effective tax rate for the entity for the entire financial year, the disclosed tax expense might provide interesting clues as to management's assessment of prospects for the remainder of the financial year.

- For example, if the effective tax rate is low, this could indicate an expectation of a greater proportion of profits originating in low-tax-rate jurisdictions.

- Alternatively, if capital gains are taxed at lower rates than other gains, it might indicate an anticipated higher level of fixed asset disposals.

EXAMPLE: INTERIM FINANCIAL REPORTING

EXAMPLE 35.1

The following three basic recognition and measurement principles are stated in IAS 34:

A. An entity should apply the same accounting policies in its interim financial statements as it applies in its annual financial statements, except for accounting policy changes made after the date of the most recent annual financial statements that are to be reflected in the next annual financial statements. However, the frequency of an entity's reporting (annually, semiannually, or quarterly) should not affect the measurement of its annual results. To achieve that objective, measurements for interim reporting purposes should be made on a year-to-date basis.

B. Revenues that are received seasonally, cyclically, or occasionally within a financial year should not be anticipated or deferred as of an interim date if anticipation or deferral would not be appropriate at the end of the entity's financial year.

C. Costs that are incurred unevenly during an entity's financial year should be anticipated or deferred for interim reporting purposes if, and only if, it is also appropriate to anticipate or defer that type of cost at the end of the financial year.

EXPLANATION

Table 35.1 illustrates the practical application of the above-mentioned recognition and measurement principles.

Table 35.1 Principles and Application of IAS 34

Principles and Issues	Practical Application
A. Same accounting policies as for annual financial statements	
A devaluation in the functional currency against other currencies occurred just before the end of the first quarter of the year. This necessitated the recognition of foreign exchange losses on the restatement of unhedged liabilities, which are repayable in foreign currencies.	In the interim financial statements, these losses are recognized as expenses in the first quarter in accordance with IAS 21.
Indications are that the functional currency will regain its position against the other currencies by the end of the second quarter of the year. Management is reluctant to recognize these losses as expenses in the interim financial report and wants to defer recognition, based on the expectation of the functional currency. Management hopes that the losses will be neutralized by the end of the next quarter and wants to smooth the earnings rather than recognize losses in one quarter and profits in the next.	The losses are recognized as expenses on a year-to-date basis to achieve the objective of applying the same accounting policies for both the interim and annual financial statements.

Principles and Issues	Practical Application
B. Deferral of revenues	

An ice cream manufacturing corporation recently had its shares listed on the local stock exchange. Management is worried about publishing the first quarter's interim results because the entity normally earns most of its profits in the third and fourth quarters (during the summer months).	It is a phenomenon in the business world that some entities consistently earn more revenues in certain interim periods of a financial year than in other interim periods, for example, seasonal revenues of retailers.
Statistics show that the revenue pattern is more or less as follows:	IAS 34 requires that such revenues are recognized when they occur, because anticipation or deferral would not be appropriate at the Statement of Financial Position date. Revenue of $254,000 is therefore reported in the first quarter.

First quarter   = 10 percent of total annual revenue

Second quarter = 15 percent of total annual revenue

Third quarter   = 40 percent of total annual revenue

Fourth quarter = 35 percent of total annual revenue

During the first quarter of the current year, total revenue amounted to $254,000. However, management plans to report one-fourth of the projected annual revenue in its interim financial report, calculated as follows:

$254,000 \div 0.10 \times 1/4 = \$635,000$

C. Deferral of expenses	

An entity that reports quarterly has an operating loss carry forward of $10,000 for income tax purposes at the start of the current financial year, for which a deferred tax asset has not been recognized.	According to IAS 34, §30(c), the interim period income tax expense is accrued using the tax rate that would be applicable to expected total annual earnings, that is, the weighted average annual *effective* income tax rate applied to the pretax income of the interim period.
The entity earns $10,000 in the first quarter of the current year and expects to earn $10,000 in each of the three remaining quarters. Excluding the carry forward, the estimated average annual income tax rate is expected to be 40 percent. Tax expense for the year would be calculated as follows:	This is consistent with the basic concept set out in IAS 34, §28 that the same accounting recognition and measurement principles should be applied in an interim financial report as are applied in annual financial statements. Income taxes are assessed on an annual basis. Interim period income tax expense is calculated by applying to an interim period's pretax income the tax rate that would be applicable to expected total annual earnings, that is, the weighted average annual *effective* income tax rate.

40 percent $\times$ (40,000 − 10,000 tax loss) = $12,000

The effective tax rate based on the annual earnings would then be 30 percent (12,000 ÷ 40,000).

The question is whether the tax charge for interim financial reporting should be based on actual or effective annual rates, which are illustrated below:

This rate would reflect a blend of the progressive tax rate structure expected to be applicable to the full year's earnings.

This particular issue is dealt with in IAS 34, Appendix B §22.

Income Tax Payable		
Quarter	Actual Rate	Effective Rate
First	0*	3,000
Second	4,000	3,000
Third	4,000	3,000
Fourth	4,000	3,000
	$12,000	$12,000

* The full benefit of the tax loss carried forward is used in the first quarter.

Chapter Thirty Six

Accounting and Reporting by Retirement Benefit Plans (IAS 26)

36.1 OBJECTIVE

IAS 26 prescribes the information that a retirement benefit plan should include in its financial statements for all participants. The standard specifically distinguishes between the information requirements for defined benefit and defined contribution plans.

36.2 SCOPE OF THE STANDARD

This standard should be applied in retirement benefit plans' financial statements that are directed to all participants. The standard's requirements apply to both defined contribution and defined benefit plans that are

- funded by a separate trust or from general revenues,
- managed by an insurance company,
- sponsored by parties other than employers, and
- documented by formal or informal agreements.

36.3 KEY CONCEPTS

36.3.1 **Retirement benefit plans** include both defined contribution plans and defined benefit plans.

36.3.2 **Defined contribution plans** are retirement benefit plans under which amounts to be paid upon retirement are determined by contributions to a fund together with investment earnings thereon. An employer's obligation is usually discharged by its contributions. An actuary's advice is therefore not normally required.

36.3.3 **Defined benefit plans** are retirement benefit plans under which amounts to be paid upon retirement are determined by a formula that is usually based on employees' earnings, years of service, or both. Periodic advice of an actuary is required to assess the financial condition of the plan, review the assumptions, and recommend future contribution levels. An employer is responsible for restoring the level of the plan's funds when deficits occur in order to provide the agreed benefits to current and former employees. Some plans contain characteristics of both defined contribution plans and defined benefit plans. Such hybrid plans are considered to be defined benefit plans for the purposes of IAS 26.

36.3.4 Participants are the members of a retirement benefit plan and others who are entitled to benefits under the plan's distinctive characteristics. The participants are interested in the activities of the plan because those activities directly affect the level of their future benefits. Participants are interested in knowing whether contributions have been received by the plan and whether proper control has been exercised to protect the rights of beneficiaries.

36.3.5 Net assets available for benefits are the assets of a plan less liabilities other than the actuarial present value of promised retirement benefits.

36.3.6 Actuarial present value of promised retirement benefits is the present value of the expected payments by a retirement benefit plan to existing and past employees, attributable to the service already rendered.

36.3.7 Vested benefits are benefits the rights to which—under the conditions of a retirement benefit plan—are not conditional on continued employment.

36.4   ACCOUNTING TREATMENT

Defined Contributions Plans

36.4.1 The **financial statements of a defined contribution plan** should contain a statement of net assets available for benefits and a description of the funding policy.

36.4.2 The following principles apply to the valuation of assets owned by the plan:

- Investments should be carried at fair value.
- If carried at other than fair value, the investments' fair value should be disclosed.

Defined Benefit Plans

36.4.3 The financial statements of a defined benefit plan should contain either

- a statement that shows the net assets available for benefits, the actuarial present value of retirement benefits (distinguishing between vested and nonvested benefits), and the resulting excess or deficit; or
- a statement of net assets available for benefits including either a **note** disclosing the actuarial present value of retirement benefits (distinguishing between vested and nonvested benefits) or a **reference** to this information in an accompanying report.

36.4.4 Actuarial valuations are normally obtained every three years. The present value of the expected payments by a defined benefit plan can be calculated and reported using either current salary levels or projected salary levels up to the time of the participants' retirement.

36.4.5 Retirement benefit plan investments should be carried at fair value. In the case of marketable securities, fair value is market value. If the plan holds investments for which an estimate of fair value is not possible, the financial statements should disclose why fair value is not used.

36.4.6 The **financial statements** should explain the relationship between the actuarial present value of the promised retirement benefits and the net assets available for benefits, as well as the policy for the funding of the promised benefits.

36.5   PRESENTATION AND DISCLOSURE

36.5.1 A **description of the plan** which requires information such as the names of the employers and the employee groups covered, number of participants receiving benefits, type of plan, and other details.

36.5.2 **Policies** including

- significant accounting policies,
- investment policies, and
- the funding policy.

36.5.3 The **statement of net assets** available for benefits showing the amount of assets available to pay retirement benefits that are expected to become payable in future. It includes

- assets at year-end, suitably classified;
- basis of valuation of assets;
- a note stating that an estimate of the fair value of plan investments is not possible, if any plan investments being held cannot be valued at fair market price;
- details of any single investment exceeding either 5 percent of net assets available for benefits or 5 percent of any class or type of security;
- details of any investment in the employer's securities; and
- liabilities other than the actuarial present value of promised retirement benefits.

36.5.4 A **statement of changes in net assets** available for benefits, which includes

- investment income,
- employer contributions,
- employee contributions,
- other income,
- benefits paid or payable (analyzed per category of benefit),
- administrative expenses,
- other expenses,
- taxes on plan income,
- profits and losses on disposal of investments and changes in value of investments, and
- transfers from and to other plans.

36.5.5 Actuarial information (for defined benefit plans only), which includes

- the actuarial present value of promised retirement benefits, based on the amount of benefits promised under the terms of the plan, on service rendered to date, and on either current salary levels or projected salary levels;

- description of main actuarial assumptions;

- method used to calculate the actuarial present value of promised retirement benefits; and

- date of the most recent actuarial valuation.

36.6 FINANCIAL ANALYSIS AND INTERPRETATION

See chapter 24 for a discussion of analytical issues related to retirement benefit funds.

EXAMPLE: ACCOUNTING AND REPORTING BY RETIREMENT BENEFIT PLANS

EXAMPLE 36.1

The financial statements of a retirement benefit plan should contain a statement of changes in net assets available for benefits.

EXPLANATION

The following extract was taken from the *World Bank Group: Staff Retirement Plan–2004 Annual Report*. It contains statements that comply with the IAS 26 requirements in all material respects.

Statements of Changes in Net Assets Available for Benefits (in thousands)		
	Year ended December 31	
	2004	2003
Investment Income (Loss)		
Net appreciation in fair value of investments	881,325	1,348,382
Interest and dividends	262,406	265,212
Less: investment management fees	(45,193)	(43,618)
Net investment income	1,098,538	1,569,976
Contributions (Note C)		
Contributions by participants	77,224	76,280
Contributions by employer	184,228	85,027
Total contributions	261,452	161,307
Total additions	1,359,990	1,731,283
Benefit Payments		
Pensions	(293,908)	(271,399)
Commutation payments	(41,218)	(32,099)
Contributions, withdrawal benefits, and interest paid to former participants on withdrawal	(28,312)	(23,586)
Lump-sum death benefits	(622)	(1,671)
Termination grants	(2,375)	(3,048)
Total benefit payments	(366,435)	(331,803)
Administrative Expenses		
Custody and consulting fees	(4,516)	(4,985)
Others	(8,083)	(5,902)
Total administrative expenses	(12,599)	(10,887)
Net increase	980,956	1,388,593
Net Assets Available for Benefits		
Beginning of year	10,276,705	8,888,112
End of year	**11,257,661**	**10,276,705**

Chapter Thirty Seven

Insurance Contracts (IFRS 4)

37.1   OBJECTIVE

Accounting practices for insurance contracts have been diverse, often differing from practices in other sectors. The objective of IFRS 4 is to address improvements to accounting for insurance contracts by insurers and require disclosure that identifies and explains the amounts related to insurance contracts. It helps users of financial statements to understand the amount, timing, and uncertainty of future cash flows from insurance contracts.

37.2   SCOPE OF THE STANDARD

Entities should apply this IFRS to

- ▪ insurance contracts (including reinsurance contracts) that it issues,
- ▪ reinsurance contracts that it holds, and
- ▪ financial instruments that it issues with a discretionary participation feature.

It does *not* apply to financial assets and financial liabilities within the scope of IAS 39.

This IFRS does *not* address

- ▪ accounting aspects related to other assets and liabilities of an insurer,
- ▪ product warranties,
- ▪ residual value guarantee embedded in a finance lease, or
- ▪ financial guarantees.

IFRS 4 is the first international standard to deal with insurance contracts. It is, therefore, a stepping-stone to be used until all relevant conceptual and practical questions have been investigated.

37.3   KEY CONCEPTS

37.3.1 An **insurance contract** is a contract under which one party (the insurer) accepts significant insurance risk from another party (the insured).

37.3.2 **Insurance liability** is an insurer's net contractual obligations under an insurance contract.

37.3.3 **Insurance risk** is risk, other than financial risk, transferred from the insured to the insurer. **Financial risk** is the risk of a possible future change in one or more of a specified interest rate, financial instrument price, commodity price, foreign exchange rate, index of prices or rates, credit rating, credit index, or other variable.

37.3.4 An **insured event** is an uncertain future event that is covered by an insurance contract and that creates insurance risk.

37.3.5 An **insurer** is the party that has the obligation under an insurance contract to compensate a policyholder if an **insured event** occurs.

37.3.6 A **policyholder** is a party that has a right to compensation under an insurance contract if an **insured event** occurs. A **cedant** is a policyholder under a reinsurance contract.

37.3.7 **Guaranteed benefits** are payments or other benefits to which a particular policyholder or investor has an unconditional right that is not subject to the contractual discretion of the issuer. A **guaranteed element** is an obligation to pay guaranteed benefits, including guaranteed benefits covered by a contract with a discretionary participation feature.

37.3.8 **Fair value** is the amount for which an asset could be exchanged or a liability settled between knowledgeable, willing parties in an arm's-length transaction.

37.4   ACCOUNTING TREATMENT

37.4.1 IFRS 4 provides a temporary exemption from the IAS 8 hierarchy—the main reason why the IFRS has been issued. It exempts an insurer from applying those criteria to its accounting policies for

- insurance contracts that it issues (including related acquisition costs and related intangible assets), and
- reinsurance contracts that it holds.

37.4.2 Insurers must, however,

- not recognize as a liability any provisions for possible future claims that arise from insurance contracts that are not in existence at the reporting date, and
- remove an insurance liability from its Statement of Financial Position only when the obligation is discharged.

37.4.3 An insurer should assess at each reporting date whether or not its recognized **insurance liabilities** are adequate, using current estimates of future cash flows under its insurance contracts.

37.4.4 A **liability adequacy test** should consider current estimates of all contractual and related cash flows and recognize the entire deficiency in profit or loss. Where a liability adequacy test is not required by its accounting policies, the insurer should

- determine the carrying amount of the relevant insurance liabilities less the carrying amount of related deferred acquisition costs, as well as intangible assets; and
- determine whether the amount is less than the carrying amount that would be required if the relevant insurance liabilities were within the scope of IAS 37, and if so, account for the difference in profit or loss.

37.4.5 If a cedant's **reinsurance asset is impaired,** the cedant should reduce its carrying amount accordingly and recognize that impairment loss in profit or loss. A reinsurance asset is impaired if

- there is objective evidence that the cedant might not receive all amounts due to it under the terms of the contract, or

- an event has a measurable impact on the amounts that the cedant will receive from the re-insurer.

37.4.6 An insurer might **change its accounting policies** for insurance contracts if the change makes the financial statements more relevant (but not less reliable) to the users' economic decision-making needs. Greater reliability should not be at the expense of relevance.

37.4.7 When an insurer changes its accounting policies for insurance liabilities, it might **reclassify some or all of its financial assets at fair value** through the Statement of Comprehensive Income (profit and loss account).

37.4.8 The following principles apply when considering a change in accounting policies:

- **Current market interest rates.** An insurer is permitted to change its accounting policies so that it remeasures **designated insurance liabilities** to reflect current market interest rates. Changes in those liabilities must be recognized in profit or loss. This allows an insurer to change its accounting policies for designated liabilities without applying those policies consistently to all similar liabilities, which IAS 8 would otherwise require. If an insurer designates liabilities for this election, it should continue to apply current market interest rates consistently in all periods to all these liabilities until they are extinguished.

- **Continuation of existing practices.** An insurer might **continue** the following practices, but the **introduction** of any of them is not allowed:
    - Measuring insurance liabilities on an undiscounted basis
    - Measuring contractual rights to future investment management fees at an amount that exceeds their market-comparable fair value
    - Using nonuniform accounting policies for the insurance contracts of subsidiaries, except as permitted by this IFRS

- **Prudence.** An insurer need not change its accounting policies for insurance contracts to eliminate excessive prudence. However, if an insurer already measures its insurance contracts with sufficient prudence, it should not introduce additional prudence.

- **Future investment margins.** An insurer need not change its accounting policies to eliminate future investment margins. However, there is a presumption that an insurer's financial statements will become less relevant and reliable if it introduces an accounting policy that reflects future investment margins in the measurement of insurance contracts, unless those margins affect the contractual payments. Two examples of accounting policies that reflect those margins are
    - using a discount rate that reflects the estimated return on the insurer's assets; and
    - projecting the returns on those assets at an estimated rate of return, discounting those projected returns at a different rate, and including the result in the measurement of the liability.

- The insurer might make its financial statements **more relevant** by switching to a comprehensive investor-oriented basis of accounting that involves
    - current estimates and assumptions,
    - a reasonable adjustment to reflect risk and uncertainty,
    - measurements that reflect both the intrinsic value and time value of embedded options and guarantees, or

- a current market discount rate.

- **Shadow accounting.** An insurer is permitted to change its accounting policies so that a recognized but unrealized gain or loss on an asset affects those measurements in the same way that a realized gain or loss does. The related adjustment to the insurance liability or other Statement of Financial Position items should be recognized in equity if the unrealized gains or losses are recognized directly in equity. This practice is sometimes called shadow accounting.

37.4.9 An insurer need not separate and measure at fair value a policyholder's embedded derivatives, such as an option to surrender an insurance contract for a fixed amount or interest rate, or both, even if the exercise price differs from the carrying amount of the host insurance liability. IAS 39 does apply to certain put options.

37.4.10 Some insurance contracts contain both an insurance component and a deposit component. In some cases, an insurer is required or permitted to **unbundle those deposit components.** Unbundling is prohibited if an insurer cannot measure the deposit component separately.

37.4.11 An insurer should, at the acquisition date of a business combination, measure the insurance contracts at fair value. The **subsequent measurement** of such assets should be consistent with the measurement of the related insurance liabilities.

37.4.12 The issuer of an insurance contract that contains a **discretionary participation feature** as well as a guaranteed element could recognize all premiums received as revenue without separating any portion that relates to the equity component. The resulting changes (in the guaranteed element and in the portion of the discretionary participation feature classified as a liability) should be recognized in profit or loss.

37.5 PRESENTATION AND DISCLOSURE

37.5.1 An insurer should **disclose** the following information to **identify and explain the amounts** arising from insurance contracts in its financial statements:

- Its **accounting policies** for insurance contracts and the **assets, liabilities, income, and expenses** related thereto

- **Recognized** assets, liabilities, income, and expenses

- **Cash flows** on the direct method—optional

37.5.2 If the insurer is a **cedant,** it should **disclose**

- gains and losses recognized in profit or loss on buying reinsurance;

- amortization of deferred gains and losses for the period;

- unamortized amounts at the beginning and end of the period;

- the process used to determine assumptions underlying measurement of recognized profits and losses;

- the effect of changes in assumptions; and

- reconciliations of changes in insurance liabilities, reinsurance assets, and related deferred acquisition costs.

37.5.3 An insurer should disclose information that helps users to understand

- the amount, timing, and uncertainty of future **cash flows** from insurance contracts;

- risk management policies and objectives;

- material terms and conditions affecting the amount, timing, and uncertainty of the insurer's future cash flows;

- insurance risk, including

  - the sensitivity of profit or loss and equity to changes in applicable variables,

  - concentrations of insurance risk, and

  - actual claims compared with previous estimates, up to a maximum period of 10 years (claims development);

- interest rate risk and credit risk detail required by IAS 32; and

- exposures to interest rate risk or market risk under embedded derivatives that are contained in a host insurance contract, where the embedded derivatives are not measured at fair value.

37.6 FINANCIAL ANALYSIS AND INTERPRETATION

37.6.1 Traditionally, insurance accounting has varied between countries because insurance is highly regulated by national government regulators. There is often a strong focus on prudence because stakeholders have demanded certainty about insurance companies' abilities to pay out cash on contracts as required.

37.6.2 From the analyst's perspective, all financial instruments should be measured, recognized, and reported at their fair value. A fair value approach greatly improves the transparency of financial information, while enabling users of financial statements to predict more reliably the amounts, timing, and uncertainty of an entity's future cash flows. Fair values overcome the historical cost deficiency of not incorporating sensitivity to financial risk exposures, such as interest rate risk and credit risk.

37.6.3 Many insurance firms currently manage their financial assets and financial liabilities using fair value techniques to determine which products to underwrite, which investment strategies to adopt, and how best to manage overall risks. Moreover, those firms actively acquiring insurance firms or blocks of insurance business analyze and determine the fair value of those targets as part of their decision-making process. In addition, current and prospective investors of those insurance firms pursue similar information for making their investment decisions.

37.6.4 Fair value accounting better reflects economic reality by showing the volatility inherent in the values of financial instruments, given changes in market conditions and operations of the entity. Historic cost-based accounting facilitates smoothing these effects, thus obscuring this volatility and masking the actual economic impact of various positions held in financial instruments. Fair value accounting therefore unmasks, but does not create, the real volatility.

37.6.5 One would expect less volatility or distortion of results once all financial instruments are recognized at fair value, assuming that a firm is effectively managing its risks and exposures to those risks. At present, however, there is still a distortion in reported financial performance because of an accounting model where some financial assets are marked-to-market and others are not, and where financial liabilities are not measured using fair value techniques.

Chapter Thirty Eight

Financial Reporting in Hyperinflationary Economies (IAS 29)

38.1   OBJECTIVE

In a hyperinflationary economy, reporting of operating results and financial position without restatement is not useful. Money loses purchasing power at such a rapid rate that comparison of amounts from transactions and other events that have occurred, even within the same accounting period, is misleading.

38.2   SCOPE OF THE STANDARD

IAS 29 should be applied by entities that report in the currency of a hyperinflationary economy. Characteristics of a hyperinflationary economy include the following:

- The general population prefers to keep its wealth in nonmonetary assets or in a relatively stable foreign currency.
- Prices are normally quoted in a stable foreign currency.
- Credit transactions take place at prices that compensate for the expected loss of purchasing power.
- Interest, wages, and prices are linked to price indexes.
- The cumulative inflation rate over three years is approaching or exceeds 100 percent (that is, an average of more than 26 percent per year).

IAS 29 requires that the financial statements of an entity operating in a hyperinflationary economy be restated in the measuring unit current at the reporting date.

IAS 21 requires that if the functional currency of a subsidiary is the currency of a hyperinflationary economy, transactions and events of the subsidiary should first be measured in the subsidiary's functional currency; the subsidiary's financial statements are then restated for price changes in accordance with IAS 29. Thereafter, the subsidiary's financial statements are translated, if necessary, into the presentation currency using closing rates. IAS 21 does not permit such an entity to use another currency, for example a stable currency, as its functional currency.

38.3   KEY CONCEPTS

38.3.1 A general **price index** should be used that reflects changes in general purchasing power.

38.3.2 **Restatement** starts from the beginning of the period in which hyperinflation is identified.

38.3.3 When **hyperinflation ceases,** restatement is discontinued.

38.4 ACCOUNTING TREATMENT

38.4.1 The financial statements of an entity that reports in the currency of a hyperinflationary economy should be **restated** in the measuring unit current at the Statement of Financial Position date; that is, the entity should restate the amounts in the financial statements from the currency units in which they occurred into the currency units *on the Statement of Financial Position date.*

38.4.2 The restated financial statements **replace** the financial statements and do not serve as a supplement to the financial statements. Separate presentation of the nonadjusted financial statements is not permitted.

Restatement of Historical Cost Financial Statements

38.4.3 Rules applicable to the restatement of the **Statement of Financial Position** are as follows:

- Monetary items are not restated.
- Index-linked assets and liabilities are restated in accordance with the agreement that specifies the index to be used.
- Nonmonetary items are restated in terms of the current measuring unit by applying the changes in the index or currency unit to the carrying values since the date of acquisition (or the first period of restatement) or fair values on dates of valuation.
- Nonmonetary assets are not restated if they are shown at net realizable value, fair value, or recoverable amount at Statement of Financial Position date.
- At the beginning of the first period in which the principles of IAS 29 are applied, components of owners' equity, except accumulated profits and any revaluation surplus, are restated from the dates the components were contributed.
- At the end of the first period and subsequently, all components of owners' equity are restated from the date of contribution.
- The movements in owners' equity are included in equity.

38.4.4 All items in the **Statement of Comprehensive Income** are restated by applying the change in the general price index from the dates when the items were initially recorded.

38.4.5 A **gain or loss on the net monetary position** is included in net income. This amount can be estimated by applying the change in the general price index to the weighted average of net monetary assets or liabilities.

Restatement of Current Cost Financial Statements

38.4.6 Rules applicable to the restatement of the **Statement of Financial Position** are as follows:

- Items shown at current cost are not restated.
- Other items are restated in terms of the rules above.

38.4.7 All amounts included in the **Statement of Comprehensive Income** are restated into the measuring unit at Statement of Financial Position date by applying the general price index.

38.4.8 If a **gain or loss on the net monetary position** is calculated, such an adjustment forms part of the gain or loss on the net monetary position calculated in terms of IAS 29.

38.4.9 All **cash flows** are expressed in terms of the measuring unit at Statement of Financial Position date.

38.4.10 When a foreign subsidiary, associate, or joint venture of a parent company reports in a hyperinflationary economy, the financial statements of such entities should first be **restated** in accordance with IAS 29 and then translated at the **closing rate** as if the entities were foreign entities, per IAS 21.

38.5 PRESENTATION AND DISCLOSURE

The following should be disclosed:

- The fact of restatement
- The fact that comparatives are restated
- Whether the financial statements are based on the historical cost approach or the current cost approach
- The identity and the level of the price index or stable currency at Statement of Financial Position date
- The movement in price index or stable currency during the current and previous financial years

38.6 FINANCIAL ANALYSIS AND INTERPRETATION

38.6.1 The interpretation of hyperinflated results is difficult if one is not familiar with the mathematical processes that give rise to the hyperinflated numbers.

38.6.2 Where the financial statements of an entity in a hyperinflationary economy are translated and consolidated into a group that does not report in the currency of a hyperinflationary economy, analysis becomes extremely difficult.

38.6.3 Users should consider the disclosures of the level of price indexes used to compile the financial statements and, where provided, should consider the levels of foreign exchange rates applied to the translation of financial statements.

38.6.4 When inflation rates and exchange rates do not correlate well, the carrying amounts of nonmonetary assets in the financial statements will have to be analyzed to consider how much of the change is attributable to structural issues such as hyperinflation and how much is attributable to, for example, temporary exchange rate fluctuations.

38.6.5 As accounting standards increasingly require use of fair value measurement, users of the financial statements of entities that operate in hyperinflationary economies must consider the reliability of fair value measurements in those financial statements.

38.6.6 Hyperinflationary economies often do not have active financial markets and could be subject to high degrees of regulation, such as price control. In such circumstances, the determination of fair values, as well as discount rates for defined benefit obligations and impairment tests, is very difficult.

EXAMPLE: FINANCIAL REPORTING IN HYPERINFLATIONARY ECONOMIES

EXAMPLE 38.1

Darbrow Inc. was incorporated on January 1, 20X2, with an equity capital of $40 million. The Statement of Financial Positions of the entity at the beginning and end of the first financial year were as follows:

	Beginning $'000	End $'000
Assets		
Property, plant, and equipment	60,000	50,000
Inventory	30,000	40,000
Receivables	50,000	60,000
	140,000	150,000
Equity and Liabilities		
Share capital	40,000	40,000
Accumulated profit	–	10,000
Borrowings	100,000	100,000
	140,000	150,000

The Statement of Comprehensive Income for the first year reflected the following amounts:

	$'000
Revenue	800,000
Operating expenses	(750,000)
Depreciation of plant and equipment	(10,000)
Operating profit	40,000
Interest paid	(20,000)
Profit before tax	20,000
Income tax expense	(10,000)
Profit after tax	10,000

Additional Information

The rate of inflation was 120 percent for the year.

The inventory represents two months' purchases, and all Statement of Comprehensive Income items accrued evenly during the year.

EXPLANATION

The financial statements can be restated to the measuring unit at Statement of Financial Position date using a **reliable price index,** as follows:

Statement of Financial Position	Recorded $'000	Restated $'000	Calculations
Assets			
Property, plant, and equipment	50,000	110,000	2.20/1.00
Inventory **(Calculation a)**	40,000	41,905	2.20/2.10
Receivables	60,000	60,000	
	150,000	211,905	
Equity and Liabilities			
Share capital	40,000	88,000	2.20/1.00
Accumulated profits	10,000	23,905	Balancing
Borrowings	100,000	100,000	
	150,000	211,905	
Statement of Comprehensive Income	**$'000**	**$'000**	
Revenue **(Calculation b)**	800,000	1,100,000	2.20/1.60
Operating expenses	(750,000)	(1,031,250)	2.20/1.60
Depreciation **(Calculation c)**	(10,000)	(22,000)	2.20/1.00
Interest paid	(20,000)	(27,500)	2.20/1.60
Income tax expense	(10,000)	(13,750)	2.20/1.60
Net profit before restatement gain	10,000	5,500	
Gain arising from inflationary adjustment		18,405	Balancing Figure
Net profit after restatement gain		23,905	

Calculations

a. **Index for inventory**
    Inventory purchased on average at November 30
    Index at that date $= 1.00 + (1.20 \times 11/12) = 2.10$

b. **Index for income and expenses**
    Average for the year $= 1.00 + (1.20 \div 2) = 1.60$

c. **Index for depreciation**
    Linked to the index of property, plant, and equipment $= 1.00$

Printed in the United States
154219LV00001B/31/P

9 780821 377277